Incident at Howard Beach

Incident at Howard Beach

THE CASE FOR MURDER

Charles J. Hynes
and Bob Drury

G.P. PUTNAM'S SONS / NEW YORK

Published by G. P. Putnam's Sons,
200 Madison Avenue, New York, NY 10016.
Published simultaneously in Canada

The text of this book is set in Gael.

Library of Congress Cataloging-in-Publication Data

Hynes, Charles J.
    Incident at Howard Beach : the case for murder / Charles J. Hynes
and Bob Drury.
        p.   cm.
    ISBN 0-399-13500-6
    1. Murder—New York (N.Y.)—Case studies.   2. Homicide
investigation—New York (N.Y.)—Case studies.   3. Trials (Murder)—
New York (N.Y.)   4. Race relations—New York (N.Y.)—Case studies.
I. Drury, Bob.   II. Title.
HV6534.N5H96 1989   89-33669 CIP
364.1'523'09747243—dc20

Printed in the United States of America
1 2 3 4 5 6 7 8 9 10

This book has been printed on acid-free paper.
∞

For Regina Catherine Drew Hynes
and Patricia L. Pennisi Hynes,
the two most important women in my life;
and for my children,
Kevin, Sean, Patrick, Jeanne, and Lisa.
—C.J.H.

For Bob and Syl.
—B.D.

CONTENTS

The Trial

ACKNOWLEDGMENTS

A general is only as good as his troops, and I am forever indebted to the staff of the New York Special State Prosecutor's Office for harnessing the thought processes that went into this book. I also owe a debt of gratitude to Governor Mario M. Cuomo, who appointed me to the position. I would also like to thank Richard Emery, who believed that the tragedy in Howard Beach was a story worth telling, and my agent, Jay Acton, who turned that belief into a reality.

Bob Drury wishes to thank the following individuals for their time, recollections, and analyses: Ed Boyar, Helman Brook, Sonny Carson, John Cotter, David Dinkins, Don Forst, Matt Greenberg, James "Hap" Hairston, Det. (Ret.) John Hammond, Dennis Hawkins, Pamela Hayes, Hillel Hoffman, Det. (Ret.) Robert Howell, Murray Kempton, Larry Kurlander, Gabe Leone, Doug LeVien, Bryan Levinson, Bill Lynch, Richard Mangum, Mike McAlary, Gene McPherson, Stephen Murphy, Marty Steadman, Ronald Rubinstein, Bill Tatum, Jitu Wateusi, and Brad Wolk. In addition, dozens of people were interviewed for this work on the condition of anonymity. You know who you are, and I thank you.

Special thanks to the reporters who did such a thorough job covering the incident at Howard Beach, to Karen Van Rossem and Christine Baird in the New York Newsday Library, and to Fran Koenig of Washington Computer Services, who made us computer literate.

Incident at Howard Beach

PROLOGUE

There was still a half-hour until dinner, on the Saturday after Christmas 1986, and I was browsing idly through the shelves of the library of the Eastover Inn in the Berkshires. I glanced at the well-thumbed copies of Melville and Fenimore Cooper, at a few volumes of Faulkner encased in tiny white cobwebs. My wife, Pat, was right about this, as she was about so many things. I needed these quiet moments, in a place far from the world I knew in Brooklyn: that squalid world of crooked cops and sleazy politicians, that dark and slippery little universe that I examined each day on my job as special prosecutor and tried hard not to bring home to Pat and the children. I had learned that it was a world with almost no heroes. Heroes usually existed only in books, and I took down a volume, looking for a comfortable chair where I could sit and read and smell the hickory fires curling up from the valley below.

And then I heard a chant, distant and blurred, coming from the world we'd left behind:

Howard Beach, have you heard? This is not Johannesburg! Howard Beach, have you heard, this is not . . .

It was coming from the tiny black-and-white television set in the corner of the room, and I moved closer, the book in my hand, drawn like a moth to a flame. On the screen, black protesters and white onlookers were exchanging the language of anger and bitterness. The blacks were marching through a small Queens hamlet called Howard Beach. Exactly one week earlier, the lives of dozens of human beings had been changed forever on its streets. I didn't know it yet, but my life was about to be changed too.

The black-and-white images were like a ghostly replay of scenes from the civil rights struggles of the late 1950s and early seventies, except for the accents and cadences of the players. Once again, black marchers were asking for justice. Once again, white faces were contorted with fury, snarling obscenities. Once again, police stood between them while reporters and cameramen recorded the seething drama. It suggested Selma; Birmingham; Albany, Georgia. The difference was that this was happening in the liberal North, in a city that prided itself on its sophistication, that offered to the world some of the ornaments of our civilization.

And here were the voices. *Black:* "I don't need a passport to walk through Howard Beach. This is 1986!" *White:* "Don't *I* need a passport to walk through Bed-Stuy?" Whites were stuffing five-dollar bills into a large cardboard box. "We want to show those white kids that the white people in the neighborhood are sticking behind them," an elderly female crossing-guard told the camera. "The marchers are doing what they think is right, we're doing what we think is right." A television reporter read a statement from a black lawyer named Alton Maddox: "There is certainly an official policy in this city never to convict a white person for killing a black person." When several black photographers climbed to an overpass for a better view of the march, whites began chanting: "Jump, jump, jump." Several hundred surged against barricades, tried to get past a group of Guardian Angels to join the march; some black marchers turned around and one of them pointed at the whites and yelled: "We're marching the wrong way! Bigotry and hatred are the other way. Eye for an eye. Out the window with peace and justice. Let us young guys do it our way."

The Reverend Timothy Mitchell, pastor of the Ebenezer Baptist Church in Flushing, Queens, and one of the protest organizers, rushed to intervene from the front of the parade. "All you black folks," he shouted, "I've been to Selma, I've been to Mont-gomery. I know these folks. If you're in the march, don't stay with them. Let's go. These are some mean people here. They already killed Michael Griffith. What do you think they'll do to you? *I want black people out of here!"*

The clergyman's plea worked. The last of the black marchers turned and walked north, across the bridge spanning the Belt Parkway, out of Howard Beach. But the camera continued to provide details of life in New York City, 121 years after the Civil War: the departing blacks, with raised fists, some with pickax handles; whites staring sullenly after them, waving the stars and bars of Jefferson Davis's Confederate States of America.

"What the fuck do they want now?"

The voice came from behind me in the library, and I instantly recognized the unmistakable accent of South Boston. For a mo-ment, I was reminded of childhood summers with my mother's relatives in Dorchester, Massachusetts. The gentle voice of Aunt Minnie. The raucous shout and quick laugh of Uncle Jack. But the voice at my back was angry and frustrated. I turned from the television set to see a young man in his late twenties. Except for the angry red tide rising in his eyes, the ruddy Celtic face could have been that of my cousin, Kilday. The man's muscles were barely concealed by a shamrock-green sweatshirt bearing the words, in large white script, THE FIRE DEPARTMENT OF THE CITY OF BOSTON.

He walked across the room and kicked the off button on the television set. "Goddamn creeps," he shouted. "They want fuc-kin' everything." Quickly he turned and looked to me for a reaction. The look was a challenge. If I didn't like the way he turned off the set, I could try to do something about it. At fifty-three, alas, my best fistfighting days were long behind me. But I could feel the blood surging as we stared at each other across the musty gothic library. I was shocked and angry. The poison-ous fevers of Howard Beach had reached into this quiet room in the hills of Massachusetts. Part of me wanted to strike out at the man, at his swaggering stupidity, at his unstated alliance with the snarling young men of Queens. But I was a man of the law. For thirty years, I'd dedicated my life to the belief that irrational human passion must be tamed by the law. *His* passions, and mine.

Then a voice on the hotel's public address system broke the tension. "Mr. Hynes, telephone."

I left the library and walked to the lobby of the inn. The caller was Larry Kurlander, who was director of criminal justice for Governor Mario Cuomo. He was calling from the state capitol in Albany.

"Joe," he said, "have you been following the incident out at Howard Beach?"

"A bit, Larry. In fact I'm watching something now on the news. Why?"

"The governor may want you to take a look."

I ended up taking more than a look. But when Kurlander called, I wasn't ignorant of the events in Howard Beach. They were being discussed on local talk-shows and the national network news. They were filling columns in the newspapers. People spoke knowingly or angrily or despairingly about The Incident. And everyone knew that Howard Beach was becoming more than a mere incident. It was a stark and ugly metaphor for the racial tension that was eating away at every city in America. As a citizen of the United States, as a New Yorker, as a man of the law, I was concerned and disturbed by The Incident and its terrible implications. But I was the Special Prosecutor for the State of New York, the head of an investigative office that had been established back in 1972 for the express purpose of ferreting out government corruption. Racial problems were not part of my mission.

Still, that night I telephoned my First Assistant, Helman Brook, and gave him Monday's assignment: to begin collating all the contradictory stories, charges, countercharges, eyewitness accounts, statements, and complaints that made up The Incident.

He was as puzzled as I was about the assignment. "Boss, what's this got to do with us?" he said. "That's why we have the police, and the district attorney. Where's the corruption angle in a street killing?"

"I don't know. There doesn't seem to be any," I replied. "But

I have a strange feeling we are about to expand our area of expertise."

That feeling came from my twenty-five years of experience in government. I had been a Marine. I'd worked in the racket squad of the Brooklyn District Attorney's Office. I'd been the city's fire commissioner. And since the year before, after months of excruciating boredom in private practice, I'd been the state's special prosecutor, taking over a staff of ten attorneys, twenty-three investigators, and two lonesome accountants from two floors of cramped office space in the permanent shadow of the twin towers of the World Trade Center. We had successfully exposed and prosecuted some major cases of police corruption; we were looking at others. But this I knew: when superior officers suggested that a subject, a case, or an incident deserved attention, they were considering action.

As I read through the first spare reports about The Incident, I realized that we were looking at more than a fatal combination of race and violence. We were looking at a tragedy. And that tragedy would consume the next year of my life.

The
Incident

1

HEART OF DARKNESS

Cedric Sandiford listened absently as a news broadcast interrupted the reggae music blaring from the car radio. The lead story that day was about an alleged cop-shooter named Larry Davis. Sandiford wasn't interested. It was not quite nine o'clock, Friday evening, December 19, 1986. The air was crisp, the darkness of the sky heightened by the brilliance of a gibbous moon and a billion glistening stars. Sandiford was then thirty-six years old, the oldest of the four men in the car. He was tall and laconic, a construction worker who had left Guyana as a teenager for the good jobs and better life in New York. Some of that life had been good; but much had been bad, and for fourteen years now, Sandiford had been addicted to cocaine. On this night, as the music of the islands played on the radio, he was in the backseat, behind the driver of the souped-up 1976 Buick.

The car's owner, a nineteen-year-old named Curtis Sylvester, was driving. He was a part-time auto mechanic who had just arrived in the city a few days earlier on a visit from Tampa, Florida. Beside Sylvester was his cousin, twenty-three-year-old Michael Griffith, a lean five feet, ten inches with smooth mahogany skin, who also did construction work. Griffith's mother, Jean, was an immigrant from Trinidad, and had a five-year-old daughter, Brenda, with Sandiford. Later, Sandiford said that he was engaged to Griffith's mother and thought of the younger man as

his stepson. They had at least one characteristic in common.
Michael was hyper that evening, described by one friend as "full
of life." His autopsy later would show that some of his liveliness
was the result of an earlier snort of cocaine.

Completing the foursome was a moody, tense young man
named Timothy Grimes, who, at eighteen, already had been
convicted of several violent felonies, including a particularly
nasty armed robbery. Grimes was fifteen years old when he and
three companions, including his fourteen-year-old cousin, surrounded an elderly couple in the Park Slope section of Brooklyn.
As his three accomplices threw a choke hold on the seventy-
five-year-old man, Timothy jabbed a .38-caliber revolver behind
the right ear of the man's seventy-four-year-old wife.

"You've got three seconds to give me your money or I'll blow
her fuckin' head off," Timmy Grimes said, according to court
documents. Caught and convicted, Grimes spent three years in
the Spofford Correctional Institute for Juveniles. Out of jail for
only a little more than a year, he was now an unemployed furni-
ture mover and a hopeless addict of crack cocaine. The three
New Yorkers had all picked up the virus of drugs; the young man
from Tampa, the city where Mets pitcher Dwight Gooden got
in so much trouble, was apparently not immune. Earlier in the
year, police raided the Tampa public housing project where
Sylvester lived. Under the park bench where he was sitting with
a girl, they found nine grams of brown cocaine. A police report
said that, although they could not prove this cocaine was Sylvester's, they did believe he was a major cocaine supplier in the
project. So on this cold December night, the four men in the car
had two factors in common: color and cocaine.

Sylvester was driving his tan Buick Skylark west on the six-
lane Belt Parkway. As a newcomer, he had no way to know that
at various points the parkway forms a frontier between the small
sylvan pockets of Queens and the vertical Calcutta of Brooklyn's
housing projects. There were very few excursions in either direction across this steel and concrete racial border. But he drove
on, seeing the sights, his guides excited and cheerful.

Several hours earlier, the four had met in Brooklyn, at the
apartment of Cheryl Sandiford. She was Cedric's niece and

Timmy Grimes's girlfriend. The men decided to go for a ride to show Sylvester, the country boy, a bit of the big city.

"I didn't want them to go," Cheryl said later. "If they hadn't taken that ride, Michael would be alive today."

But as a sight-seeing adventure, the journey seemed peculiarly without direction. Timmy Grimes asked them first to make a stop in St. Albans, Queens, at the home of his sister-in-law, Dorothy Wood. He didn't invite the new arrival inside. Nor did he ask Sandiford and Griffith to join him. Later, Grimes said that the stop was merely to "say hi." Investigators believed that he was really there to *get* high. At any rate, they seemed not to know how to find their way back to Brooklyn, and Wood gave them directions. Along the way, they stopped at a Jamaican bakery in St. Albans to buy wine, bottles of Heineken beer, and several Jamaican beef patties.

As Sylvester drove west on the Belt Parkway, steam began seeping and then flowing from under the hood. It was very hard for Curtis Sylvester to see through the billowing steam clouds, but he was a stranger, he didn't know where he was or what to do. Grimes shouted for him to get off the parkway at Rockaway Boulevard, and he began maneuvering into the right-hand lane. His red indicator light was flashing. Then he saw the large green and white sign, marked EXIT 17-S, CROSS BAY BOULEVARD. THE ROCKAWAYS.

It was the wrong exit.

"Michael said something about the smoke, and Curtis saw the word 'Rockaway' and thought that was our exit," Sandiford later told the police. "The rest of us weren't paying too much attention. I figured we were almost home free."

With smoke and steam rising over the Buick, Sylvester eased the car on to the Exit 17-S ramp. He drove slowly down the exit ramp and headed southbound along Cross Bay Boulevard. "The Boulevard," as it is called by local residents, is a long, six-lane roadway that bisects Howard Beach, separating an older, less-affluent neighborhood on the Kennedy Airport side to the east from a newer neighborhood to the west. But both sides were part of a tightly knit, isolated enclave of the working class in southern Queens. It was 98 percent white.

Through the car windows, the four black men could see aging single-family homes, draped with blinking ropes of colored Christmas lights. "Fairy lights," Sandiford called them. American cars stood in driveways next to lighted plastic crèches connected by extension cords to kitchen outlets. Sylvester pressed the accelerator down to compensate for the car's loss of power. Driving south, away from Brooklyn, the group passed two all-night service stations in the otherwise darkened business district of Howard Beach.

Seven minutes after leaving the Belt Parkway, Sylvester's car crossed the Joseph P. Addabbo Memorial Bridge and rolled to a halt along a slight incline at the foot of the span. They were next to a small enclave of bungalows called Broad Channel, a tiny community nestled in the center of Gateway National Park. They were three and a half miles south of Howard Beach. The bridge, spanning Jamaica Bay and named for a former Queens congressman, separates the Queens mainland from the Rockaway Peninsula, the southern end of Long Island. The car had stopped in a corner of the National Park called the Bird Sanctuary. There were no highway lights. The area was desolate.

The Buick's transmission and water pump were both broken, a fact unknown at the time to Sylvester and his passengers. It was just after 9:30 P.M. Sandiford, the eldest, attempted to assume control. He told Griffith and Grimes to go and find water for the radiator while he "tumbled with the engine."

At six feet, four inches and a steel-trim 175 pounds, Sandiford is an imposing figure. Although he had once applied for United States citizenship, he had never followed up on the paperwork. That did not stop him from serving two years in the United States Army, as a medic stationed at hospitals in West Germany and Virginia. Most of the patients were veterans of the Vietnam war. Honorably discharged in 1971, he held a succession of well-paying heavy construction jobs. Among other things, he was a skilled crane operator. But he was out of work often, partially because of the erratic nature of the construction industry and partially because since his second year in the service he had been addicted to cocaine.

Personally, he is a gentle, dignified man, with considerable charm. There is almost nothing to suggest that he was once convicted of attempted murder. But as we all learned later, Sandiford had a past. Shortly after his discharge from the Army, while he was living in Virginia, Sandiford's second wife called the police and said he was trying to kill her. Specifically, she claimed that he attempted to blow her head off with a sawed-off shotgun. After a two-day trial, Sandiford was convicted by a jury and sentenced to ten years. But during the summation, the prosecutor referred to Sandiford as an "alien." This was the basis for a reversal of the verdict by an appellate court after Sandiford had already served two years. He was scheduled to go on trial all over again.

Then his court-appointed attorney informed him that if he pleaded guilty to the lesser charge of criminal possession of an illegal weapon, he would be sentenced to "time served" and immediately released. Sandiford insisted on his innocence. He *had* slapped his wife, but he'd never threatened her with a gun. Still, he accepted the deal to gain his freedom. His record would haunt him in the year after The Incident.

While Sandiford and Sylvester stayed with the useless car, Griffith and Grimes somehow decided to walk south into the dark, the direction in which the car was pointed, rather than double back to Howard Beach. An hour later they returned, Griffith carrying a milk carton filled with water given to him by toll collectors at the Cross Bay Bridge, another span one mile away. Sandiford quickly filled the radiator. Sylvester turned the ignition key. The car would not start.

Sandiford suggested they leave the car and walk to the nearest subway station. They could make their way back to the neighborhood, find someone with a car, and return; or simply come back in the morning with a mechanic.

"Not me," said Sylvester. "I got three hundred dollars in new stereo equipment and all my clothes in this car. I can't afford to get it stolen."

So Michael Griffith, Cedric Sandiford, and Timothy Grimes agreed to return to Brooklyn, borrow a car, and come back for Curtis Sylvester. They left Curtis locked in his car, already drifting off to sleep, and they went off on foot to find the subway.

There was an H-train subway station a few blocks from where their Buick had sputtered to a halt. But the stop was unlighted, and the three black men, unaware of its existence, walked right past it. They knew there was a station on Liberty Avenue, five miles up the darkened causeway that ran through Howard Beach. They walked into the heart of darkness.

2

THE GAUNTLET

As the black men began their fatal walk, a woman named Ida Bendetto was a mile away, slowly peeling down to her bra and panties before a slavering crowd. This was her fourth and final performance that evening. Bendetto, alias Edna Bennet, alias Cindy the Cop, was tired. She had spent the evening doffing her costume—a police officer's uniform—at private parties in neighboring Nassau County. Each show brought her $115. Now she was in Howard Beach, where her employer, Hot Bodi Grams and Talent Agency, had booked her last show of the night. This was an eighteenth birthday party for a kid named Steven Schorr.

The party was in the home of the Schorrs at 158th Avenue and 80th Street, in the newer, more prosperous side of Howard Beach. The young man's sister, seventeen-year-old Diane, had made all arrangements, including the hiring of Cindy the Cop as a special present for her brother. The Schorrs' paneled basement was packed with teenagers. Everybody was drinking.

Midway through her routine, Bendetto noticed an especially boyish-looking teenager waving a twenty-dollar bill at her.

"What would you do for this?" said the kid named Jon Lester.

Bendetto was a pro. She ignored him and finished her act. And at 11:20, she left the party. Three of the boys walked with her to her car.

At this precise moment, one mile away, Cedric Sandiford,

Timothy Grimes, and Michael Griffith, walking north on Cross Bay Boulevard, stepped into Howard Beach.

At the same moment, Simone Berritto and her cousin, Romi Shulman, were cruising "the Boulevard" in a bright-red 1986 Nissan ZX, driving north and south "looking for boyfriends." They stopped for a traffic light near the Surf Side Motel and heard shouting. They noticed the three black men. They claimed later that the one named Michael Griffith called out to them, "Hey, white girls, come over here." The young women ignored him and continued cruising, passing the three men twice more. On each occasion they said they heard similar remarks. Finally, Simone and Romi stopped for coffee at the Esquire Diner. From there, they said, they went home.

Moments after Berritto and Shulman walked into the Esquire Diner, Dean Lewis, a youth counselor from Brooklyn, pulled his car into the parking lot of the Blue Fountain Diner, several blocks north on Cross Bay Boulevard. He noticed Sandiford, Grimes, and Griffith walking north. "Hey, you guys," shouted Lewis, who is black, "for your own good you should get out of this area." The three didn't answer, but Sandiford made a motion with his hands as if to say, "We know."

As Lewis was entering the diner, a car pulled up near the three blacks. Lewis paused. A white man stuck his head out of the window on the passenger side and shouted, "Get out of here, niggers." Lewis shook his head and entered the diner.

After Cindy the Cop's performance, Salvadore DeSimone, eighteen, left Steven Schorr's party to drive a girlfriend home. Jon Lester, sixteen, and William Bollander, seventeen, went with him for the ride. DeSimone made a left turn off Cross Bay Boulevard onto 157th Avenue, one-half mile north of the Blue Fountain Diner, when he jammed on the brake and stopped. Sandiford, Grimes, and Griffith were standing in a crosswalk between a bowling alley and the New Park Pizzeria, a red-brick, one-story restaurant with a façade that juts out like a roadhouse porch. DeSimone blew his horn and flashed his high beams. DeSimone, Lester, and Bollander started yelling at the three black pedestrians. Sitting next to Lester in the backseat, the fourth passenger, Claudia Calogero, said nothing.

"The black guys were fooling around as we were crossing, pulling the ski hats off each other's heads," Calogero recalled later. "Sal said, 'Hey, get out of the way, we almost hit you.' "

Then Lester rolled down his window. "Fucking niggers," he shouted.

"White motherfucker," Sandiford replied.

"Wait here, wait here, we'll be back," yelled Lester.

"Don't worry, we'll be here," Sandiford shot back.

The exchange lasted perhaps five seconds. When the three teenagers dropped Calogero off at her home, she implored them, "Go back to the party. Don't start nothing."

The young men didn't listen.

After covering nearly four miles in an hour and a half, San-diford, Grimes, and Griffith were hungry. Grimes and Griffith suggested they eat at Lenny's Clam Bar, a restaurant on Cross Bay Boulevard. But Sandiford, seeing what he called the "fairy lights" of Christmas strung across the façade of the establishment, thought the place "too ritzy" for the crew. Instead, the three settled on the New Park Pizzeria.

As they walked into the pizza place, a white man named John Laffey was watching from across the street. He was an off-duty short-order cook from a nearby Kentucky Fried Chicken. He walked to a nearby pay phone and dialed 911, the number used for emergencies. Laffey thought the black men were "suspicious" and acting intoxicated. He called the cops because he was afraid they "were going to start up."

"I thought they were going to stick up the pizza place," Laffey told police later. "They looked like they had no place to go. They were very shady-looking. They looked like stickup men to me. They looked like muggers."

It was true that the three men weren't dressed for a fancy-dress ball; Sandiford thought they weren't even dressed for Lenny's Clam Bar. Sandiford himself was wearing a sheepskin jacket, blue jeans, and black combat boots. Grimes had on dark pants and a ski jacket. Griffith was clad in a brown leather jacket and brown leather pants. All three wore ski hats. They were dressed, in short, like workingmen. The reason they might have looked like muggers to Laffey was simple: they were black. And there were (and are) people who want to believe that all crime in American cities is black crime.

So there were other eyes watching as Sandiford, Griffith, and Grimes entered the small pizza parlor. They sat at a picnic table covered with a red-and-white checked tablecloth, and ordered four slices of pizza before changing their minds and deciding they wanted only three. Grimes paid for one slice, the counterman taking $1.50 out of his $20 bill. Griffith paid for the two others.

The New Park Pizzeria lies in the southern end of the 106th Precinct, and as the three black men ate, Officers Steven Braille and Ronald Siegel were working the midnight to 8:00 A.M. tour, cruising Sector E of the 106th in a radio car. They responded to Laffey's 911 call at 12:39 A.M. Braille entered the pizzeria alone, saw the three black men, and asked, "Is there a problem in here?" One of the two countermen, Nick Palladino, shook his head no. Braille left and reported the call as a "1090-X"—unfounded. He waved off two more arriving officers.

As Braille and Siegel drove away from the pizzeria, heading north on Cross Bay Boulevard, Sal DeSimone, Jon Lester, and William Bollander were approaching from the opposite direction. Lester spotted the three blacks eating pizza.

"We saw them," he later told police investigators. "They saw us."

They did not, however, get out of the car. Instead, the three teenagers rushed back to Schorr's party. People were milling around the driveway, saying goodbyes, boisterous with youth.

"Fight, fight," DeSimone shouted as he got out of his car.

Followed by the others, he moved into the paneled basement. Lester shouted, "There's some niggers in the pizza parlor, and we should go back and kill them."

Bollander added, "Some niggers started with us at the pizza parlor."

That was all it took.

The trio had no trouble recruiting volunteers for their courageous patrol against the men in the New Park Pizzeria. DeSimone popped back into his car and was joined by half a dozen other teenagers—Lester, Scott Kern, Jason Ladone, Michael Pirone, Tommy Farina, and James Povinelli. Harry Buonocore, who was leaving the party with his girlfriend, Laura Castagna, was intercepted by another teenager, a hulking, half-drunk Robert Riley.

"There's niggers on Cross Bay," Riley told Buonocore. "Let's go."

Buonocore, Castagna, Bollander, and John Saggese, who was too drunk to drive his own car, piled into Riley's white Buick Electra. The odds were now acceptable. There were three black men. Twelve white teenagers should be enough to teach them a lesson.

With the radio in the car blasting so loudly that members of the group could not hear each other speak, DeSimone drove to a Gulf service station on the east side of Cross Bay Boulevard, parking between a Waldbaum's supermarket and the New Park Pizzeria. Riley arrived a moment later, a metal baseball bat in his car. Thomas Gucciardo, alone and driving Saggese's car, arrived last. That made it thirteen whites.

As the whites pulled up, the three black men were leaving the restaurant. They looked up and saw twelve white teenage boys coming at them carrying baseball bats and tree limbs. One of them, seventeen-year-old Scott Kern, began banging a bat on the pavement.

"Niggers, get out of the neighborhood," yelled Jason Ladone, the sixteen-year-old son of a city sanitation worker. "You don't belong here."

Sandiford was clearly frightened. He screamed, "God, don't kill us," as one of the teens lashed a bat across his thighs. With that, the three black men began to run.

Grimes jumped over a wall in the parking lot of the adjacent Home Federal Bank and began sprinting north along Cross Bay Boulevard, toward the Belt Parkway. Someone in the mob hurled a flashlight at him, bouncing it off his shoulder blade. Grimes did not stop to turn and see the wolf pack on his tail. But luck was with him. Bollander, who had taken off after Grimes, had recently undergone hip surgery. He fell near the Boulevard's center divider, and when his friends stopped to help him, Grimes escaped.

Griffith and Sandiford were not so lucky. They ran east across Cross Bay Boulevard and into the parking lot of the Tile-O-Rama Housewares store. They were pursued by the main body of the shrieking, bat- and stick-wielding horde. And Sandiford, wearing his heavy combat boots, was gradually falling behind the younger, swifter Griffith.

After stopping to help the fallen Bollander, Farina returned to the battle. He doubled back and was the first to spot Griffith and Sandiford running south on 156th Avenue, the street parallel to the Belt Parkway.

"Get the fuck out of our neighborhood, take your friends and leave," yelled Farina. But the warning came much too late. Sandiford had already slowed to a walk. He was too old for this. He'd had too many good times, used too much coke. He was panting and exhausted, gasping for air. Sandiford did not notice the Howard Beach Public Library, with the sign announcing that the return bookslot was permanently closed due to vandalism. Nor did he see the intermittent warnings tacked to telephone poles at each corner of the street: WARNING—AREA PATROLLED BY ARMED GUARDS. On a sloping lawn at the corner of 87th Street and 156th Avenue a cheeky plastic Santa held open a green gift bag, with Frosty the Snowman standing guard nearby. Sandiford ran right by it.

And Michael Griffith was now out of sight.

At 85th Street, where 156th Avenue bumps into the Belt Parkway and then veers left, Sandiford was finally cornered. He was backed against a seven-foot-high chain-link fence by the white youths, who began piling out of their cars or arriving on foot. Lester passed Farina, ran up to the tall black man, and began slugging him with a baseball bat. Ladone arrived next and began punching the cowering black man. Kern grabbed a tree limb and started pummeling his legs. Sandiford dodged, moved, turned, pleaded; the frenzy went on.

At least a half-dozen residents of 156th Avenue witnessed parts of the attack, which took place over a quarter-of-a-mile stretch along the street.

Theresa Fisher was drinking tea in her sister's kitchen at 86-20 Shore Parkway, the fancier name for 156th Avenue. Her sister,

Angela Romanelli, had just finished perming Theresa's hair as they watched *Late Night with Joan Rivers*. Suddenly they both heard screaming outside.

Looking out the kitchen window, which faces east, the two women saw a black man across the street being chased by several white teenagers. The women ran to the front door, flung it open, and stepped out onto the front stoop. Now the tall black man was leaning against the chain-link fence that separated Shore Parkway from the Belt Parkway, and the whites began to batter him. They were pummeling him with what looked to be tree branches and tire irons. He broke away and ran toward the two women, crying for help. Theresa pulled Angelina back inside and slammed the door. Fisher then dialed 911.

Immediately, at 12:37 A.M., a police dispatcher sent a message over the radio. He said there was a racial assault under way at 156th Avenue and 84th Street. This was a mistake, for he was off by a block, placing the scene of the attack across the Belt Parkway from Angelina's home. But Theresa Fisher didn't wait for the police. After calling 911, she went to her car, followed by her sister and her brother-in-law, and drove through the neighborhood looking for the battered black man.

"The man is hurt," she told her sister. "We have to help him." They cruised the area for the next thirty minutes, fruitlessly shouting into the dark. She never found Sandiford nor saw the whites again that night.

At 12:55 A.M., George Toscano, with his wife, Dr. Maria Toscano, were watching television in his mother-in-law's house on Shore Parkway when he heard his dogs barking. Toscano, who is nearsighted, was not wearing his glasses. He went to the front window and saw what looked to be a black man staggering down the sidewalk in front of the house and, farther away, another black man near the center divider of the Belt Parkway.

Toscano watched as the taller black man limped to the berm across from his mother-in-law's front door. Fifteen seconds later his jaw dropped as several white youths surrounded the black man, who was leaning against a tree, gasping for air. One of the whites swung a baseball bat and hit the black in the stomach.

Toscano went to the front door. By the time he opened it the street was empty. Toscano's wife, Maria, was nearly hysterical as she dialed 911. When she did not get an answer, she hung up and did not dial again.

Braille and his partner, Siegel, were vouchering an abandoned, stolen car when they heard the radio report of a racial assault in progress in the vicinity of "156th Avenue and 84th Street." The officers rushed to the location, as did another patrol car, driven by officer Frank Murphy and his partner, Chris O'-Brien. The two cruisers converged at the spot at 12:57 A.M. The area was quiet, deserted, and the four officers departed at 1:02 A.M., recording their second "unfounded" report of the evening.

One minute after they left, an unidentified caller dialed 911 from a pay phone and told the operator: "There is a body in the westbound lane of the Belt Parkway."

That was Michael Griffith.

The running skirmish had lasted perhaps twenty minutes. It began on Cross Bay Boulevard and ended eight blocks away, at the corner of 84th Street, where the Shore Parkway meets the Belt. No one was quite sure yet how the black man had ended up dead in the far-left lane, the "hammer lane," of the Belt Parkway. Adding to the confusion was the discovery of an exhausted and bloodied Cedric Sandiford staggering toward Brooklyn beside the westbound lanes of the Belt Parkway, throwing orange construction cones behind him into the path of any possible pursuers.

By the time he reached the parkway, Sandiford need not have worried anymore. The teenagers had already begun to return to Schorr's party. Michael Pirone's sixteen-year-old girlfriend, Martha Vanegas, would remember "the boys" walking back in at about 1:10 A.M. "They were all very quiet," she remembered, "and talked in groups among themselves."

She saw her boyfriend sitting on the ground in Schorr's backyard, rubbing his knees. Both of Pirone's legs had been broken in a 1985 car accident, and he appeared to be in pain. She asked him what had happened.

"Nothing happened," he snapped. "Don't worry about it."

But a remark from Lester, who was standing over Pirone, carried a more ominous tone. "Don't worry about anything, Martha," he said. "Mike didn't do anything."

As the teens gathered back at Schorr's house, officers Braille and Siegel responded to the report of an accident on the highway. Police cruisers from the 75th Precinct, a car assigned to the Highway Patrol, and an ambulance were already on the scene when they arrived. A few moments later, Braille noticed two highway patrolmen accompanying a lanky black man to the body in the road. The officer recognized the man as one of the people he had seen earlier in the New Park Pizzeria. Sandiford knelt over the crumpled corpse, its head split open like a ripe melon.

"Oh my God," wailed Sandiford. "This is Michael. Oh my God."

3

CONFUSION

It was after eight o'clock on Saturday morning, December 20, and Detective Bobby Howell was late for work. As Howell pulled his car up to his customary parking spot in front of the 106th Precinct in Ozone Park, Queens, his sour mood was further aggravated by the young plainclothes officer directing him to park a block and a half away from the station house.

Uh-oh, more Internal Affairs, thought Howell. *Who's in trouble now?*

He nosed his Plymouth into a parking space. His initial reaction wasn't casual. The 106th Precinct had recently been the target of a gut-wrenching investigation by the department's Internal Affairs Division and the Queens County District Attorney's Office. The results had been brutal and disheartening: five white officers had been arrested, charged, and convicted of torturing an alleged drug dealer with electrical stun guns. The victim was black. During a period when black activists were accusing the New York City Police Department of treating minorities like animals, here was the ultimate proof: using a cattle prod on a black man who was later revealed to be innocent. For months, the story was aired on television newscasts and in the city's newspapers. Howell, with a street cop's innate distrust of Internal Affairs, was not looking forward to the airing of more departmental dirty linen.

On this Saturday, it was Howell's job to open up the squad room for the day. No detectives had worked the One-Oh-Six overnight. It was department policy to assign a "Night Watch" of detectives from Queens Borough headquarters in Forest Hills to handle any homicides that occurred in the county between 4:00 A.M. and 8:00 A.M. Lesser crimes and complaints—assaults, muggings, burglaries—were handled by uniformed officers until precinct detectives opened their respective squad rooms in the morning.

When Howell entered the station house, he was surprised to see a sergeant from the Night Watch, accompanied by several other Night Watch detectives, walking up the back stairs of the building toward the precinct commander's office.

"Whaddya got, Sarge?" asked Howell.

"We're not sure yet," replied the officer. But from the look on the detectives' faces, Howell's intuition told him that something major had occurred. His instincts were confirmed the moment he stepped into the empty detective squad room on the second floor. The phones were beeping insistently. Howell picked up one receiver and heard a familiar voice at the other end of the line.

"Well, Robert," said Detective Frank Coletti, who was based in the adjacent 101st Precinct, "I understand you've got multiple homicides over there. If you need a hand, give us a call."

"I just walk in the door and you're talking multiple homicides," muttered Howell, running his hand through his full head of blond hair. "I knew I never should have gotten out of bed today."

Howell told Coletti he'd get back to him when he sorted things out. He hung up and walked over to the squad room's coffeepot. Blanching at the sight of the cold, day-old dregs from the Friday-evening tour, Howell turned to wash out the pot. He found himself chest to chest with Deputy Chief Joseph Borelli, at the time the borough's highest-ranking detective and the officer in charge of all Queens detective operations. Standing behind Borelli was a grim-faced Robert Colangelo, Borelli's boss and the head of the department's detective bureau. *You do not rub elbows with these guys on ordinary assignments,* thought

Howell. Both wore blue suits and pleated worry lines around their eyes. Howell wondered: *Who the hell got killed last night? The Pope?* He asked what was going on.

"Homicide in Howard Beach, looks like a bias incident," responded Borelli, who ordered Howell to get on the phone and contact everybody in the squad, everybody he could find. "And bring in everyone *not* scheduled to work, too." Days off were suspended. Colangelo moved to a corner of the squad room, watching, saying nothing.

The first person Howell reached was his partner, Detective John Hammond, who was on a 10:00 A.M. to 6:00 P.M. Saturday shift. Within forty-five minutes the two detectives were sitting at their desks, poring over the previous night's Detective Division Form 5s—"DD-5's" or just plain "Fives," in police parlance. The forms list every crime or complaint that police investigate, as well as the circumstances surrounding the event. As the detectives flipped though the pages of the reports, they could hear the mutterings of their bosses in the next room.

Most of the Fives were the routine mayhem of the big city and had been handled by the Night Watch. The one that mattered, the Five that had brought the brass into this squad room, had been copied and was now being circulated throughout the precinct. It described one black male DOA on the Belt, another assaulted nearby. The dead black man was a twenty-three-year-old named Michael Griffith, the reports told Howell and Hammond. The survivor, Cedric Sandiford, was thirty-six years old and engaged to be married to Griffith's mother. Sandiford, picked up wandering aimlessly on the Belt Parkway by Highway Patrol officers, told uniformed officers that another friend, a fellow named Timothy Grimes, had become separated from the group, and no one had any idea what had happened to him.

At first, the Traffic Division's Accident and Investigation Squad had control of the Griffith case. Then the brass realized that this was more than a tragic highway accident.

By the time Howell and Hammond finished reading the Fives the squad room was in total chaos. There was more brass in the station house than either of them had ever seen during their combined sixty years of service. Uniformed officers from the nearby 75th Precinct were floating in and out of the room, filing reports. Patrolmen from the One-Oh-Six were working overtime downstairs. Accident and Investigation officers were penning highway reports next door in the lieutenant's office. And rumor had it that Mayor Edward I. Koch and Police Commissioner Benjamin Ward were on their way to the precinct, Koch driving in from Manhattan, Ward being flown down by a police helicopter from an upstate vacation. *The panic whistle,* Hammond thought, *is blowing full steam.*

Hammond and Howell were constantly interrupted by a steady stream of ranking officers blowing into the squad room and demanding to be briefed. As soon as they briefed one boss, another arrived, wanting to know everything that was going on. By two o'clock, they knew their task. No other crimes in the precinct were related to what happened to Griffith, Grimes, and Sandiford in Howard Beach. No other had such enormity for the precinct, for the department, and for the city itself.

At that moment, Griffith's body was on a slab in the basement morgue of Jamaica Hospital in Queens. Sandiford was at the same hospital, having his wounds treated and identifying the body of the young man he considered his stepson. He'd spent most of the night giving statements to uniformed patrolmen on the highway and, later, in the precinct. Detectives from the department's Bias Unit were out searching for Grimes.

From reports filed by the uniformed officers who had spent the night with Cedric Sandiford, the detectives began to piece together a sketchy outline of Michael Griffith's final moments. The words came from Sandiford's statements:

"Michael tried to climb the fence, but they dragged him down and beat him bad. Then they came after me. I pleaded with the young one with the bat, I told him I had a son his age. But he just lashed me in the head. I saw Michael escape through a hole in the fence. They went after him in cars. I pretended I was dead. Then I heard a *boom,* and saw Michael get hit."

The detectives noted that Griffith apparently had been run down by an off-duty court officer named Dominick Blum. Sandiford insisted to the patrolmen that the twenty-four-year-old Blum was part of the white gang, but the detectives doubted this. Blum was older than the attackers described by Sandiford. And he had an airtight alibi: his father was a city cop and vouched for his son's whereabouts. *Well,* thought Hammond, *we'll check that one out.*

They did. Blum said that three hours before Griffith's death he was applauding as the curtain fell on a Brooklyn College Theatre Group production of *Top Girls.* Blum, who worked in Manhattan's Family Court, attended the play with his girlfriend, Martine Channon, his parents, and another couple. At 10:30, Blum's mother and his father, police officer Paul Blum, drove home together to the Flatbush section of Brooklyn. Blum, Channon, and the other couple, riding together in Blum's 1979 blue Dodge Aspen, drove to a Brooklyn diner, where they ate and chatted for about an hour. Then Blum and his girlfriend dropped their friends off at their respective apartments—the woman in Flatlands, Brooklyn, and the man in Flushing, Queens.

Driving back to Brooklyn at about 12:30 A.M., with Channon asleep next to him in the passenger seat, Blum told police he was in the left lane of the westbound Belt Parkway when the brake lights of the car in front of him suddenly flashed red. He looked over his right shoulder, trying to swerve into the center lane to avoid a collision.

Suddenly, Blum said, something careened off his Aspen's left front fender, crashed into the windshield, and flew over the car. Blum said he thought he'd hit a tire, or perhaps an animal. His girlfriend, he said, never woke up.

Blum said he pulled over on the shoulder of the road about three hundred feet down the roadway, looked back, and saw nothing. After dropping Channon at her apartment, he drove the Aspen home. It was now without a front left headlight. The windshield was smashed. There were dents in the left front fender and hood. He told his father what had happened, and his father insisted they return to the scene of the accident. They set off together, not in the damaged Aspen, but in Paul Blum's blue Dodge Colt.

Meanwhile, the reports said, Robert Napolitano, an off-duty Port Authority policeman, had been driving home to Brooklyn after finishing his shift at Kennedy International Airport. Just beyond the Cross Bay Boulevard overpass, he noticed a body in the left lane. Napolitano pulled over to the right shoulder, parked his BMW, and walked across the highway toward the prone figure, flicking a cigarette lighter to ward off traffic. The victim appeared to be dead. Napolitano hurried back to his car, turned on his flashers, and drove it across the road to shield the body of Michael Griffith. He was waiting there when police arrived.

The first officers from the Accident Investigation Squad to reach Griffith's body discovered a beeper and a toy gun not far from the scene. They started playing with the gun, passing it back and forth, effectively negating any successful fingerprint check. Howell and Hammond were appalled at the lack of professionalism in those first moments by the AIS men. Much worse was their treatment of Sandiford.

4

"TREATED LIKE A ROBBER"

I will go to my grave believing that there is no better cop than a New York City cop. Investigative lawyers—and I'm one of them—like to think they're really detectives at heart; big, rough, tough city detectives. But the truth is that I've never heard of a lawyer who can hold a candle to a New York City detective, who is, as a rule, smart, thorough, imaginative, and often gifted with a knack for brilliant intuitions.

But no one has ever accused New York City cops of possessing a huge gift for tact and sensitivity. When you patrol a town where nearly two thousand murders a year are heaped on top of literally hundreds of thousands of assaults, rapes, and robberies, good manners are generally a rare luxury. Detectives usually operate with a gruff efficiency. Some might think them rude.

There is, however, a difference between the tony precepts of Miss Emily Post and simple civility. Too often, even simple civility is forgotten. This is exacerbated by the fact that more than 75 percent of the city's police are white, many of them living in the middle-class suburbs. And they are policing a city where much of the routine crime is committed by the black or Latin poor.

As a result, I sometimes find myself agreeing with the acerbic

H. L. Mencken, who covered cops as a police reporter on the streets of Baltimore at the turn of the century and could have been describing cops in any American city today.

"They are badly paid but they carry on their dismal work with unflagging diligence," Mencken wrote. "And they love a long, hard chase almost as much as they love a quick, brisk clubbing. Their one salient failing, taking them as a class, is their belief that any person who had been arrested, even on mere suspicion, was unquestionably and *ipso facto* guilty."

The uniformed cops who first arrived on the scene at Howard Beach seemed to take Mencken's precept one step further: they believed that the victims of the crime, because they were black men traveling through a white neighborhood, had to be *ipso facto* guilty of something. This attitude nearly set the city on fire and almost destroyed the case.

After Michael Griffith was chased to his death, a passing motorist named Steven Wiener doubled back to the cordoned-off accident scene. He told police that he'd just seen a black man staggering down the Belt Parkway about a mile away. Weiner thought this man might be connected to the dead body sprawled across the road. He was asked to help identify the staggering black man, and he went with several officers down the highway in a patrol car. They spotted Sandiford walking west, picked him up, and took him back to Griffith's body.

There the worst happened. Blood was dripping onto the highway from Sandiford's head as he tried to explain what had taken place back in Howard Beach. But he was pushed against a patrol car. He was spread-eagled. He had his coat roughly ripped off his back. Finally, bleeding and shivering in the December cold, he was frisked. The police began peppering him with questions about a completely different homicide that had taken place nearby. Not the death of Griffith, who was lying at their feet. A different death. And then Sandiford got angry, explaining to the officers that he was a victim of a crime, not a perpetrator. The officers told him it was their duty to search anyone they put in a patrol car. True enough according to the police handbook, but their attitude and the manner of their search was obviously incendiary. It's doubtful they'd have behaved the same way if Sandiford had been white.

Once in the patrol car, the officers sat for nearly three hours listening skeptically to Sandiford's story. He told it over and over again. And Griffith's broken body, the gray matter of his brains seeping off the Belt Parkway's concrete divider, lay a few feet away. Sandiford, with his own wounds still untreated, watched all of this in an unbelieving daze.

"They chased us on foot and then got into their car and ran Michael down," Sandiford told police, adding that he believed he could identify the driver of the car who had smashed the life out of the man he called his stepson.

While Sandiford and the uniformed officers were talking, Blum and his father drove up. The two got out of their car and passed in front of Sandiford, who made no sign of recognition. The Blums then began speaking to officers Braille and Siegel. Dominick Blum said he thought he was the one who had hit the man, but not with the car in which he had just arrived. His Aspen, he told the patrol officers, was damaged, and he had left it at home.

Braille and Siegel told all of this to the highway patrolmen, who at this point were in charge of the investigation. For some unfathomable reason, they neglected to mention to their fellow cops that Paul Blum's Dodge Colt was not the automobile involved in the accident.

Looking back and forth from Griffith's body to the elder Blum's undamaged car, the police decided that Blum could not have caused so much trauma to Griffith's body. They concluded that Blum must have been one of several drivers who hit the black man on the busy parkway, if indeed he had hit the dead man at all. It was not until the next morning that homicide detectives, collating the Fives, realized the mistake. They called Blum and asked him to bring his damaged car to the 106th Precinct.

When they finished reading the Fives, Howell and Hammond were faced with a blurred scenario. They had a dead black man on the highway. He was a friend of another black man who may

or may not have been in deep shock when he told his tale of
being attacked by a white mob. They had a white court officer
who may or may have not driven the car that killed Griffith and
may or may not have been part of the white gang that chased
him to his death. Most important, they had no suspects.

But the detectives felt their priorities were clear: find those
responsible for this homicide before half the commanding officers of the New York City Police Department were brought
down by coronaries. For the heat was on. By 10:00 A.M. Saturday, Koch and Ward had arrived at the 106th Precinct, as had
dozens of reporters and cameramen. During an impromptu
press conference in the roll-call room, the mayor made various
remarks that did not strike the detectives as "useful" in calming
down the emotions surrounding what was swiftly becoming
known as The Incident in Howard Beach.

"They were chased like animals through the streets," said
Koch, who offered a $10,000 reward for information leading to
the arrest of the attackers. "This attack rivals the kind of lynching party that existed in the Deep South."

While the mayor talked to the press, a group of high-ranking
officers joined Commissioner Ward in Squad Lieutenant Sean
Driscoll's office. Chief Borelli, somber and erect, sat behind Driscoll's government-issue, gunmetal-gray desk. Richard Dillon,
the handsome commander of all Queens County uniformed officers, stood off to one corner. Commanders from the Bias Unit
and a plethora of uniformed bosses who had been covering the
borough over the weekend squeezed into the tiny room. Someone asked if the district attorney was coming.

He wasn't. From his home one-half mile away from the 106th
Precinct, Queens DA John Santucci dispatched Brad Wolk, an
assistant district attorney, to represent his office. When I reviewed the record later, this detail astonished me. In the days
when I was the Rackets Bureau chief in the Brooklyn DA's office,
a crime of this magnitude would have brought District Attorney
Eugene Gold and most of his top assistants to the relevant precinct within hours, if not minutes, of the first report. Obviously,
Santucci worked in a different style.

As the investigative strategy session began, the door to Driscoll's office stood slightly ajar. From the squad room next door, Hammond and Howell sidled up to eavesdrop on the conversation. So far, only a few uniformed officers from several different commands were involved in the case, and no detectives had been technically assigned to take over.

Benjamin Ward appeared agitated. He obviously had received the first reports that the uniformed officers on the scene had crudely mishandled Cedric Sandiford. Ward is a complex man. As police commissioner, he had many predecessors in certain respects; not only did he feel responsible for the fight against crime, but he also felt a duty to prevent the department from appearing inept, stupid, or—worse—racist in the eyes of the public. But as a black man, Ward must have been torn by this case. He had publicly agonized over the recent deaths of several black citizens in encounters with the police, most notably a grafitti artist named Michael Stewart and an emotionally disturbed grandmother named Eleanor Bumpurs.

In both cases the courts had relieved the police of criminal culpability. But there was a simmering belief in the city's black community that cops had murdered both Stewart and Bumpurs—and gotten away with it.

In that context, the callous police treatment of Sandiford was alarming. At best, it was an obvious example of police insensitivity. At worst, it could be viewed as racism. When the reporters got the details, there would be much bad publicity. Ward knew this. So did his boss, the mayor.

An uncertain silence fell over Lieutenant Driscoll's office as the men grasped the enormity of The Incident. Finally, Borelli stood and banged his fist on the metal desk. "All right," he said, "who's gonna catch this case?"

Outside the door, Howell thought for a moment, made his decision, and pushed his senior partner inside.

"Okay, Hammond, you just made Second Grade," Borelli said with a snarl. "Now you're going to have to earn your money. You got it." Hammond gave Howell a you'll-pay-for-this look and snapped to attention. Borelli assigned fifty officers from throughout the borough to assist in the investigation.

As the meeting adjourned, Ward grabbed Chief Dillon, and

the two went to a quiet office near the back of the precinct. Then, according to my sources at the scene, the commissioner exploded. He charged the uniformed officers on the scene with misconduct. He wanted to know what kind of command Dillon was running.

"Sandiford was treated like a goddam perp!" Ward shouted. "Those white uniforms laughed in his face at his story. The man was bleeding from the head, his body all busted up, and he was made to sit in a patrol car, next to the body of his dead stepson, *for nearly three hours!* Who went to look for the white kids? How did the patrol car miss them at the pizza parlor? Just what the hell was going on? Why the hell wasn't anything done about Blum? The papers are going to have a field day with this."

Dillon, the loyal commander, defended his men. And finished himself politically in the New York Police Department. He was soon transferred to a command in the Bronx—the department's Elba—and several months later he retired. The Incident would destroy many people in different ways.

By Saturday noon, accompanied by detectives from the Queens Borough Task Force, Cedric Sandiford and Michael Griffith's older brother, Chris, had arrived at the 106th Precinct from Jamaica Hospital, where they had identified Michael's body and consoled his mother, Jean. Now they were to be asked to help find the young men responsible, the whites who had done this. Detectives Hammond and Howell met Sandiford in the Squad Room, took him aside, and walked him across the corridor to a small, empty, Anti-Crime office.

"Cedric, I'm Detective Hammond and this is my partner, Detective Howell" is how Hammond described the conversation to me later. "We're investigating Michael's death. We're sorry for your loss, but Cedric, now we need you to tell us everything. Where were you coming from? Where were you going to? Who came after you? Why? When? Everything that happened, Cedric. Don't leave anything out. Are you ready to start?"

Sandiford told the story again. He glossed over the original exchange with the whites outside the pizza parlor. He described the chase, the beatings. He told the detectives about the white woman who opened the door across the street and how he begged her to help him. He recalled, with bitterness, how he saw the door closed in his face. He described Michael Griffith climbing the fence and the white kids pulling him down and beating him.

"Then the mob turned on me," he said, and a hypnotic daze, like a dark cloud, appeared to descend on his face. "I fell to the ground near the fence and watched Michael crawl through a hole in the fence. The baby-faced one stood over me and began swinging a baseball bat. I looked up at him and begged, 'Please, I have a son your age, please don't kill me.' He hit me in the head with the bat. Others began kicking and punching. I faked that I was unconscious. They were trying to kill both of us. It was like a lynch mob, like something that would happen in the days of slavery, not something that would happen in modern times."

A car belonging to one of the whites tore down the service road after Michael, Sandiford continued, the rest of the mob began running after the car. "Then," said Sandiford, "I heard the horrible noise. *Boom* . . ."

Sandiford said he then got up and crawled through the same hole in the fence Griffith had used to escape. He crossed the eastbound lane of the Belt Parkway, hopped over the divider, and began walking west, in the Brooklyn-bound lane. He ducked down behind the highway divider and began throwing orange construction cones on the roadway behind him "so they couldn't hit me, couldn't run me down."

He was picked up by police and "treated like a robber," he said, even after returning to the station house. His attempts to call Jean Griffith were rebuffed. When he was finally allowed to use the phone it was almost dawn. Mustering up what little strength he had left and dredging up a West Indian expression to break the horrible news, he spoke into the receiver:

"Jean, band your belly, I have bad news for you. . . ."

5

THE BREAK

While I absorbed the details of The Incident, the official investigation was under way, such as it was. Under heavy political pressure, and a climate that approached hysteria among the police brass, the department was beginning to lose control of the case. Queens district attorney Santucci never seemed to want control. I sensed that the governor would be forced to step in. Soon.

Not surprisingly, Hammond and Howell were relieved to escape the confusion of the station house that first Saturday afternoon, accompanying Cedric Sanford back to Howard Beach to retrace with him the scene of the attack. Sandiford had several stitches in his head, his right eye was swollen nearly shut, and cuts, scrapes, and deep bruises mottled the trunk of his body. Howell recalled one detective passing through the Squad Room and remarking that Cedric looked like "he'd been rode hard and put away wet." Yet the police felt he was well enough to cooperate, and at that point the dazed Sandiford still seemed willing. That would change.

As the trio drove through Howard Beach, cruising up and down Cross Bay Boulevard and Shore Parkway, the detectives became convinced that Sandiford would make a more than credible witness. Although he was extremely shaken, his story never varied. At one point, Sandiford stood beneath the leafless tree where he had stopped to rest and heard the dogs barking. He had not imagined them, had not used them as embellishment. The dogs, in fact, belonged to the mother-in-law of George Toscano, whom two detectives from the "Howard Beach Task Force" had already interviewed. Toscano, a pharmacist from Manhasset, Long Island, told them he was watching television in his wife's mother's home a little before 1:00 A.M. when he, too, was roused by the dogs. He repeated for the detectives his story: the barking, his nearsightedness, the tall black man staggering down the sidewalk in front of the house, and, farther away, another black man near the center divider of the Belt Parkway.

Next Sandiford pointed Hammond and Howell to the house where he had seen the two women come to the front porch. This, too, had checked out.

Finally Sandiford led the detectives to the break in the fence beside the Belt Parkway.

"That's where we ran to the highway," Sandiford said each time. "They caught Michael and was beating him all over with everything they had. He started running again to the highway. He crawled through the hole. Then they drove around and caught him on the highway. Michael got up to run away, but the car turned around and rammed him."

The area on the Belt Parkway where the body of Michael Griffith was discovered was some eight hundred feet from the hole in the chain-link fence. In order to catch him on the parkway, the attackers would have had to drive back seven blocks on Shore Parkway, make a left on Cross Bay Boulevard, drive across the overpass, and head down the entrance ramp at the exact moment Griffith was jumping the concrete divider. Not inconceivable, thought the detectives, considering the time it would have taken Griffith to run from the hole in the fence to the spot where his body was found. But it seemed highly unlikely and extremely coincidental. The timing would have had to be perfect. In addition, they had other doubts about this part of Sandiford's account. From Sandiford's position, he couldn't have seen the accident that killed Griffith. The distance was too great, and a hedge of shrubbery made a clear sightline difficult.

Later I learned that Hammond and Howell discussed Sandiford's story over coffee that night. Hammond told his partner:
"The guy was on the mark about everything else, so I don't see
where we can do anything else but believe him about this. He
was getting the crap knocked out of him at the time, after all.
He might just be off by a couple of yards."

"I don't know," replied Bobby Howell. "It's like he shot a roll
of film, and he's got thirty-six photos lined up in his head, but he
doesn't have them in the right sequence."

At that point, that image could have been applied to the entire
investigation.

The detectives spent the remainder of the afternoon driving
Sandiford through Howard Beach in their unmarked cruiser,
hoping to spot one of the cars involved in the attack. As they
rode through the suburban streets, peering into driveways and
garages, Sandiford became curious about how the media were
reporting the attack. At his request, the detectives turned on
their radio and, between news reports, flicked the dial back and
forth to a New York Football Giants playoff game.

Meanwhile, Task Force detectives found Sylvester at a Rockaway Beach garage, where his ten-year-old, souped-up Buick
Electra had been towed. The transmission and the water pump
were shot, Sylvester told the investigators, adding that he had
woken Saturday morning and had no idea what had happened
the previous night. Throughout the night, as he slept in his car,
he remained completely unaware of the attack. But the story
Sandiford had related to Howell and Hammond was checking
out. There *had* been car trouble. The three black men *had*
decided to walk to the subway, a journey that would take them
into Howard Beach.

A different team of Brooklyn detectives found Grimes in the
Bedford-Stuyvesant apartment of Sandiford's niece, Cheryl Sandiford, the woman Grimes was dating. Grimes told detectives he
could add little more to what they already knew about The
Incident. He appeared edgy and not at all pleased to make their
acquaintance. After the confrontation at the pizza parlor, he said
he had run to the Belt Parkway, where two black men in a
late-model sedan, "brown, maybe a Cadillac," picked him up as

he hitchhiked and drove him home to Brooklyn. No, he said, he
didn't know the names of the Good Samaritans, nor had he ever
seen them before. He said he didn't know what had happened
to Griffith and Sandiford until he heard the news reports Saturday morning.

Then Grimes reluctantly agreed to accompany the Brooklyn
investigators to the Howard Beach command post at the 106th
precinct. During an obligatory search, an ice pick was discovered in his pocket. It was was duly noted and vouchered. When
Hammond and Howell returned to the station house with Sandiford, Grimes was still there.

Sandiford may have been upset at his treatment at the hands
of police the night before, but he seemed willing enough to
cooperate with Hammond and Howell. Grimes, on the other
hand, made it clear he wanted nothing to do with the investigation.

"I didn't see nothin', I can't identify nobody, and I don't know
what happened," he told Hammond and Howell as they drove
the mile and a half to the neighboring 112th Precinct to view
mug shots culled from local high-school yearbooks. The only
time Grimes perked up at all was when the detectives offered
to buy the two black men dinner. Sandiford refused, saying he
was too upset by the gruesome memory of Griffith's body lying
on the highway. But Grimes was a trencherman, shoveling away
a large portion of fried rice and egg rolls purchased from a
Chinese restaurant on Cross Bay Boulevard. When the mug shot
search proved fruitless, the detectives drove Sandiford and
Grimes home to Brooklyn.

Day one of the Howard Beach investigation had been a disas-
ter. What Chief Borelli described as the department's "shotgun
investigation" had yet to find a target. But in a crime of this
magnitude, there is always a break. It came the next morning,
Sunday, December 21.

One of the many tips called in to the precinct was from a
Howard Beach teenager not involved in the attack. He named
sixteen-year-old Jason Ladone as a member of the mob. Detective Frank Paulson and his partner, Richie Mandel, went to the

Ladone home, where Jason's mother, Joanne, told the investigators she knew nothing of her son's whereabouts the previous
evening. At that moment, Jason was out working at his part-time
job, pumping gas at a Brooklyn service station, and Joanne Ladone led them to her son. After agreeing to be interviewed,
Ladone sat in the back of their squad car and haltingly said he
knew nothing at all about the racial attack. The detectives did
not find him convincing.

The columnist Murray Kempton was to write that the only
people who carry any real authority in Howard Beach, "the
people its residents look to in times of trouble, are the Mafiosi."
This was not hyperbole. Three bosses of the city's Five Families
lived in Howard Beach, and the new boss of all the bosses, John
Gotti, also called the community home. By example, or through
fear, the Mob guys enforced the old codes, including the
"omertà," or code of silence. At first, Jason Ladone appeared the
perfect example of a young man being true to the code. He
played the part of a regular junior g-man, as in "gangster," as he
attempted to stonewall the detectives with false bravado.

But the investigators were an experienced pair, and they
pounced on the inconsistencies of his story. Ladone, who turned
out to be merely a scared little boy in trouble with the law, soon
found his memory returning, like a sheet of film in a developer.
Under a rapid-fire cross-examination in the back of the investigators' unmarked cruiser, Ladone admitted to being with the
group who had "gotten into a fight with the black guys." He said
he had even "punched the tall black guy." But as to the death
of Michael Griffith, he drew a blank. Maybe, he said, his friends
would know something about that.

"And who would they be?" asked Paulson.

Ladone named all eleven of his companions. Then he was
taken back to the precinct. At the station house, the youngster
attempted to armor himself with his swaggering street-pose,
passing off the confrontation as nothing more than one of the
many street fights that occurred in the neighborhood. Fine, said
his interrogators, then we'll treat it like that if you just tell us
about it. After several hours of relentless questioning, Ladone
dropped his surly attitude. He was scared, he said. He hadn't

done anything illegal, he knew that. Tears were forming in his eyes when he told detectives he was ready to talk about it. He gave Paulson and Mandel a full statement.

The case broke wide open.

Ladone told about the party at Schorr's house, Cindy the Cop stripping, the reports about "niggers on the Boulevard," the departure for the New Park Pizzeria, and, finally, the fierce pursuit of the black men. "I threw a few punches myself," he said in a whisper. And he saw "the medium-sized black guy" running eastbound on the Belt Parkway, starting to climb over the highway divider. Ladone said he turned away at that moment. An instant later he heard a loud "boom" and turned back to see Michael Griffith flying twenty feet through the air.

That was all the police needed. For the remainder of Sunday evening, Paulson, Hammond, and a sergeant from the Bias Unit drove Ladone through Howard Beach in an unmarked van outfitted with two-way mirrors, attempting to persuade the teenager to locate and identify his accomplices. Ladone had been in police custody for several hours by this time. And as they canvassed the little urban hamlet he called home, Ladone again assumed his tough-guy attitude. He barely deigned to look out the windows. But Ladone's lack of cooperation didn't really matter: all afternoon and evening, the neighborhood's usual teenage haunts were eerily empty.

As the evening dragged on, the investigators were in a quandary. What should they do about Ladone? Arrest him? Book him? Or wait until they had the others in custody? Near midnight, Chief Borelli called the head of Santucci's Homicide Bureau, Gregory Lasak, and presented him with the problem. Lasak immediately ordered Assistant District Attorney Brad Wolk down to the station house, telling him: "They got a kid down there named Ladone and he's apparently giving everybody up." He also cautioned Wolk: "I think they're planning on releasing him, treating him as a witness rather than a suspect. So get down there right away."

ADA Brad Wolk had drawn beeper duty for the weekend. Every month to six weeks, one member of Santucci's staff was on call for seven consecutive days, twenty-four hours a day. Wolk, reed-thin and a week shy of his twenty-seventh birthday, had been in Santucci's office for two years and had handled just over two dozen homicides. Most were garden-variety murders: drug deals gone awry and domestic squabbles that had gotten out of hand. In a way, sending him to Howard Beach was like sending a rookie out to pitch the seventh game of the World Series. But Wolk had already been to the precinct once that weekend, also on orders from Lasak, to wait for arrests and monitor the situation. He had, in fact, pulled up to the station house just in time for Koch's impromptu Saturday news conference.

As Koch labeled the death of Michael Griffith the most heinous homicide he had ever seen, Wolk had grimaced. *The last thing you need when you're just beginning to conduct an investigation is inflammatory statements like this,* he thought. *We don't even have a suspect yet, and already the mayor's stirring the pot.*

Thus, the Sunday-night phone call from Lasak came as no surprise. When Wolk arrived this time, Ladone was sequestered in a small chamber off the squad room, sitting on a cot, chain-smoking Marlboro cigarettes. Although Ladone had never in his statement admitted to any involvement in Griffith's death, Wolk realized immediately, as Lasak had over the phone, that the youth had incriminated himself. The ADA advised Borelli that he had probable cause to arrest Ladone on a variety of charges. He also advised the officers gathered in Driscoll's office that although Ladone's statement naming the eleven other alleged attackers provided probable cause for their arrest, a conviction would be nearly impossible in the absence of corroborating evidence.

"New York State law says you can't be convicted on a statement of a codefendant," Wolk explained to Borelli and his staff. "If all you have is Ladone saying Lester, Kern, Gucciardo, or whoever also committed this crime, sure you can go out and pick them up. But I don't think we'll have a prosecutable case."

It was nearly three o'clock in the morning when Wolk came up with a plan. Why not ask these eleven teenagers to come down to the precinct voluntarily?

"There's a statute on the books," explained Wolk, who later recalled the conversation nearly word for word, "that says if you arrest someone inside their house without a warrant, the fruits of the arrest can be suppressed. In other words, whatever statements they make can be thrown out of court. So why not approach their parents? Tell them your men are investigating leads. Ask them to bring the kids down here. Ask the parents to drive down themselves. Get voluntary statements, and we can use them. And you better do it now. Considering the kind of defendants you're dealing with in this case—middle-class white kids—if you wait until morning, you can be sure they'll all march in here with attorneys and you won't get anything out of them."

Borelli agreed to try the tactic. He gave the order, and in the pre-dawn hours of Monday, December 22, a division of two dozen detectives swarmed out of the 106th Precinct and descended upon Howard Beach.

Throughout the morning, between midnight and 6:00 A.M., the teenagers straggled in: Jon Lester, Scott Kern, Michael Pirone, Tommy Farina, James Povinelli, Harry Buonocore, John Saggese, William Bollander, Sal DeSimone, Robert Riley, and Thomas Gucciardo. Jason Ladone, who was still being held, made an even twelve. This dirty dozen, so brave wielding bats in the dead of night, looked like a high-school detention class shuffling into the precinct. Ten of the eleven arrived with their parents. James Gucciardo, an attorney, accompanied his nephew Tommy.

The Monday newspapers were also in, and Sandiford was quoted extensively. Photographed wearing a large white bandage over his right eye, he'd talked with reporters Sunday afternoon in the fourth-floor Brooklyn walk-up he shared with Jean Griffith.

"In the South I heard of things like this happening," Sandiford told the media crowded into the small apartment. "But I never thought it could happen in New York." He also complained that no witnesses had yet stepped forward.

"Perhaps a half-dozen people saw us being attacked," Sandiford said. "But worst of all, I don't see how those people could stand by and see a vicious act like this go on and not do anything." Sandiford had not, so far, publicly aired any complaints about the police. His mood may have been tempered by Jean Griffith's composure. A forty-two-year-old nurse's aide, the dead boy's mother had to be devastated. Yet somehow she managed to retain her dignity, even as her son was being prepared for burial.

"It still doesn't sit in my mind what whites did to my son," she said. "But I don't feel that whites are all the same. I've worked with children, and most of the kids are white. I worked with one white child that I loved so much that when I got home at night I called his house to see how he was doing."

Throughout that Sunday evening, scores of friends, many of them Caribbean immigrants, streamed through Jean Griffith's Bedford-Stuyvesant apartment to offer condolences.

"The truth will eventually come out," said Michael's brother, Christopher, standing sentry in the stairwell outside the apartment. "No racist remarks are coming out of our family, which is great. We weren't brought up like that. My mother's being very strong about this, partly because of her devout Catholic faith. She's been trained to accept death." Then he paused. "Although not like this."

Monday morning's tabloids were strikingly similar. The words "horror" and "hell" fit nicely with Howard Beach for the headline alliterationists. Even the staid *New York Times* carried the story of the racial attack on page one.

Meanwhile, while the pairs of detectives had been sent into Howard Beach to round up the unusual suspects in the pre-dawn hours of Monday, December 22, John Hammond and Bias Unit Detective Harry Knorr were given a photo spread for Sandiford to view that included pictures of Lester and Ladone. On the way to Sandiford's Brooklyn apartment, Knorr pointed to the chain-link fence separating the Shore Parkway from the Belt Parkway. Within twenty-four hours, in a city where potholes linger for years, the holes in that fence would be repaired. They arrived at Jean Griffith's door at 1:05 A.M. on Monday. The reporters had long since departed, and Christmas decorations hung from the

walls of the clean, well-maintained flat. Jean Griffith offered the
detectives coffee, and they asked if they could speak to Sandiford alone in the apartment's tiny kitchen. They showed Sandiford the photographs. His eyes were so swollen that he had to
stand under a bulb hanging from the ceiling and peer up, squint-
ing at the pictures. Sandiford made an honest effort, the detectives reported, but his injuries made it impossible for him to see
clearly enough to identify anyone.

By the time Hammond and Knorr reported back to the 106th
Precinct, the building was crawling with people. If the previous
forty-eight hours had thrown the station house into confusion,
the scene was now utter pandemonium. Suspects were stashed
everywhere in an effort to keep them sequestered; no one
wanted concocted stories. Lester was sitting in a large, walk-in
closet used by the precinct clerks to store paper stock. There
were teenagers in the interview room, in the anticrime room, in
the lieutenant's office, in the coffee room, in the conference
room, and in the juvenile offenders' room. Milling about were
angry parents becoming more irate by the moment. Everyone
was being held for lineups.

"Is my son under arrest or are we free to go?" Harold Kern,
Scott's father, asked Wolk after he had been at the precinct for
nearly five hours.

"Look, nobody's under arrest, but we want you to just be
patient," Wolk said. "We're sorting this out, so sit tight. And as
soon as we have word for you, we'll give you the word."

Everyone was willing to play by those rules except James and
Tommy Gucciardo, and Joseph Riley and his son Robert. Gucciardo's uncle told Wolk that they would remain, but his nephew
would make no statement. Joseph Riley, a corrections officer
whose eldest son was a city cop and who knew from experience
how this game usually ended, went further. "If my son's under
arrest, place him under arrest," he told Wolk. "If he's not under
arrest, we're leaving." He wasn't, and they did.

Oddly enough, when Hammond returned to the station
house, he immediately recognized one of the teenagers. He had
once had a run-in with the big, dopey-looking kid. Ironically,
that too was a bias case. The kid had knocked the yarmulke off

a rabbi's head on a High Holy day. The rabbi didn't want the kid arrested, he merely demanded an apology. It was grudgingly proffered.

"See the big marshmallow walking through the door?" Hammond asked Knorr while pointing to Riley, who was leaving with his father. "Real wise guy. Won't surprise me if he was involved."

Lester was the sole suspect with a prior criminal record. He was awaiting sentencing for unlawful possession of a weapon, a loaded .32-caliber handgun. He and a friend had been arrested the previous August in a stolen car with the loaded gun and burglary tools. He had plea-bargained to a sentence of five years' probation. Once a defendant has counsel, as Lester did, he cannot legally be questioned without the presence of his attorney, even if the suspect waives that right and even if the interrogation involves a separate crime, as in this case. Lester had, in fact, asked his mother to telephone his lawyer when she dropped him off at the station house. Detectives had been warned not to question him.

But at one point, as Wolk was speaking to Harry Buonocore across the hall from the stock closet, Lester shouted through the open doorway, "I know a lot of people are giving me up. I won't give anyone up, but I will tell you what I did." Legally, Wolk was forced to ignore him.

But the other teenagers had no criminal records. And aside from Riley and Gucciardo, they all volunteered statements. The investigators tried to fit them together like the pieces of a jigsaw puzzle.

Kern, for instance, said that he met Lester, Farina, and Bollander at Gino's Pizza on Cross Bay Boulevard after Schorr's party broke up. They all boasted to a delivery boy about beating up blacks. "Lester told the delivery guy he hit the black guy with the bat. I said I hit the guy with a tree limb just to brag that I did something, but I really didn't hit the black," Kern told investigators, professing complete innocence.

"John Lester was hitting the black guy in the legs," he said, referring to Sandiford. "Tommy Gucciardo was hitting the black guy in the back of the legs with a stick. I didn't do anything. Back at the party, Lester said we shouldn't have hit the niggers, and Gucciardo also said we shouldn't have done it."

Buonocore described tending to Bollander, who had fallen down on Cross Bay Boulevard as he chased "the one that escaped" (Grimes). Povinelli remembered pushing Riley's car home because the battery had died. Bollander said he heard Gucciardo boast about "swinging the tree limb like Conan the Barbarian." And Farina portrayed himself as Sandiford's protector: "The black guy started walking and eventually I was within five or six feet of him and I told him to take his friends and leave," he said. "As I was talking to him, Jon Lester came from behind me and hit him twice with the bat. I turned and grabbed Lester by the lapels and told him to stop hitting the guy. I turned back towards the guy, who I thought had run, but he was still standing there. Lester broke away from me and swung at the black guy with the bat, at his legs."

Farina then mentioned the death of Michael Griffith, a subject the others had studiously avoided. "At this time Sal DeSimone drove up and started to get out of the car," he told Detective John Jessen. "I said, 'Stay in the car and let's get out of here.' Just then, before I got into the car, Mike Pirone came up to me crying and said that he thought the other black guy got hit by a car. I don't know where Mike came from. Then Sal and me drove back to Cross Bay Boulevard."

Michael Pirone had originally refused to speak to detectives when they arrived at his house at 5:00 A.M. But Vito Pirone spoke to his son in private and then drove the sixteen-year-old to the precinct. Once there, Michael Pirone insisted he knew nothing about anyone being hit by a car.

Someone was obviously lying. Someone had to know something about the death of Michael Griffith. Kern had even mentioned that he, Lester, and DeSimone drove back to the Belt Parkway after meeting at Gino's and spotted three police cruisers on the far side of the highway.

"See," Kern quoted DeSimone as telling the others. "I told you the black guy got killed."

Soon the station house resembled a crowded subway train. Scores of detectives from all over the borough shuffled in and out of rooms, comparing notes, attempting to paint a complete picture of The Incident.

One detective, Peter Fiorillo of the 106th, walked past Lester carrying the *New York Post,* whose headline screamed the words HOWARD BEACH.

"That ain't the way it happened," yelled Lester. "That's all bullshit."

Intrigued by the unsolicited comment, and unaware in the confusion that the youth's attorney had already been contacted, Fiorillo asked Lester to elaborate.

"All of us were whacked, only on alcohol," said the baby-faced sixteen-year-old. Then he told Fiorillo about leaving the Schorr party to drive his girlfriend home, seeing the black men going to the New Park Pizza, the exchange of curses, the promise to come back. That exchange had lasted perhaps five seconds, he said. When the three teenagers dropped Claudia Calogero off at her house, she implored them, "Go back to the party. Don't start nothing." That was good advice. Naturally the kids ignored her. They saw the blacks, returned to the party, uttered the war cry: *There's niggers on the Boulevard. Let's kill them.* Then went to the pizza parlor.

"The black guys came towards us," Lester told Fiorillo, "and this is where I want to clear up the bullshit. They had knives and a gun."

No weapons were ever found at the scene of the attack, so Fiorillo asked Lester if he had actually seen Sandiford, Griffith, or Grimes holding a knife or a gun. "Not exactly," he replied, adding that he had picked up that fact from several of his friends. Then, in chilling detail, he described how he had fought with one of those "friends" for control of a baseball bat. True to his word, he wasn't giving up anyone.

"I saw some guys by the hill, I thought they were hitting the black guy," said Lester. "I knew there was a bat in the backseat of my friend's car and I went to get it. My friend also wanted the bat. My friend and I fought for the bat, him pulling on his end, me on the other. I wanted a piece of the action. I got the bat and I went over to the guy called Sandiford."

Lester admitted smashing Sandiford with the bat but denied

any knowledge of Michael Griffith's death. As Fiorillo scrawled Lester's statement onto a yellow legal pad, the sixteen-year-old grabbed him and asked him to amend his phrasing. "Don't use the word 'kill,' " he told the detective, "it's just an expression for fight." Lester then told the detective that his career goal in life was to become a capo in the Mob.

As Lester was repeating his story at Fiorillo's request, Wolk received a call from Alan Zuckerman, counsel for Lester, who told Wolk that the family had retained his services and that Lester should give no statements. By the time Wolk found Lester, his statement to Fiorillo was complete. It was also inadmissible as evidence. This mistake would later prove quite embarrassing to the Police Department.

But by eight in the morning, the investigators now had nine other halting statements from the Howard Beach suspects. Only Riley and Gucciardo had left the precinct without speaking.

In the traditional game of playing one suspect off against another, the investigators were slowly corroborating parts of Sandiford's story. But it was obvious to Wolk that only fragments of The Incident had been accounted for. That Monday morning, shortly after 9:00 A.M., Lasak appeared at the station house. Wolk made his preliminary report.

"They're telling us what happened at the pizzeria, and we have one guy saying he chased Sandiford and another guy saying he punched Sandiford, and another guy saying he hit Sandiford and so forth" is how both Lasak and Wolk remember their conversation. "But we're certainly not getting anything relative to a homicide. Not even close to a homicide."

None of the initial statements were videotaped, because, as Santucci later explained, he was waiting for arrests to be made before he taped anyone's confession. That was another mistake. They were beginning to pile up.

While the suspects were being interviewed, detectives were sent out to round up "fillers," white teenagers from the area who could be integrated into lineups for Sandiford and Grimes to view. Many of the fillers knew the suspects from high school, and the station house became even more chaotic.

The last thing a prosecutor wants is a compromised lineup, with suspects and fillers chatting and laughing. The job is too serious for that. Wolk wanted the fillers to stay on one side of the station house, the defendants to remain on another. "Look," he said to Lester, the obvious leader. "I haven't given you a hard time. I haven't given anyone a hard time. I'm treating all the families with respect, and I'm treating all you guys with respect. Man to man, keep your guys over there and the fillers over here."

Lester looked him right in the eye and nodded. There was no more mixing.

At the same time, Lasak ordered detectives to pick up Sandiford, so he could look at the lineups. Paulson and Mandel drove to Jean Griffith's apartment. And discovered that Sandiford was not alone. Sonny Carson, a Brooklyn-based black activist who had once served time for kidnapping, was waiting for them. The detectives were surprised to see Carson. He was a self-proclaimed "enemy of the state." His presence alone was the first hint that The Incident was beginning to shift into another gear.

Carson was the founder of The Black Men's Movement Against Crack, an open critic of the Police Department, and a conduit between the city's mean streets and the paneled offices of two activist black attorneys: C. Vernon Mason and Alton Maddox. He first learned of the Howard Beach attack early Sunday morning, in a phone call from Jitu Wateusi, another Brooklyn activist. Putting aside preparations for a citywide Black Power conference, by 8:00 A.M. that Sunday he was listening to Sandiford recount details of the attack and its aftermath: the frisking, the rude treatment, the questions about his motives.

"Michael's lying there on the street, his head smashed right in front of me, and all the cops wanted to do was question me about a murder committed somewhere in the area," Sandiford told Carson and Peter Noel, a friend of Christopher Griffith's and a freelance writer for several of the city's black newspapers. "Then when we tried to find the guys, they're more concerned about the football game than the death of Michael."

Outraged, Noel and Carson advised Sandiford to speak with Alton Maddox. Carson called the attorney and left, promising Sandiford he would return early the next morning. He kept his promise, and was waiting when Paulson and Mandel came for their witness.

"I don't want Cedric going out with the cops alone today," Christopher Griffith told Carson. "I don't trust them, they're treating him like a suspect. But I can't make it. I have to go to the funeral home to take care of Michael."

Carson volunteered to go with Sandiford.

The detectives, naturally, didn't like the idea. But Sandiford was adamant. "If Mr. Carson can't go with me, then I'm not going," he told them. Paulson and Mandel, having no choice, relented. When the group reached the station house and met with a befuddled Lasak, he looked at Carson and asked: "Who are you?"

Carson's ego was probably stunned by the homicide chief's failure to recognize him.

"My name's Carson. Sonny Carson."

"Oh."

"I'm a member of Mr. Sandiford's community," said Carson. "And I'm here to make sure he's treated right."

"Fine," said Lasak.

As detectives took statements from the teenagers downstairs, Lasak and Sandiford sat in a second-floor office and for thirty minutes once again went over the story of the attack. Finally, Lasak asked Sandiford to accompany him to Howard Beach. Carson followed in his car. By three that afternoon, Sandiford, Lasak, Hammond, and Howell were all standing before the Toscanos' house—Carson trailing a few feet behind in his ramshackle sedan—when, as if on cue, the dogs began barking. Then a white woman in a black Cadillac drove by and screamed out the window, "Leave us whites alone!"

Carson, who had heard the epithet, got out of his car and told Sandiford that it was time to assist with Michael Griffith's funeral arrangements. Before he left in Carson's car, Sandiford promised to be at the precinct for a five-o'clock lineup.

When Lasak returned to the station house, he found Alton

Maddox waiting for him. The scowling, potbellied defense attorney, dressed, as always, in a blue three-piece suit, informed Lasak that he was now representing Sandiford. The two, with Detective John Daly in tow, repaired to a back office on the first floor of the precinct. Lasak told Maddox that the police had twelve suspects in custody, and he would like Sandiford back later that day to view lineups.

Without a word, recalled witnesses, Maddox jabbed his finger into Lasak's chest. Then he did it again. Daly tensed and began to move forward. Lasak waved the detective back. Unlike Lasak, Daly knew Maddox had developed a reputation as an attorney who would literally fight for his clients. Two years earlier, Maddox had been charged with jumping onto a huddle of court officers as they grappled with one of his clients. Arguing that he was merely trying to stop the court officers from beating his client, he was acquitted of charges of obstructing government administration.

"Sandiford's my client," Maddox finally said to Lasak, "and he'll do what I tell him to do."

Lasak was astonished by the attorney's belligerence.

"The man's a victim of a crime," Lasak said. "We want to get these guys locked up."

"You want him, then subpoena him," said Maddox. "You and Santucci, you're both white racists. You and I both know Santucci's going to cover this up. It's your investigation. Do it yourself without our help."

Maddox jabbed his finger into Lasak's chest one more time before wheeling out of the room. The gauntlet had been dropped. Later that day Maddox told black reporters that Sandiford would not cooperate in the investigation until the governor appointed a special prosecutor.

At seven that evening, Hammond, Howell, and Harry Knorr of the Bias Unit returned to Jean Griffith's apartment in the hopes of coaxing Sandiford into viewing a lineup. Two Housing Police officers were stationed in the stairwell of the apartment house, and the detectives trudged past them only to encounter Christopher Griffith, who came out of his mother's apartment to tell the detectives that Sandiford was resting, under medication. "Cedric will not be available," Griffith told the investigators, and before turning to walk back inside he handed them Alton Maddox's card.

From there the detectives went to Cheryl Sandiford's apartment, looking for Grimes, who told them he wouldn't be able to identify anyone associated with the assault. He refused to come to the precinct.

On Tuesday morning, the authorities made one final try. Three detectives from the Queens Homicide Task Force attempted to serve a subpoena on Sandiford. Chris Griffith met them on the sidewalk outside his mother's house.

"The only way Cedric Sandiford is going down to that police station," Griffith told the detectives, "is in handcuffs."

The case was falling apart.

6

MASON AND
MADDOX

On Monday afternoon, December 22, at a news conference at
police headquarters, Commissioner Benjamin Ward and Mayor
Edward I. Koch announced the arrests of Jon Lester, Jason Ladone, and Scott Kern for the murder of Michael Griffith. District
Attorney John Santucci ordered the trio charged with second-
degree murder, or murder with depraved indifference, as well
as second-degree manslaughter and assault. The anonymous assistant district attorney who typed up the arrest reports added
the charge of reckless endangerment on his own, apparently out
of habit and contrary to Santucci's orders.

"The persons who drove Griffith across the highway committed murder," Koch proclaimed to the assembled media. He
added that the incident was a "ghastly, unbelievable scene that
you could describe as hellish, and that wouldn't describe it at
all." Since no one yet had a clear idea of what exactly had happened during this "ghastly" scene, Koch was closer to the mark
than he realized when he said that it couldn't be described at all.

Ward was oddly sullen at this moment when The Incident
seemed to have been solved. He said only that he hoped further
investigation would result in more arrests. Afterward, some reporters commented on the subdued demeanor of the usually
garrulous police commissioner. They were unaware that six

more teenagers from Howard Beach had been arrested Monday, but, without Sandiford to identify them, the arrests had been voided. Ward also knew that, without Sandiford's cooperation, there was a good chance Lester, Kern, and Ladone would soon walk free too.

Ward wasn't alone in his depression. Lasak and Wolk returned to the district attorney's headquarters in Kew Gardens to inform Santucci of this strange turn of events. Sitting at the head of a conference table on the third floor, surrounded by his staff, the Queens DA finally decided to become a player in the Howard Beach case. His delayed interest struck some members of his staff, and more than a few police officers, as a case of too little, too late.

Over the next six hours Santucci and his aides discussed their options.

"We've charged these kids on murder-two, depraved indifference,' I was later to learn Santucci had muttered. "That means they knowingly chased Griffith onto the Belt Parkway. But none of them admit to that in their statements. Our case is riding on Sandiford, and he's not talking to us. Is that the way I read it?"

No one at the table felt it necessary to answer. There was nothing left to do but pull out the records, the Fives, the statements, and pore over them yet again, searching for what prosecutors call a "hook" upon which to hang this case. For the moment, at least, it appeared to his subordinates that Santucci had decided to bluff his way through. Lester, Ladone, and Kern were arraigned that evening and ordered held without bail. Santucci explained to reporters that, despite the fact that Sandiford was refusing to cooperate, the three youths had been "identified in other ways."

Afterward, wading through a throng of reporters on the courthouse steps, he took a verbal shot at Maddox. "We are the people in charge of prosecuting an action," he told the assembled media. "Not Mr. Maddox or any other attorney."

On December 23, Michael Griffith was buried in an unmarked grave at a Catholic cemetery in Brooklyn, the Borough of Churches. A tombstone bearing his name has since been

erected. Only family and close friends attended the service. A
member of Mayor Koch's staff called the family and asked if the
mayor could attend. He was told no. Alton Maddox, C. Vernon
Mason, and Sonny Carson sat silently through the memorial
service.

Christmas passed. The stalemate did not. And Jon Lester,
Scott Kern, and Jason Ladone spent their holidays behind bars.
More and more I began to hear the calls for a special prosecutor
to take over the case.

In order to indict, a prosecutor normally presents his evidence
to a grand jury, a secret panel of citizens which decides whether
the facts warrant the handing up of an indictment. But without
Sandiford to describe the case or identify suspects, Santucci realized that a grand jury would have little evidence with which to
make a judgment. Searching to save face, Santucci decided to
bypass the grand jury proceedings and convene a rare public
hearing. His stated reason was that, since this was a highly controversial case, the facts should be aired in a public forum rather
than in the secrecy of the grand jury room. His unstated reason
was to take the heat off his office should there be no indictment.
The hearing was scheduled for December 29.

Maddox and Mason, now also representing Timothy Grimes,
howled to reporters. They characterized the proposed public
hearing as an example of Santucci's inability to bring the "white
murderers" of Michael Griffith to justice.

"There were people up and down that street who witnessed
the beating," Maddox argued. Mason agreed. By calling a public
hearing, they charged, Santucci was exposing potential witnesses to the hostility of their neighbors.

They were right, of course. But Santucci was one of the few
district attorneys who made a practice of holding public hearings in controversial cases. In fact, civil libertarians, Mason and
Maddox foremost among them, had long argued that closed
grand jury meetings can hide prosecutorial misconduct and do
not serve the public's need to know. In this case, however, the
attorneys were not mollified by Santucci's plan.

"DAs don't hold open felony hearings because they want to

protect their witnesses from physical retaliation," said an angry Mason. "But this one did."

Yet, in his 1984 run for the Manhattan district attorney's office, Mason had made his support of preliminary public hearings— and his opposition to grand juries—a major plank of his campaign. Consistency was not to be part of the process. Not on this one.

On the day after Christmas, three days before the crucial public hearing, publicity shifted to the tangled issue of Dominick Blum. Maddox claimed there was a cover-up because Blum's father was a retired police officer. He made Blum's name his rallying cry for noncooperation. Until Blum was arrested, said Maddox, Sandiford would remain silent.

No aspect of the Howard Beach case was as confusing as the conflicting accounts of the fatal collision on the highway. To this day, there are people who believe Blum's was the second or even the third automobile to strike Michael Griffith. But all that was known at this point was that Blum had indeed hit Griffith. Police had disproven Sandiford's claim that Blum was part of the white mob. Yet Blum's own account of the collision—he maintained his sleeping girlfriend never awoke when the "tire or small animal" destroyed his Aspen—combined with the gentle treatment afforded him by the police (in contrast to the highhanded manner in which Sandiford was treated) to raise doubts among members of the black community. If it was a mild case of paranoia, neither Mason nor Maddox did much to relieve it.

Since he had returned within an hour of the accident, Blum was never arrested for leaving the scene. An alcohol breath test was never administered because, Santucci explained, Blum showed no sign of intoxication. The police at the scene treated Blum merely as a driver involved in an unavoidable traffic accident. Although the young man was telling the truth, days passed before detectives verified his travels that night. Later, I came to believe that if the police had acted sooner in running down Blum's account of his evening, Maddox might well have allowed Sandiford to cooperate.

Maddox tailored several erroneous accounts of Blum's complicity to suit his own agenda. Jason Ladone, for instance, had told police that he was riding in a maroon Cutlass while chasing the victims. Later, Ladone said he saw another maroon Cutlass strike down Michael Griffith. Maddox ignored the fact that Blum was driving a blue Aspen, compressed both maroon Cutlasses into one, said that Blum was their driver, and offered the story to any news organization that would print it. Several did.

"Blum's car was one of the three that were outside the Howard Beach pizza parlor as the three black men left it," he said at a news conference. "Blum followed the men as they were beaten with sticks and bats and then maneuvered onto the highway and intentionally hit Griffith."

With this erroneous accusation, Maddox was inadvertently laying a foundation for the attorneys eventually hired to defend the Howard Beach youths. They too would try to shift the blame to Dominick Blum.

Two days before the preliminary hearing, while I was in the shelter of the Berkshires watching the black protest march wind through Howard Beach, Timothy Grimes was arrested for stabbing Cheryl Sandiford in her neck and back. Cedric's niece, however, refused to press charges, stating that Timothy went berserk because of the tremendous mental strain he had been under since The Incident—"He just flipped," she said—and the case was dropped.

Meanwhile, in the days leading up to the hearing, Santucci tried desperately to persuade Maddox to allow Sandiford to testify. "You must believe me when I say that in the past several days we tried every possible way to get Sandiford to testify," the haggard-looking district attorney told reporters. "We asked mutual friends to intercede. We did not succeed. We tried to get Maddox on the phone. We did not succeed. We sent detectives to his home. We did not succeed. Sandiford is the only person who can make this case."

The prosecution still entertained hopes that Sandiford would appear at the public hearing, right up to the moment on Tuesday morning, December 29, when Judge Bianchi convened the open hearing in Part AP-6, a large courtroom on the first floor of the Queens County Criminal Court building. Black activists filled the spectator's rows. Reporters piled in. And Cedric San-

diford was not there. At the last moment, the desperate prosecutors attempted to introduce a letter from Jamaica Hospital, using
Sandiford's injuries as an excuse for his failure to appear. Bianchi
refused to accept it. He also denied a prosecution request for a
one-day postponement.

Lasak and another Santucci assistant, Jim Hubert, handled the
State's case. Wolk, who was scheduled to be called as a witness,
later recalled that he was "petrified." He had taken Lester's
"capo" statements literally. He said he envisioned a contract put
out on his life, and before the hearing began he walked into the
public lavatory and threw up.

For four hours Bianchi sparred legally with Lasak and Hubert.
Lasak revealed for the first time the statements made by Lester,
Ladone, and Kern to police. Detectives were called to the stand.
Wolk was called to the stand. And that was it. The State had no
other witnesses. Finally Bianchi ruled.

"I didn't hear anything about cause," said Bianchi as he
dropped the murder, manslaughter, and assault charges against
Lester, Ladone, and Kern. "The death of Michael Griffith must
be caused by an actor or actors. I don't see that at all in any of
the proof. All I know is that a person was hit by a car. I know
it's alleged Griffith was killed in this incident. How it happened,
I don't know."

Bianchi retained only the single charge of reckless endangerment against the youths, the charge Santucci never ordered, for
the beating of Sandiford. Kern and Ladone posted $15,000 in
bail. Lester was held on $25,000 bail, the higher figure the result
of his gun-possession case. His mother, who had given birth to
a baby boy two days before, couldn't make bail. He was ordered
held in isolation for his own protection in the city jail on Rikers
Island.

In his ruling, the judge admitted that the trio had imposed "a
risk of death upon the person of Sandiford." He strongly suggested that Sandiford's testimony would be essential in support-
ing a charge of murder in the death of Griffith. Bianchi's decision
was greeted by angry chants of "Injustice! Injustice!" from most
of the black spectators in the courtroom. "Shut up, put them out
of here," he ordered his bailiffs. After the protesters were

removed, the flustered Bianchi lashed out at the remaining black spectators.

"May I call to the attention of those loudmouths that Mr. Sandiford happens to be a Negro, a black man, who did not happen to come in to testify, so the prosecutors are bound by what they produced—or couldn't produce."

That evening, with his investigation seemingly at a dead end, Santucci convened a private brainstorming session with police at his office. All told, eighteen members of the Queens County District Attorney's Office and the New York City Police Department sat around Santucci's mahogany conference table shaking their heads in frustration. Their dwindling options were explored. The decision by Mason and Maddox seemed baffling. They said they wanted justice but refused to allow their clients to give evidence that might make justice possible. If Sandiford didn't come forward, the kids who had taken part in The Incident might literally get away with murder.

Santucci wondered out loud whether it was possible that the testimony of those who did not participate in the chase could be used against those who did. "This could circumvent our evidentiary problems," he said. Or, asked the DA, frantically throwing out ideas, what if we treated the assault at the pizza parlor and the assault on Shore Parkway as two separate incidents? Then, he concluded, we could get the "fringe players" from the pizza parlor attack to testify against the "heavy players" from the Shore Parkway attack. The notion was discussed and shelved.

Not all of the investigators were predisposed to sympathize with the Howard Beach victims. Their police records indicated that they were not the most innocent group of individuals these cops had ever come across. Even the dead man, Michael Griffith, had carried excess baggage into his grave. The police and the DA's office were well aware that Griffith's autopsy had revealed cocaine in his bloodstream. And the coroner who performed that autopsy was surprised to find a .22-caliber bullet lodged in the right side of his chest, just above the tenth rib. Indeed, that bullet had momentarily sent Hammond and Howell into states of apoplexy—until the medical examiner hastily informed them that it was an "encapsulated," or old, wound.

At one point, someone in Santucci's conference room that evening even offered a cocaine theory involving Sylvester, whose pedigree had arrived from Tampa. "Here's a guy sitting in a cold car for ten hours for no reason," this cop said. "There's probably a couple of kilos out there in the marsh somewhere. That's what they were doing in St. Albans before their car broke down."

"So what?" replied an assistant district attorney. "That has nothing to do with three guys getting attacked three miles away."

There was talk of having material-witness orders drawn up against Sandiford and Grimes. When a witness refuses to honor a subpoena, as both had, that refusal might constitute a warrant for their arrest. Santucci, anticipating the outcry in the black community at the arrest of Cedric Sandiford, squashed the idea.

The detectives at the meeting also vented their anger at Koch, whose "lynching" remarks they believed had exacerbated the situation by strengthening the noncooperative stance of the witnesses. Lieutenant Donald Burmeister of the Accident Investigation Squad said that it was impossible for anyone to have seen Michael Griffith flying twenty feet into the air, as a stricken body would have rolled off Blum's Dodge after being hit. Chief Borelli ordered every 911 tape concerning the incident to be gone over "with a fine-toothed comb." All of them must have felt they were grasping at air. Without Sandiford, everyone concluded, the case was going nowhere.

Santucci vowed that he would never "cave in" to Maddox and Mason and give up the case to a special prosecutor. The meeting was adjourned.

7

THE STANDOFF

The investigators spent the next two weeks trying to pull a rabbit out of a hat. The Toscanos were re-interviewed, as was Theresa Fisher. Attorneys for the youths not arrested were contacted and asked to supply information. One by one they declined. Blum volunteered to testify, without immunity, before a grand jury. Wolk and members of the district attorney's staff joined police out in Howard Beach, ringing doorbells, searching desperately for witnesses. Charts of 911 calls were diagrammed. Every cop who had contact with Sandiford the night of the crime was brought into the District Attorney's Office and re-interviewed. But the flurry of activity was ineffective, and tempers became frayed.

On December 30, Police Commissioner Ward publicly accused Maddox of holding back Sandiford in order to make money in a civil suit against the city. "There can be an awful lot of money in a tort action," Ward said at City Hall with Koch beaming at his side. "Here we have the potential for a wrongful-death action. He didn't kill himself. Some of the questions about why things are being done the way they are being done begin to answer themselves."

Maddox may be many things, but I believe he is a committed man. The commissioner, who holds a legal degree himself, did not explain why Maddox and Sandiford couldn't file a civil suit against the city even if they *did* cooperate with the investigation.

Maddox refused to respond to Ward's charges. But Peter Noel, the freelance writer who helped put Maddox in contact with Sandiford, wrote an eloquent defense of the attorney in the *City Sun,* a black Brooklyn weekly.

"To accuse Alton Maddox of being in this for the money is malicious defamation of character," wrote Noel. "I have known Alton Maddox for nine years, and all during that time he has tried to open the eyes of the black community to racial injustice. In most cases, he has done this for free."

On Saturday, January 3, Maddox and Mason called a news conference in the Reverend Calvin Butts's Abyssinian Baptist Church in Harlem. Sandiford spoke for the first time since taking the stance of noncooperation. "My attitude has nothing to do with my lawyer," he said. "Until Governor Cuomo assigns someone to this case, I will not cooperate, period."

The Police Department ordered Detective Hammond to attend the meeting and answer reporters' questions at the Abyssinian Church. "No, that's wrong," he told his squad commander, Lieutenant Driscoll. "What happens if I answer a question one way, it turns out to be the wrong answer, and then this thing comes up in court and I have to testify. We might blow the case. With all due respect, sir, I'm not going."

Hammond was right, but the brass were furious. Only a telephone call from Lasak to police headquarters, explaining the legal damage that could be done, saved Hammond from charges of insubordination. The request itself, however, was highly unusual for a police department which has a trained public relations staff at its disposal and frowns upon its detectives' ever speaking to newspaper reporters, much less the general public. It was a sign of the department's desperation, a desperation several detectives would witness firsthand.

On January 7, Hammond, Frank Paulson, and Harry Knorr of the Bias Unit were ordered to Ward's fourteenth-floor office atop police headquarters. As the three walked into the commissioner's office, with its panoramic views of lower Manhattan, they lugged a milk carton of Fives, official reports, and statements from the suspects. Ward was sitting on the corner of his oak desk, personally crafted at the turn of the century for New York City Police Commissioner Theodore Roosevelt. He was fingering a set of worry beads.

Once more the three were surrounded by brass. There was a hush as Ward held the floor, dissecting the case with surprising acuity, for the former foot patrolman was not known for his analytical mind. Suddenly a side door opened and Chief of Department Robert Johnston burst into the room. Johnston was an old-line Irish cop, the second-most powerful officer in the department. He is most noticeable for wearing an outlandish helmet when he shows up at street encounters such as hostage negotiations or, as he had been doing a lot lately, racial rallies. His penchant for wearing the helmet, which looks like something lifted from a World War II German army officer, has earned him the derisive sobriquets "Patton," "McFührer," and "The Irish Rommel" among the rank and file.

"Who has the case?" Johnston barked. His blue uniform trousers were neatly creased, his white uniform shirt, with four stars on each shoulder, rolled up at the sleeves.

"Detective Hammond," answered Lieutenant Driscoll, nodding to the man seated on the commissioner's leather couch between Paulson and Knorr.

Johnston hovered over Hammond and demanded to know if Hammond knew why he had been called downtown.

"No, sir," Hammond said.

"You don't know why you're here? Did you read today's papers? Do you *read* newspapers, Detective Hammond?" The veins on Johnston's rose-colored nose appeared about to burst.

"No, sir, I haven't read today's papers."

With that, Johnston stalked out through Ward's side door. He returned a moment later with a stack of newspapers and dumped them on Hammond's lap. The detective, a twenty-six-year veteran and a former Marine, felt like a little boy being scolded. He looked down at the headlines.

POLICE ERROR COULD INVALIDATE STATEMENT IN RACE ATTACK.

The story under the headline in *New York Newsday*, written

by Mike McAlary, went on to explain how Lester's statement was obtained improperly and would probably be inadmissible in court.

Why isn't Fiorillo here to take this guy's crap? Hammond wondered. But he kept his mouth shut. He knew that the loss of Lester's statement, coupled with Sandiford's refusal to testify, could cripple the prosecution's case. Johnston turned to Ward and began blustering.

"See, that's the problem, Commissioner," he said. "I want the detectives in each squad room to get the papers every morning. They should know what's in those newspapers when they get to work."

The room was silent, its occupants incredulous. They had severe problems with the case. But the department's second-ranking commander's main concern was to have his detectives read the newspapers. Even Ward looked embarrassed.

"Let's not get into this now," he said. "Put it aside."

Johnston took a seat across from the detectives, and for the remainder of the meeting gave them his evil eye.

Hammond took the newspapers home and read them. The following day a captain from Johnston's office telephoned Lieutenant Sean Driscoll, telling the squad commander the chief wanted his newspapers back.

Two days after Johnston's explosion, Santucci was still reeling from the Lester botch-up. That afternoon, Friday, January 9, the district attorney invited two dozen members of the black leadership in Queens to his office in an attempt to "pry Sandiford loose" from Maddox. Those invited had been the district attorney's friends for twenty years. They were ministers, legislators, Catholic priests. They were the people he had represented as a state senator before he was elected to the district attorney's post. Cake, cookies, and coffee were served. Lasak gave the visitors a general rundown of the case. But this was not a cordial meeting. Booming voices more accustomed to the pulpit echoed angrily off the plaque-encrusted walls of the conference room.

"John, you're white, you're Italian, and my people look upon white Italians as racists," one of the preachers said to Santucci.

The district attorney had expected support from these people. He was not prepared for this.

"That's why I called you here," replied Santucci lamely. He was trying to hide his anger, but his face turned red and the words poured from his mouth a touch too haltingly. "I've represented you for twenty years. You know I'm not a racist."

It was Santucci's last gasp, and it failed. After two hours, the black leadership of Queens handed the district attorney the same message he had been reading daily and hearing nightly on the news from Maddox and Mason: give up the ghost and cede the case to a special prosecutor.

That weekend Santucci came to the office dressed casually, in pressed blue jeans and a crewneck sweater. On Sunday, Lasak walked into his boss's office and found him sitting with his feet up on his desk, blowing rings of cigar smoke. Lasak felt that, for the first time since the Howard Beach attack, the district attorney looked relieved.

"Greg," he said, "I'm thinking of giving up the case. I think it might be the best thing for us."

"You're the boss," said Lasak."

"Yes," Santucci said in a distracted way.

Two hours later he called Lasak at home. "What are you doing tomorrow? Have you ever been to Albany?"

"No," Lasak answered.

"Well, you're going tomorrow. We're going to the governor's office. Meet me at LaGuardia at seven o'clock."

8

CUOMO'S DECISION

The next day Mario Cuomo casually studied the draft of his Budget Message to the New York State Legislature as the noisy blades of the Sikorsky six-passenger helicopter sliced through the thick winter clouds. Below him lay the great Allegheny plateau, rising in the southwest to meet the Catskill ridgeline. The governor was flying to New York City, which exactly twenty-four days before had been shaken by a racial incident that seemed to come out of another time and another place. On this morning, however—it was Tuesday, January 13, 1987— Cuomo's mind was at ease. For he had finally cut the Gordian knot that ensnarled New York's criminal justice system.

He was going to Manhattan to announce my appointment as special prosecutor, charged with investigating and prosecuting the case of The Incident at Howard Beach.

He told me later that in the past three weeks, Howard Beach had never been far from his mind. Even as he prepared his fourth State of the State Address, he was aware of the simmering fury in the city's black community. He was also aware of the implications of The Incident to race relations in the city and state. And as the victims refused to cooperate and the investigation stalled, the confidential reports he was receiving had gone from bad to worse. He was extremely disappointed in John Santucci, the district attorney of his home borough, whose blurred, timid approach to the investigation had succeeded only in further polarizing the city.

But now, through a combination of gentle persuasion and the DA's own self-doubts, John Santucci was out; I was in. Cuomo knew that the appointment was not yet de jure, but it was certainly de facto. He believed he would convince the city's black leadership at their meeting today that I was the man for the job, as he had hinted to Manhattan borough president, now mayor, David Dinkins during a telephone conversation several nights earlier.

Sitting beside Cuomo on the helicopter was the man whose planning had made this trip possible, Lawrence Kurlander, the State's director of criminal justice, and Cuomo's first appointee four years earlier. The stocky, bespectacled Kurlander chatted with Marty Steadman, the governor's chief press officer, as the Sikorski banked and New York City came into view.

Kurlander had followed the Howard Beach case from the day the news broke, and had spent much of the past month in New York City, in direct communication with Santucci and the ranking officers of the New York City Police Department. From the start, Kurlander's instincts told him Howard Beach was going to be huge. He had reported to the governor about the investigative errors and community-relations disasters. He had urged Santucci to become more aggressive. And he'd set up today's meeting. The case was getting hotter by the day, and part of Kurlander's job was to deflect the heat.

"You don't call a meeting unless you know the outcome before you call the meeting," was a Kurlander truism. No governor could be put on the spot by surprises. If this meeting fell apart, it would be Kurlander's fault. So he had prepared well. The participants could dance around for a short while, but the bottom line was simple: If there was going to be a special prosecutor for Howard Beach, it would be me.

That's why C. Vernon Mason and Alton Maddox, the contentious attorneys for the Howard Beach victims, had been subtly disinvited. They were not high on me.

And he had little sympathy for Santucci. The truth of the

matter is, the Queens district attorney never wanted this case. The police were far more aggressive in trying to get to the bottom of the race attack than the DA's office had been. Kurlander, in fact, had been urging Santucci for weeks to arrest Cedric Sandiford as a material witness. He was the only one who could identify the attackers, and he wasn't cooperating. Kurlander pleaded with Santucci: "Lock the sonofabitch up."

"Oh no," the district attorney replied. "I can't do that. The black community would crucify me."

"Then simultaneously arrest the driver of the car, the white court officer who killed the other black man," Kurlander said. "Everybody's going to come down on your head, sure. But the reflective people, the opinion makers, they'll see it as an even-handed approach. John, you have to get aggressive."

Santucci didn't listen and it became clear to Kurlander, and subsequently to Cuomo, that the district attorney couldn't carry this fight.

I've spent day and night on this thing, I lived this thing, thought Kurlander as the chopper veered toward the Battery Park Heliport in lower Manhattan. He had visited the attack scene with detectives, sat in on the district attorney's brainstorming sessions, met secretly with the city's black leaders. All in a futile attempt to avoid what was about to happen. He shared the governor's view on special prosecutors: they really had no place in a democratic system. But, he thought, neither do frightened district attorneys. Kurlander was absolutely convinced Santucci was incapable of doing the job. At first, he hadn't told the governor this. After all, he thought, *Who the hell am I to recommend replacing an elected official? The people of Queens chose this man.* Cuomo had reminded him of that on several occasions. "It would be legally wrong and morally wrong," was the phrase the governor used. Unless fraud or malice were found. And they hadn't been. Just what they felt was bungling. Thus, the appointment of a special prosecutor was not the governor's choice. Until now.

As Cuomo and his staff walked from the helicopter to the limousine that would take them to the governor's Manhattan offices at 2 World Trade Center, Kurlander reviewed the previous forty-eight hours, the two days that had changed everyone's mind:

It began Sunday afternoon, with a call from a reporter. Kurlander was relaxing in front of the television set at his home in the Albany suburb of Loudonville, looking forward to the New York Football Giants playoff game against the Washington Redskins. Just as the Redskins were kicking off, the State phone line buzzed. It was Fred Dicker, the Albany reporter for the *New York Post. How did he get this number?* Kurlander wondered as the journalist identified himself.

"Larry, I'm hearing that John Santucci is going to request a special prosecutor in the Howard Beach case."

"Who did you hear that from?" asked Kurlander.

The reporter wouldn't divulge his source.

"That's really interesting that you're hearing that," Kurlander said. "Because I ain't hearing that."

Kurlander hung up to give himself time to think.

Then *Newsday* called. And the *Times.* Finally, the *Daily News.* Each reporter was "hearing" the same rumor. One of the reporters told Kurlander that its source was Santucci himself. Kurlander's initial anger quickly focused. *A trial balloon,* he thought. *He wants to see how he'll look if he abdicates.*

Perhaps this was the solution they needed—the governor, New York City. Relations with Santucci, though cordial, were stalled. Kurlander wanted one thing: Santucci's resignation. But the district attorney was familiar enough with Cuomo's thinking to realize that, as the chief elected law enforcement officer of Queens County, he held all the cards.

Now, however, Santucci was breaking the rules. He was going to the press.

Kurlander dialed the Executive Mansion.

"Governor, look, here's what's happening," he began. Cuomo said nothing as Kurlander outlined the latest development in the Howard Beach fiasco. "I'm going to keep my analysis short," Kurlander concluded. "Santucci and I have been in touch four times a day for the last two, three weeks. And now he's getting cute."

"Get the goddamn guy up here tomorrow morning, first thing," said Cuomo. "Send the helicopter down for him."

Kurlander called Santucci. "You got a hell of a nerve. You're leaking."

"No, I'm not."

"John, don't bullshit me. There'll be a helicopter for you at LaGuardia Airport at seven in the morning. There's a meeting scheduled with the governor. Be here."

"Larry, I can't come up at that time."

"John, there are no options. The governor is sending for you. You will be on the second floor at eight o'clock tomorrow morning. You do not have a choice." Santucci didn't catch the reference at first. Around the state capitol, the term "second floor" inspires fear in the governor's enemies and envy in his supporters. State senators and government administrators do not dally when called to the second floor. It is Albany patois meaning "business of the highest importance."

The conversation was by turns nasty and pathetic, with Kurlander harshly accusing Santucci of leaking, and the district attorney lamely denying the charge. Kurlander worked the rest of Sunday night. He spoke with David Dinkins, perhaps the most influential black leader in New York City. Then the governor spoke with Dinkins, feeling him out about my appointment.

The following morning John Santucci's limousine disgorged the district attorney, his executive assistant Thomas Russo, and his chief of homicide, Gregory Lasak, at the helipad at La-Guardia Airport. It was a bumpy, noisy flight. Santucci sat through it pensively, smoking a cigar. Lasak, bouncing around the wind-buffeted cabin, clearly not enjoying his first flight in a helicopter, was seen handling a set of rosary beads. Russo laughed at the homicide chief. It was the only time any of the three smiled. There was no conversation.

A state trooper picked up the Queens contingent at the Albany Airport and drove them to the Statehouse. Santucci spent the next three hours in room 245, Kurlander's office, behind closed doors. Then he saw Cuomo, who perfunctorily informed him that he wanted me to take over the prosecution of The Howard Beach Incident. It was said that Santucci was smiling as he walked out of the governor's office. The group flew back to Queens with a rabbi as company, a friend of the governor's. Lasak felt better. Then the aircraft returned to Albany, in order to fly Cuomo to New York the same day.

I left my house in Brooklyn at about the time Mario Cuomo was stepping into his helicopter. My Albany sources had told me about the governor's scheduled meeting with the city's black leadership. But it wasn't time yet for me to make an appearance. It was 6:45 A.M., the sun had not yet risen, and I jogged the four blocks to Bob Keating's home for our daily three-mile run. Robert G. M. Keating, a National Merit Scholar at Georgetown University and a graduate of Duke University's School of Law, was the chief administrative judge of the New York City Criminal Court System. We started our law careers together in the Criminal Division of the Legal Aid Society in Brooklyn. Keating joined the Brooklyn District Attorney's Office in April 1969, four months after I was appointed an assistant district attorney. He has been one of my closest friends ever since.

Over the past several weeks, as we jogged each morning, Keating and I had often discussed the investigation's implications. But today he must have sensed that I felt my duties were about to be expanded. Keating's jovial demeanor disguises an iron toughness, the result of losing his father, a city firefighter, at the age of five. In some way, his father's fatal heart attack left Keating with a gift for making judgments that were totally unclouded by emotion. His advice was always direct and incisive.

I told Keating what I knew about Cuomo's meeting with the black coalition. Characteristically, Keating went directly to the basic point.

"I think Mario's in deep shit on this one," he grunted. "You should stay out of it."

Mario Matthew Cuomo, elected as New York State's fifty-sixth governor in 1982, graduated first in his class from St. John's University School of Law in 1956. I was a junior in the university's undergraduate liberal arts department at the time. And although I graduated from the same law school five years later, another decade was to pass before I met Cuomo.

One Friday in 1971, after leaving the DA's office, Keating and I stopped for a beer at a Brooklyn lawyers' oasis on Court Street known as The Brewery. Keating was then Brooklyn district attorney Eugene Gold's chief of the Supreme Court Bureau, and I was Gold's Rackets Bureau chief. We were still on our first beer when a tall, somewhat chubby guy began to talk to us about Gold's operation. He introduced himself as Mario Cuomo, a partner in a prestigious—by Brooklyn standards—law firm.

The three of us hit it off right away, and over the next four years we met almost weekly, solving the world's problems at our own version of the Algonquin Round Table at The Brewery. Despite Cuomo's rather patrician standing in private practice, he always seemed to be "one of the guys." Over the years, as he assumed the governorship and became a national leader of the Democratic Party, our relationship had not changed.

After my run with Keating that morning, I stopped to buy the city's four newspapers. Howard Beach filled the news sections. The tension caused by the incident and its aftermath had begun to escalate around New Year's Day. Now, New York City was holding its collective breath.

In *The New York Times* I read a story in which Larry Kurlander was hinting at the imminent appointment of a special prosecutor. A *New York Newsday* editorial demanded: "Name a Special Prosecutor."

Even more than Keating, my wife, Pat, has been my most insightful adviser for twenty-five years. When I walked into the house, the newspapers under my arm, I didn't have to say a word. She read the look on my face.

"If they want you to be involved in this," she said, "just make sure you want it"

"What do you think?"

A wry smile crossed Pat's face. "It's your decision."

At 8:30 A.M. I arrived at my office, and five minutes later I placed my first call, to Joe Bellacosa, an associate judge of the New York State Court of Appeals. Joe, an ex-seminarian, has been a friend since our law school days; he's godfather to my second son, Sean, and I'm godfather to his second boy, Peter.

I've relied on Joe for sound advice for thirty years. Unlike Saul of Tarsus, the ex-Pharisee who wove his legalistic training into his proselytizing, Bellacosa's law judgment has not been influenced by his youthful stint in the seminary.

I asked Joe, "What if I was offered the Howard Beach case as special prosecutor?"

"I think you'd be nuts to take it," was Bellacosa's firm and immediate reply.

That made it two negatives, one assent (I liberally counted my wife's smile as an aye).

As I did every morning, I convened a nine o'clock meeting of my senior staff, sometimes referred to around the office as the "Sanhedrin," after the sixteenth-century supreme council of the post-exile Jews. I may have been appointed the high priest of the Special State Prosecutor's Office, but I'm the opposite of a loner and I prefer to "talk things through" with my staff and friends. Some call it the collaborative approach to leadership. Our office is something like the locker room of a winning football team, complete with nicknames, good-natured ethnic needling, and shouting matches, in this case, over legal theory.

S. Michael Nadel served as my counsel. The former director of personnel for the City of New York under Mayor Koch, Nadel was also a former deputy counsel to Governor Hugh Carey, who subsequently left my office to become a Criminal Court judge. Nadel has the body of a small linebacker and the smarts of a head coach. His political judgment is as fine-tuned as any person's I know. I always counted on Nadel to locate the land mines before I stepped on them.

Helman Brook, another member of my inner council, has been a friend since my Brooklyn district attorney days. Brook's thin, wiry frame and ever placid demeanor disguises a toughness bred on the streets of Birmingham, Alabama. He served as Gene Gold's chief of the Appeals Bureau before joining my office as my First Assistant. Before that, Brook also served as the chief legal adviser to the Appellate Division of the State Supreme Court, where he had the final responsibility for advising the judges on the law. He was, obviously, the man I went to when I had to straighten out the office's thorny legal questions.

Hillel Hoffman, another old friend, and Matt Greenberg were

Brook's main support staff. Hoffman, always in perpetual motion, looked the kind of man any mother on the street would immediately come over to cuddle, served with me when I held a statewide position as the special nursing home prosecutor. And the gray-haired and bookish Greenberg, a former professor at New York Law School, also worked for me during the nursing home investigations. The three are considered among the brightest appellate attorneys in the State of New York.

The Sanhedrin also included Dennis Hawkins, our resident longhair, whose face has broken a thousand hearts. Hawkins was my counsel when I was New York City fire commissioner. Finally, the group was completed by Richard Mangum, a burly black man possessed of a quick wit and an iron will who is a former Queens County prosecutor and holds a master's degree in social work. Hawkins and Mangum were the pragmatic members of my tribunal, the street-hardened counterpoints to the appellate eggheads.

For the next hour, we debated the pros and cons of accepting the Howard Beach case. There was a tremor of excitement rumbling through the office, and if Cuomo was indeed going to call on us, we wanted to be prepared to hit the street running. Possible legal strategies were discussed, potential assignments kicked around.

"During that entire meeting you acted as if accepting the position was still up in the air," Mangum told me later. "But every one of us sitting at that table knew you had already made your decision. No one was going to talk you out of the job."

Since my appointment in 1985, the legal staff of the Special Prosecutor's Office had been doubled, the result in large part of the 77th Precinct scandal, which reminded many people of the abuses the Knapp Commission uncovered in the early 1970s. In addition to the six members of the Sanhedrin, I called in three other lawyers to work with me should the Howard Beach case be assigned to our office. And I hand-picked fifteen investigators, including my chief investigator, Al Pica, a former sergeant in the New York City Police Department's Internal Affairs Division, and Detective Doug LeVien, who was on loan to me from the department. LeVien, one of the best police officers I have ever met, had worked with me at various times since I headed the Rackets Bureau.

I spent the rest of the morning dividing my time between routine office work and preparation for an afternoon disciplinary hearing. For the past four years I had been a member of the Disciplinary Committee of the First Judicial Department of the Appellate Division in Manhattan, a committee that hears and resolves allegations of attorney misconduct and makes recommendations to the Appellate Court. Today's session was scheduled for 2:00 P.M.

At noon, Keating called to invite me to lunch at Joanna's, a yuppy restaurant on Manhattan's Lower West Side. The "Irish Mafia," another group of close friends who have particularly sound judgment, was convening. The group included Bob Tierney, an executive with AT&T and former Counsel to Mayor Koch, and Timothy J. Russert (always referred to as "Timothy J."), a political wizard who had worked for both United States Senator Daniel Patrick Moynihan and Governor Cuomo, and was now an executive vice-president at NBC News. The four of us would be joined by Nadel, our token non-Gael.

On the drive to Joanna's my beeper went off. Catherine Schauf, one of my secretaries, informed me on the car phone that I had an urgent call from Larry Kurlander. I like Kurlander, but he is a character right out of a Graham Greene novel, a spy with a high-collared trenchcoat speaking in muted, breathless tones. On occasion I've found myself leaning so close to hear this quiet American's conspiratorial whispers that I've been sprawled across a table. Some day he'll make CIA director by virtue of his delivery alone.

"Joe, is this a safe phone?" he asked.

"No."

"Then take this number, and call right away."

I recognized it as Governor Cuomo's direct line in Manhattan. Without thinking, I blurted, "Holy shit."

My driver, an ex-cop by the name of Tom Mulvihill, swiveled his head slowly. "Pardon me?"

"Nothing, Tom. Get me to a pay phone fast, please."

The phone rang twice. "Governor? Joe."

"Joe, how would you feel about letting someone supervise your staff in the Howard Beach case?"

I could feel the anger instantly well up inside me, but I managed to reply in a controlled voice: "You're the governor, and I will do whatever you want. I believe I have the best lawyers and the best investigators in the system. But I was the one who hired them, and they're loyal to me. I think it would be a mistake to put somebody else in charge—but, as I say, you're the boss."

"Goodbye," Cuomo said. I knew his curtness wasn't a sign of peevishness. He just doesn't go in for small talk.

Whatever his intention—and I still wasn't sure—he got his answer. I was honest and gave him my gut reaction. If the case was going to the special state prosecutor's staff, I wanted to control it. Over lunch, as I related the governor's call and the purpose of his meeting to the Irish Mafia, Keating got to the Machiavellian heart of the matter (I believe he carries *The Prince* in his briefcase). "You should have told him yes," he said. "If they come up a winner with someone else in charge, it's your hand-picked staff that handled it. If it's a loser, whoever's in charge takes the fall."

Classic Keating. Russert, on the other hand, seemed to sense that Cuomo was facing a dilemma.

"I think he wants you to head the investigation," said Timothy J. "But I'll bet the blacks don't want you because there's some problem. Maybe Breezy Point."

For nearly twenty-five years I have had a summer home in Breezy Point, a sandy tract of dunes and scrub grass at the rump end of Long Island (or the opposite end from the fashionable Hamptons). Until fifteen years ago, it was known as the Irish Riviera, an oceanfront mecca for city firefighters and cops. Today the community's composition is half Irish and half Italian, thanks, I like to think, to my marriage to Patricia Pennisi. Sixteen Jewish families summer in Breezy Point, as well as two families of Hispanic descent and several Asian families. There are no blacks in Breezy Point, a vestige of the tribal geography and sociology of New York City that rankled some of my critics.

Russert suggested that, because of the summer cottage, I would be perceived as "biased," whether I was or not, and the black leaders would have no choice but to reject me when Cuomo threw my name out.

My combative juices were flowing now. "What about Flatbush?" I asked. For fifty-one of my fifty-three years I have lived in the Flatbush section of Brooklyn, a neighborhood with the largest collection of Victorian-style homes in the United States. Flatbush was lily-white until 1970. Then black families began moving in and white flight resembled the roads to Dunkirk. By 1980 the neighborhood was 70 percent black. Today, I live on a rainbow block with six black families, four Jewish, two Italian, two Asian, two Latin, and two Irish.

Russert's keen reaction to my Flatbush defense theory was typical: "It probably doesn't matter anyway. Whatever Cuomo's going to do, he's already done, at least in his own mind."

I started pondering the scene in Cuomo's conference room. I knew who had been invited, and I was optimistic. I had a close relationship with Dinkins and a mutual respect existed between me and both former New York secretary of state Basil Paterson and his son, State Senator David Paterson. I hardly knew the Reverend Herbert Daughtry, a Brooklyn-based civil rights activist and outspoken opponent of the Police Department, and I had never met Brooklyn state assemblyman Roger L. Green, chairman of the Black and Puerto Rican Legislative Caucus. The Reverend Calvin Butts, pastor of the Abyssinian Baptist Church, was the wild card at this meeting, for I had been told he represented the interests of the recalcitrant attorneys Mason and Maddox.

My beeper interrupted my thoughts once again. I called my office and spoke with Rose Marie Pastore, who has been my secretary for eighteen years and treats my younger secretary, Catherine Schauf, like a daughter. As frenetic as I am, Rose is unflappable. "Mr. Kurlander wants you to call his number right away."

I did.

"Joe," Kurlander whispered into the phone, "where will you be this afternoon?"

My hearing at the Departmental Discipline Committee was

scheduled to begin at two, so I gave Larry the phone number
and told him I would arrange for any calls to be put through
immediately. "What's going on?" I asked him. And in his best
conspiratorial tone he replied, "I can't talk–talk about it."

The crew at Joanna's finished lunch speculating about the
outcome of Cuomo's meeting. Russert came around to Tierney's
way of thinking; he now felt the governor was probably selling
my case to the black leadership. He looked at me steadily.

"Joe," he said, "are you sure you want this?"

"Hey, it will be an adventure."

My answer was partly bravado and partly fact. To be honest,
I really didn't know. What I did understand was that it was going
to be one bitch of a case, primarily because of the involvement
of Mason and Maddox. I thought they would have to be handled
very carefully. Ironically, that was the part about which I was
dead wrong.

As I was to discover later, while the Irish Mafia played speculative games over our nouvelle cuisine, a dozen representatives of
the movement for a Howard Beach special prosecutor filed into
the governor's conference room on the fifty-seventh floor of 2
World Trade Center.

Singly and in pairs they entered: David Dinkins and his chief
of staff, Bill Lynch; the Patersons, father and son; Charles
McKinney, the director of Manhattan's Riverside Park; Assemblyman Green, whose caucus had a week earlier formally urged
Cuomo to appoint a special prosecutor to investigate the Howard Beach assault; the Reverends Daughtry and Butts. The coalition was received by Cuomo, Kurlander, Marty Steadman, and
Leonard Dunston, the head of New York State's Division for
Youth Agency, who for the past several weeks had acted as a
conduit between Kurlander and the city's black community.
Dunston had attended many of the protests staged around the
city, and he had even set up a secret preliminary meeting between Kurlander and Butts the previous week.

Cuomo's Manhattan offices are located in the southwest corner of 2 World Trade Center. The majestic conference room has
magnificent southern views of lower Manhattan, the Statue of

Liberty, Battery Park, and Governors Island. In 1983, when Governor Mario M. Cuomo succeeded to the statesmen's chair once held by Alfred E. Smith, Franklin D. Roosevelt, Thomas E. Dewey, and Nelson A. Rockefeller, the Italian government sent a ceremonial delegation to meet with the United States's first elected Italian-American governor. Cuomo's new offices were as yet bare, not even carpeted, and the Italians were clearly disappointed by the lack of pomp and ceremonial circumstance. To impress the disappointed delegation, Cuomo drew back the curtains in his conference room.

"And there's Governors Island," he proclaimed. The Italians were awed. Today's delegation would not be so easily impressed.

Coffee was served, as I learned later, and the governor, clad as usual in his standard blue pin-striped suit, greeted each guest with a handshake before taking his seat at the head of the table. He bantered with some of his guests about their old sandlot days. McKinney had once been a teammate of Cuomo's, and the two swapped baseball lies. Steadman, an avid fan, joined them as they recounted their gilded exploits on the diamonds of Queens, and Basil Paterson listed his favorite players. This informal aura didn't last long.

As the meeting opened, Cuomo asked each person to speak: "I'm here to listen to what's on your minds."

As expected, the black coalition renewed its demand for a permanent special prosecutor to investigate and try bias incidents. David Paterson was particularly eloquent, citing a litany of past racial crimes. "First," he said, "we had Michael Stewart. Then Eleanor Bumpurs. And now we have a black man named Michael Griffith sprawled dead across the highway in Howard Beach. The black community is still not receiving justice."

Paterson ceded the floor to Dinkins.

"Survival for blacks in New York is a daily struggle," the Manhattan borough president told the governor. "They have nowhere to go; there is uselessness and despair. Dealing with the criminal justice system sometimes seems to blacks as if they're being taken for a ride. And at the end of the ride they know they're going to be killed. What do you have to lose during the trip if you try to escape?"

Dinkins went on: "Why does there exist this inability to prose-cute police officers who we feel are guilty of being abusive or using excessive force? There's no shock or surprise in the black community when a police officer is brutal. In the case of Eleanor Bumpurs there was not even a crime, nor was there one alleged. The woman didn't pay her rent. That's a simple civil situation. And she was killed! These things make no sense to us.

"Now it's Howard Beach, and Howard Beach is so raw," he concluded. "This guy was chased to his death. It was a lynching by a mob. Governor, there has to be a resolution."

Governor Cuomo nodded in agreement. He explained his philosophical opposition to a permanent special prosecutor: he did not want to set any precedent. What would happen next time, when a governor whose policies they mistrusted decided to appoint a special prosecutor whom they might consider ra-cially insensitive? The history of the country's law enforcement is local law enforcement, he said. Only in extraordinary circum-stances was a special prosecutor appointed. However, he assured them, he *had* given some thought to the extraordinary circum-stances surrounding the case of Howard Beach.

The meeting went on, staying narrowly within the boundaries of cordiality, as David Paterson and Assemblyman Green con-tinued to press for a permanent special prosecutor.

There was no break for lunch, but there were several cau-cuses. One occurred when the governor put my name forth to conduct the Howard Beach investigation. Calvin Butts asked if Cuomo would consider appointing an outsider who would be allowed to run my staff. As the delegation bandied about names, Cuomo and his people left the room, and that's when my beeper went off for the first time.

When the governor returned to the conference room he told the group he was leaning toward my appointment, and the Rev-erend Butts asked, "If Hynes is appointed, will he be trying the case himself?"

"That's up to Hynes," said Cuomo, who sat still for several moments as more names were thrown out. When it became apparent that a quorum could not be reached, the coalition turned to the governor once more. "If there are no objections," he said, "I'm going to appoint Joe Hynes as special prosecutor to handle the balance of the Howard Beach case."

The governor and his staff left the room once again to allow the coalition to caucus. That's when Kurlander beeped me at lunch to ask where I'd be for the rest of the day. When they returned, Butts told the governor, "I'm sorry, sir, but Mr. Hynes is unacceptable."

During the break, I was to learn, Butts had telephoned Mason and Maddox, who told him I had once defended two white firefighters accused of assaulting a black female co-worker. They told Butts that I had been rough on the woman during cross-examination, neglecting to mention that my cross-examination style is similar to Maddox's own.

Cuomo exploded. Dark eyes shining, he stood up and pounded his fist on the oak table.

"I'm not going to walk out of this room and brand Joe Hynes a racist," the governor said in a menacing tone. "This is not negotiable. It's Joe Hynes or it's John Santucci. That's your choice. No more negotiations. I will not end this man's career because somebody is going to walk out of this room and tell the media what went on, and Hynes will be branded a racist. Absolutely not."

Mario Cuomo likes to say he does not become angry, he merely becomes more forceful. I wonder if anyone in that room, after seven hours of negotiation, could have told the difference.

"Why don't you discuss it among yourselves," he told the black coalition.

Fifteen minutes later Butts addressed Cuomo: "Governor, we accept Joe Hynes."

Steadman, who had worked for Cuomo for three years, turned to Larry Kurlander and smiled. "I believe," he said, "we have just witnessed the governor's finest hour."

Cuomo called Santucci personally to formally announce my appointment, and while the governor and the black delegation met the press in the World Trade Center lobby, Kurlander called Mason.

"It's Hynes, Vernon, as you probably already know," he said.

"Listen, he's a decent guy. He's an honorable guy. Please meet with him and cooperate."

Mason, who first wanted to confer with Maddox, said he'd consider it.

The governor flew back to Albany that evening.

The proceedings of the disciplinary committee began about five after two, and I confess I had trouble focusing during the first hour. No calls for me. During a five-minute break, one of my colleagues, a black lawyer named Nick Cherot, asked rather casually, "So, are you going to get involved in that Howard Beach mess?"

I gave him my only possible reply. "You never can tell." He smiled and shook his head, as if he felt sorry for me.

At 4:00 P.M., with still no call, I decided to recess the hearing at 4:30. Suddenly the door opened and a committee secretary hurried over with a note: "Governor Cuomo is on the line."

I called a five-minute adjournment and rushed to the phone.

"Joe," said the governor, "will you take over the Howard Beach case?"

"Yes, sir."

"Joe, do the job."

He hung up.

I called my office immediately. Catherine answered. "Do we have it?"

"Yes. Tell the A-Team to be ready to meet at five-thirty," I said.

The A-Team was a subsection of the Sanhedrin: nine lawyers, each uniquely qualified by training, experience, and personality to handle tough, complicated cases and bonded by a shared appreciation of the free rein I gave them to do their jobs. They were the same lawyers with whom I had investigated and prosecuted the 77th Precinct scandal, and the nickname—after the multiracial, multiethnic television characters—had been created late one night during a particularly giddy trial strategy session. Having worked so well together on the 77th Precinct case, they had to be my choice now.

In addition to my appellate people—Brook, Hoffman, and Greenberg—and my street people—Nadel, Hawkins, and Mangum—the A-Team consists of Martin Hershey, Ed Boyar, and Pamela Hayes.

Marty Hershey's age is slowly creeping up on his golf score: he's sixty-two. He is an expert skier, spending each December vacationing and moonlighting as a ski instructor in Aspen, Colorado. The former Aspen chief of police, Marty was once the Brooklyn district attorney's chief of narcotics, and his energy level and athletic life-style combine to make him a superb investigative lawyer.

Ed Boyar, another alumnus of the Brooklyn DA's Office, is regarded as one of the best prosecuting trial attorneys in the city. He is also my rock-ribbed conservative; disappointed by the Goldwater debacle and elated by the subsequent Nixon landslide, he didn't come to terms with Watergate until Ronald Reagan's second administration. The lone right-winger among my office's eclectic collection of liberals, he is the type of guy who will consume himself for weeks preparing for a trial, and then disappear on a fishing expedition into the jungles of Brazil or the coves of Iceland when it's over.

Pamela Hayes is a young black woman who worked for a spell as the law secretary to the chief administrative judge of the Manhattan Criminal Court. The staff idealist, she believes deeply in the brotherhood of our species and spends much of her spare time working with her local Catholic parish in Harlem, where she lives. If the A-Team found its intellect in Brook, Hoffman, Greenberg, and Nadel, its legal skills in Hershey and Boyar, and its street-smart pragmatism in Mangum and Hawkins, then its soul was definitely in Pamela Hayes.

The combination is the best law firm I've ever worked with. For the year and a half prior to Howard Beach, the A-Team was responsible for twenty-four convictions and no acquittals.

By the time I arrived at 2 Rector Street at five o'clock, the block was full of television vans. Upstairs, my secretary Rose told me that the conference room was filling up with reporters. The governor had held a joint press conference with the black coalition to announce my appointment.

"This is a special episode that has lifted tensions to a special level," Cuomo had told the media. "It requires a special response."

Characteristically, when Cuomo was asked about the length of the investigation, he shrugged and answered, "Go see Hynes." They had rushed to my office that afternoon. Unfortunately, no one thought to warn me.

I gathered the A-Team, our first order of business being how to fend off the growing press corps outside the door. I don't like prosecutorial press conferences, and I refuse to hold them. They inevitably turn into carnivals of misinformation and have little to do with informing the public. Yet I do believe the public has a right to know how one of its agencies works, and the Special State Prosecutor's Office qualified as such. Now, with the Howard Beach case, we were an extremely public agency.

Balancing the two ideals is a delicate task. The staff consensus was that the most useful information I could give the press was that the victims had agreed to cooperate with the special prosecutor. Yet I wouldn't know that for sure until I spoke with the lawyers for Sandiford and Grimes. I didn't know Maddox personally, but Pam Hayes did, in a casual way, and she volunteered to call. I decided instead to phone Mason, whom I had met on occasion at lawyerlike social functions. The information operator gave me his office number and I dialed direct.

While the phone was ringing, a thought struck me. It was a simple idea, but, given the pressure-cooker atmosphere surrounding this case, it just might be the right dramatic touch. We would schedule the initial meeting with the Howard Beach race-attack victims in Vernon Mason's Manhattan office. It was something a prosecutor would never do. You always make them come to your home court.

Mason's secretary put my call through to him, and I immediately recognized the soft Southern drawl of his Arkansas boyhood. Mason, a Columbia Law School graduate, had been offered numerous jobs in wealthy corporate firms but had refused them all in order to continue his public-interest work. He is smart, he is tough, and he is cynical.

"Mr. Hynes, how are you? Looks like you got yourself a package."

"I suppose. But that's what you expect when you have a friend like the governor. Mr. Mason, I'd like to see your client and Mr. Maddox's client as soon as possible."

There was a slight hesitation before he answered, "Okay." Then I played my trump. "Mr. Mason, where exactly is your office." There was a longer hesitation before he asked why I wanted to know.

"Because I think we should meet there. My office will be crawling with reporters for the next couple of days and I don't think we should meet here."

"Let me get this straight," an apparently dumbfounded Mason replied. "You all want to come over here? Mr. Hynes, let me get back to you."

I felt confident that very soon I would be meeting Mason and Maddox, Sandiford and Grimes. There was excitement in the thought. For up until now, like the rest of New York, I had no idea exactly what had transpired at Howard Beach. And I wanted to hear the story from the men who had been there.

The Investigation

9

CITY ON FIRE

Ten minutes after I offered to meet with the Howard Beach victims in C. Vernon Mason's lower Manhattan suite, Rose's voice on the intercom found me in my private office, where I was wondering what to tell the media gathered in our conference room.

"Mr. Mason on line one, Mr. Hynes."

"Joe, how is Thursday at five o'clock?"

This was Tuesday, and I told Mason that I'd prefer an earlier introduction. But he replied that he felt he and Alton Maddox would need the two days to prepare Cedric Sandiford and Timothy Grimes. *Prepare them for what?* I wondered, but I was not in a position to argue. I told him that was fine. Then I called Santucci's office; I wanted his files as soon as possible. His secretary told me he was out but she would track him down and see that he returned my call right away.

Now I could speak to the crowd of newspeople gathered next door.

"I can only tell you," I said, "that a few minutes ago C. Vernon Mason assured me that the Howard Beach victims will cooperate with my investigation."

I mentioned that initially I was assigning nine attorneys and six investigators to the case in an effort to conclude the investigation as quickly as possible. In the middle of a somewhat fruitless question-and-answer session, Catherine Schauf snuck in behind me and passed me a note: "DA Santucci on hold." I excused myself and left the room.

"Well, Joe," Santucci said, "your friend Mario sure stuck you with a doozy."

"That's life, John. Can I see you tomorrow morning to get the file?"

With an uncharacteristic stiffness, Santucci nearly shouted into the phone, "Of course, Joe. And I want to give you my absolute assurances that you will have the fullest cooperation of my staff."

Ever the alert politician, Santucci was already covering his tracks. I was positive he thought I was taping our conversation. We agreed to meet at his offices on Queens Boulevard the following morning at 9:00 A.M. Then I returned to the conference room to inform the reporters that I didn't have a hell of a lot more to say. Most were understanding; one or two snarled as they went out, expecting me to lay out my prosecutorial plan for the press.

The A-Team—plus investigators Al Pica and Doug LeVien— began working immediately. I assigned Hershey, Hawkins, Boyar, and Mangum to gather and read every newspaper account of the Howard Beach incident. Brook, Hoffman, and Greenberg were to begin the legal research. It was important for us to know just which legal precedents, if any, existed in order to bring manslaughter and murder charges against the group that chased Michael Griffith into the path of Dominick Blum's car. I told Nadel to coordinate both groups and to prepare for an in-house meeting at 6:00 P.M. tomorrow. Then I directed Pica to select five investigators to work with him, and to begin thinking about drafting at least ten others. Joe Romano, Pica's deputy, would run his end of the office while Al concentrated solely on Howard Beach.

Then I told Jim Kohler, my chief assistant, that for the duration of the Howard Beach investigation, he would be running the rest of the activities of the Office of the Special State Prosecutor. There were several investigations pending throughout the office, including some unfinished business in the 77th Precinct.

Kohler is a superb trial lawyer, and someone had to take care of the day-to-day business of the office. Nonetheless, I wanted Kohler to stay close to Howard Beach and would use him as an idea bank, for in the back of my mind I was toying with the idea of bringing Jim in to try this case. At this stage, I had no intention at all of walking the Howard Beach case into court myself. My courtroom skills, I told myself, were too rusty.

Finally, I informed everyone in the office that there would be no time off permitted until this investigation was concluded. Evenings and weekends would be spent on the case. This one was too hot to let slide for even a day. And work we did, day and night, with only minimal grumbling, for the next twenty-eight days.

I told Pam Hayes that she would go with me the following morning to meet with Santucci's staff. At that early point in the investigation, Hayes was the only member of my staff with any hands-on experience concerning Howard Beach. She often mentioned that she would not have been shocked if the attack had taken place in her mother's hometown in north Georgia or her father's in western Virginia. But this was Queens, New York, and she'd urged me from the beginning to become involved. At the same time, she'd been monitoring the protests that followed The Incident.

The Brooklyn-based Reverend Al Sharpton was still more than a year away from a story in *New York Newsday* which charged that he trafficked with Mob figures and worked undercover for the Federal Bureau of Investigation informing on fellow black leaders. As early as Sunday afternoon, the day after the attack, Sharpton led a rally against, of all places, New Park Pizzeria.

About twenty demonstrators picketed the pizzeria, whose bewildered countermen were already receiving death threats.

"We come not with hate or anger," Sharpton was quoted as saying, "but to let the people of Howard Beach know that we are not going to run again, that we are not going to allow them to beat us into the ground." *With stale pizza crusts?* I wondered. Then, with others, he called for a citywide boycott on pizza. In New York, this was like asking for a citywide boycott of breathing.

A few days later, his pizza boycott having fizzled, the un-flappable Sharpton rallied his troops for a protest march on Ben-jamin Ward's residence in Queens. Unfortunately for the march-ers, for it was a very cold day, their leaders did not have the police commissioner's address. The demonstrators wandered aimlessly through the back roads of the borough and then drifted away.

But Sharpton's follies were far from the only reaction of the black community to The Incident. At a fund-raising rally at Brooklyn's Boys and Girls High School, which Kurlander asked Leonard Dunston to attend, Dunston recalled several speakers' telling demonstrators to "dip into your wallets and pull out money, but pretend it's a nine-millimeter that we're going to put to Santucci's head."

And three days after the Howard Beach assault, two nights before Christmas, a white teenager walking home from school through the Jamaica section of Queens was attacked and beaten by a gang of black youths chanting, "This is for Howard Beach." He told detectives that at least forty blacks had punched and kicked him to the ground, and his face on the televised news reports the next day was a bloody mess. Queens investigators soon rounded up the gang, whose leaders had also shown up on television, bragging about the revenge assault. But on orders from Santucci's office, detectives later told me, they were or-dered to arrest only three of the blacks, "because that's how many of the white kids got arrested in Howard Beach."

On the evening Judge Bianchi dropped murder charges against Lester, Ladone, and Kern at the controversial open hear-ing, Ward assigned additional patrols—thirteen uniformed of-ficers and nine plainclothes officers—to Howard Beach, citing the possibility of racial tension. Koch called the police action protection for "the people of Howard Beach, who might have a problem with other people coming in to vent their anger."

With the emotion building, the clergy attempted to step in. In a special Christmas Day plea, the Catholic churches of Howard Beach urged their parishioners to join with black Catholics at the New Park Pizzeria the following afternoon for a prayer service with "Reconciliation and Healing" as the theme. The gathering went off halfheartedly, and to this day rumors persist that at St. Helen's and Our Lady of Grace, Howard Beach's two Catholic churches, the collection plates of the more "liberal" priests dropped considerably.

At Our Lady of Charity Catholic Church in Bedford-Stuyvesant on the night after Christmas, more than six hundred people, some spilling out into the streets, heard Michael Griffith eulogized. Underscoring the tension in the Brooklyn community, Father Robert Seay, a Franciscan priest, concluded his sermon with a plea for racial harmony:

"It makes no sense to go out of here and hate. We do not know the reason this violence has been committed. And we cannot discover that tonight."

Even Mayor Koch sought to use the religious community to help quell emotions. On Sunday, December 28, the mayor made appearances at two churches, seeking to open an "honest dialogue" between the races. At Our Lady of Grace in Howard Beach, Koch was jeered by about two hundred white parishioners. "You're not the mayor of all of us," one woman screamed. In the Morningstar Missionary Baptist Church in the predominantly black St. Albans neighborhood of Queens, the polite applause that greeted the mayor's plea for racial harmony was figuratively drowned out by the rumblings in the street, where a crowd of blacks had gathered to chant, "No justice, no peace."

New York City school students were on Christmas vacation when the attack occurred. But educators cut short their holidays and rushed to open "interracial student dialogues," asking their pupils to forgo a few hours of vacation time and attend. Few did. City school officials made plans for heightened security when classrooms reopened on January 5.

"Our schools will not be turned into armed camps," then–Schools Chancellor Nathan Quinones said after a New Year's Day meeting with high school principals. "However, that doesn't mean that we shouldn't be taking necessary safeguards should something go awry."

One of those safeguards would be a "very subtle police presence" in and around the halls of academe when the new term began. "We're not coming in with the SWAT team," said a community school board president named George Russo, whose district included Howard Beach. "But we want to assure the parents that we're watching the situation."

By the first week of the new year, thirty incidents of racial bias—ranging from harassing telephone calls to physical attacks—had been reported to the police. This was an extraordinary number, and its implications were certainly being felt in Albany. For it was amid this backlash that I received my not-so-subtle warning from Albany to keep an eye on the Howard Beach case.

I therefore had thought it politic to send Pam Hayes to the news conference Maddox and Mason had staged for Cedric Sandiford at the Reverend Butts's Abyssinian Baptist Church on Saturday, January 3, the meeting Detective Hammond had nearly been forced to attend. Hayes and Maddox knew each other from the Criminal Court system, and Maddox had executed a will for Pamela's aunt. I was sure her presence at the church wouldn't be a problem, so I sent her up to Harlem with Les Smith, one of our black investigators.

"Do you want me to talk to Alton?" she asked me before leaving.

"If you can," I told her. At the time, Hayes viewed Mason and Maddox as crusaders battling for the disenfranchised. I was among those with a more realistic view of the two. But there was nothing wrong with having a preliminary parley, and Pam's idealism certainly wouldn't hurt.

That night, the second-floor meeting room in the stately Abyssinian Baptist Church, one of Harlem's oldest congregations, filled quickly with demonstrators, reporters, and cameramen. A private conversation was nearly impossible. As more and more people squeezed into the room, Maddox careened over some sort of psychological edge and began screaming at the white reporters to "get the fuck out!" This shocked both the media and Pam Hayes.

"We don't need the honky press no more!" shouted Maddox, who hinted darkly that next time steps would be taken to keep any white reporters away from his news conferences.

"I've never seen him like that," Pam told me later. "I'd always thought of him, I'd always seen him, as a diligent, low-key attorney. Here he was using all this foul-mouthed language, talking about killing all the honkies, and there just wasn't any sense in continuing our conversation. I didn't think he could get crazy like that. He was very upset."

Soon, I thought, I would be working with this man. Philosophically, I understood the point Mason and Maddox were trying to make: they were ushering in a new era of militancy and nationalism among black activists and were using the Howard Beach attack to spearhead their "black consciousness" strategy.

On the day Sandiford vowed not to cooperate with Santucci, Maddox met with a small group of black reporters in a tiny back room of the Abyssinian Baptist Church and told them that black activists throughout the city were "developing an agenda that is bigger than Michael Griffith," an agenda that included sharpening the lines between "friends" and "enemies" of the black community. "Never again will we lose our children," Maddox told them. "It would be better that we would all be eliminated today than for us to continue living like we're living in this city and this state."

That attitude, that wider agenda, was to make this more than an investigation and trial of a crime. The crime itself was being viewed by many (black *and* white) as a metaphor for the experience of blacks in New York and other American cities. At that time, Mason and Maddox were a formidable combination within the black community, pushing hard for their agenda. The Reverend Herbert Daughtry, one of the most vocal black leaders, praised the attorneys for "bringing together some of the nationalist elements" among New York blacks. And he underlined the point that many of the city's established black leaders (most of them based in Manhattan) had not yet joined in the "coalescing" around the attorneys. As was true in many other parts of the city's multiethnic crazy quilt, younger challengers were going up against the Establishment; it was part of the permanent dynamic of New York's politics. Mason and Maddox were not simply confronting the white power structure (as they called it) but the black establishment too.

This conflict was never more apparent than when the Reverend Jesse Jackson came to town the Sunday before the birthday of Martin Luther King, Jr. Mason and Maddox had organized a day-long boycott of white-owned business establishments and a march down Fifth Avenue. The object was to protest Howard Beach in particular and racism in general. Several days before this scheduled "Day of Outrage," Jackson, still a strong presidential candidate, spoke at Manhattan's historic Trinity Church.

When asked about the planned boycott and march, Jackson told a group of reporters, "I do not choose to react to that strategy. I don't want to be used as a symbol for division by those who would exploit the situation."

But the following day he "amended" his position. "If the community plans to march and boycott as a tactic, it is their right, and that right must be upheld," he said from his home in Chicago. "They have a right to resist lynching, and psychologically, it is a way of releasing their pain."

Initially, Jackson seemed leery of aligning his "Rainbow Coalition" with the ominous, sometimes separatist or nationalist tone of this new black agenda. Sonny Carson, the Brooklyn activist, hinted at the possibilities when he told a group of reporters, "People who feel they can continue to disrespect the black community are in for a surprise very soon. There are a lot of tires around this city."

At that time in South Africa, young blacks were killing those suspected of collaborating with the white authorities by placing automobile tires around their necks and setting them afire. So Carson was speaking subtly, but also making himself clear. And as I absorbed all this, I understood that the Howard Beach case was a true mine field. It seemed as if I had as much to worry about from those who wanted justice as I did from those who were insisting on their innocence.

But as I drove home that first night after being assigned to the case, I pondered more than the moral, political, and social implications of the assault in Howard Beach. I was even more concerned about the practical task of prosecuting the attackers. I was afraid that after twenty-six days, the trail might be cold. A month is a long time to give a criminal to cover himself, and I

had no doubt that the participants in that white mob were crimi-
nals. At home that evening, Pat's advice was, as always, sanguine.

"Give it your best shot. You've got terrific people. And besides," she added, "you're lucky."

10

WHY ME?

She was, of course, right. To come to this place, I'd needed more than the usual run of Irish luck. The tragic Charles Stewart Parnell once called the passion for history an Irish failing. I disagree. In the full heat of the present, I often find solace, and sometimes a solution, by examining the difficulties of the past. I suppose this is what they mean by learning from experience.

Often, the first thing I remember when I'm in a tough spot is my mother's screams. She is screaming, *You rotten bastard, you rotten bastard,* over and over again. And I see my father standing over her, swaying, the smell of cheap whiskey oozing from every pore. My mother is in her pajamas. Her face is covered with blood.

I am four years old.

I hear her yelling, *Aiken, come back, Aiken, come back.* But I'm out the door of the apartment house on Ocean Parkway and 18th Avenue in Flatbush—about ten blocks from where Pat and I now live. I hurry down the steps of our sixth-floor walkup to the ground-floor apartment of Dr. Wechsler. It is very early in the morning, perhaps two or three o'clock, and the doctor opens the door and I blurt out, *My mommy is hurt!*

That terrible night was a half a century ago, but it remains as vivid and frightening today as it was then. I never forgave my father. I suppose, like all young men, I wanted to. But he never did anything for the rest of his life that allowed me to forgive him.

My mother, Jean, was the daughter of Irish Catholic parents who landed in Boston near the turn of the century and settled in the Dorchester section of Massachusetts. I was baptized Charles Aiken Hynes, after my mother's father, Charles Cornelius Drew, who was a proud member of the Irish Republican Army back in County Cork. Aiken is a rare Irish name, and since I was not particularly fond of either of my given names, I chose Joe as my confirmation name when I was twelve years old. After that—and until the day she died, in November 1975—my mother refused to call me anything other than Joseph.

After leaving Dorchester for Brooklyn in 1928, Jean Drew became a real estate broker in an age when there were few women professionals and fewer people to complain to about gender bias. She made that one terrible mistake: she married a drunk and a wife-beater. But that experience made her an extremely tough woman, with a leathery character encompassing an iron will. She was tough; she was not, however, hard. And in her soul she never lost her deep compassion for those she called "unlucky." She and her brother Dan were the first college graduates from the Drew family, and virtually from the day of my birth, she directed me upon a path of education and Catholicism which would, of course, include college, and, if she had any say in it, law school.

Yet for all Jean Drew's inner strength, she couldn't draw blood from a stone. She moved to New York in 1938, and my academic career, from grammar school through law school, could be most charitably described by the term "undistinguished." At least that's the word an academic would employ while perusing my grades. Though that bothered me when I was a younger man, it doesn't seem to matter much anymore. I understand now that if it hadn't been for my mother's will and intelligence, I wouldn't have amounted to much of anything.

I was consoled about my own academic failings to learn later that in 1956, when Mario Cuomo graduated first in his class from St. John's University School of Law, his job application was rejected by fifty-two law firms. In those days, bigotry was not confined to matters of skin pigmentation. Five years later, graduating near the bottom of the 1961 class, the best employment I could manage was a job as a claims adjuster for the Allstate Insurance Company.

The following year, despite a second defeat at the hands of the New York State Bar Examiners, I landed a position with a small but very respected admiralty-law firm called Dorsey, Burke and Griffin. My employment on prestigious Wall Street was a sort of short-lived Valhalla. Leo Dorsey had been Governor Franklin Delano Roosevelt's patronage chief. Morgan Burke was knighted by the Italian government for settling all of the claims against the *Andrea Doria,* the liner that collided with the freighter *Stockholm* and sank off the Nantucket coast in 1956. And William Griffin was the quintessential corporate lawyer, formerly general counsel to the Baltimore and Ohio Railroad. Griffin was the partner to whom I was assigned as an associate. The firm was a classroom for me, although the lesson it taught did not fully sink in until thirty years later: specifically, that I was not fated to toil in private practice.

During the summer of 1963 I met a former law school classmate who worked for the Legal Aid Society's Criminal Division. Several weeks later I fulfilled the long-forgotten pledge of my high school yearbook and became a criminal lawyer. It was in this milieu, after seventeen years of education and another two of floundering among the corporate types, that I found myself. Becoming a criminal lawyer was, for me, what being ordained as a priest was to other Irish kids.

After spending seven months in the Lower, or Criminal, Courts in Manhattan and Brooklyn, I skyrocketed to the Brooklyn Supreme Court, fully six months ahead of the other lawyers who had joined Legal Aid with me. At this point in my life, I felt I had it all. I fell in love with and married Patricia Lee Pennisi, the daughter of a master cabinetmaker from Foggia, Italy, and a hairdresser from Ebersbach, Germany. And while I was trying cases before the Brooklyn Supreme Court, Pat, a registered nurse, became pregnant with the first of our five children. I cannot imagine what life would have become for me without her constant encouragement and incredibly precise judgment. She was and is my best friend.

During that exciting period, stalking in and out of courtrooms, representing indigents for Legal Aid, I took seventy-five jury trials to verdict over seventeen months. Added to the hundreds of misdemeanor trials I experienced in the lower courts, I attained the kind of hands-on legal experience that is impossible in today's criminal justice system, which is so densely clogged by backlogged cases.

By 1965 I had begun a private practice in Brooklyn. The money wasn't bad, but the excitement of trial was limited. The rule of thumb in this type of practice was the plea-bargain, and I would actually take a case to trial only six or seven times a year. By 1968 I was restless. As fortune would have it, that was the year I met Eugene Gold, who was to become the district attorney of Brooklyn.

Eugene Gold was one of those protean human beings about whom it is difficult to say anything brief. But this I can say clearly: After my mother, Jean, and my wife, Pat, Gene Gold was to become the third major influence in my life. Nominated to the district attorney's post in 1968 by the Brooklyn Democratic machine, Gold, an accomplished criminal-trial attorney, was determined to depoliticize and professionalize the office. Although the Brooklyn Prosecutor's Office had been directed in the past by such legal stars as William O'Dwyer (later a controversial mayor of New York), Myles F. McDonald, and Edward Silver, the Brooklyn DA's office in 1968 was the personal fiefdom of the legal wing of the Kings County Democratic Committee. As such, it was subject to the politics of the clubhouse.

Before taking the job, Gold was the junior partner in a law firm headed by William Kleinman, a retired U.S. Army colonel. "The Colonel," as he was known, was one of the last of a brilliant breed of New York trial attorneys whose ranks included Samuel Lebowitz, famous for his "Scottsboro Boys" defense in Alabama, and William Fallon, known as "The Great Mouthpiece." (Fallon, who was known to gulp a glass a bourbon or two for breakfast, once replied to a judge who smelled liquor wafting through his courtroom, "Your Honor, if your sense of justice is a keen as your sense of smell, then you will surely grant my client bail." Bail was granted.) And while Gold was only a junior partner in Kleinman's firm, he was nonetheless an integral component. It was said in the legal community that Gold supplied the brains while The Colonel supplied the bullshit.

In 1968, when Gold became the Brooklyn district attorney, he shocked more than a few observers with his independence. Since Gold had been the legal adviser to the bosses of the Brooklyn political machine, it was felt that he would be specifically obligated to two people: Stanley Steingut, speaker of the State Assembly, and Brooklyn Democratic political boss Meade H. Esposito. They would load the office with men they chose. It would be business as usual. It didn't exactly work out that way.

It was a huge surprise when, immediately after his thundering election to the district attorney's post, Gold placed an unprecedented advertisement in *The New York Law Journal* seeking quality attorneys with no connection to politics. And he was serious. Gold rejected no politically active lawyer who was otherwise qualified. But he directed each of his newly hired attorneys to take a pledge stating that he or she would refrain from political activity during the term of appointment. If not precisely Jacobin, this was certainly a radical change in the hiring practices of the Brooklyn District Attorney's Office.

In two years I went from being the Brooklyn district attorney's principal trial assistant to his confidential assistant, and, in September 1970, Gold promoted me to chief of his Rackets Bureau, where I jumped from investigating knife-wielding punks to the big-time of crime: the Mafia and police corruption. Both fell under the domain of the Rackets Bureau. My predecessors in the Rackets Bureau post had taken the Stanley Baldwin–Neville Chamberlain approach to crime-busting. Mob figures and rogue cops prevailed, and Brooklyn appeared to be controlled by the underworld. The inability and unwillingness of the Rackets Bureau to aggressively investigate both the Mob and the dirty cops had made the Rackets Bureau the joke of the District Attorney's Office and points beyond.

When I took over there were eight assistant district attorneys working Rackets, and I was stunned at their sense of complacency. They seemed satisfied with their image, and felt their dismal lack of will was a concession to political reality.

Two years later, the Rackets Bureau of Kings County contained eighteen of the best and the brightest of Gold's recruits
and an impressive list of indictments and convictions. We
smashed the police gambling pad in Brooklyn's 13th Division,
indicting twenty-four officers, or 70 percent of the command, for
accepting monthly bribes from gamblers, and soon the Brooklyn
DA's Rackets Bureau was receiving national attention, due
largely to the revelation that we had successfully planted a
court-ordered listening device in the trailer of a Canarsie junk-
yard, which was in reality the headquarters for Paulie Vario,
consigliere of the Luchese crime family. The conversations we
picked up on the "Gold Bug," as the media dubbed our microphone, involved hundreds of mobsters from all five of New York
City's organized-crime families. As impressive as our subsequent
grand jury investigation was, the Gold Bug is still largely recalled
for the fact that we went eighteen months manning the listening
device without a single leak. The Rackets Bureau notched 125
convictions off the Gold Bug, ranging from bribery to insurance
fraud to extortion.

Organized crime was not defeated. Police corruption was not
eliminated. But the bad guys surely knew that we were around.

Eugene Gold had accomplished the impossible. The politically
connected trial lawyer had removed the Democratic machine
from the DA's office. In just four years, recruiting from the
campus instead of the clubhouse, Gold had created a staff of
young men and women who would carve for him a notch in
law-enforcement history. The results were truly remarkable,
and that is how Gene Gold should have been remembered.
Unfortunately, it was not to be.

A decade later, during the summer of 1983, I took a truly
tragic telephone call from John Keenan. His voice was as serious
as a heart attack.

"Joe, have you heard about Gene Gold?" he asked. "The radio
is reporting that he was arrested in Tennessee and charged with
molesting a little girl."

The words stunned me. I could barely respond. I asked Keenan for details, but it was still too early. I dropped the phone into
its cradle and sat quietly, staring at a wall full of memorabilia

from my days in Gold's office. I heard all the charges, tried to raise money and support for my old boss, met with him, was convinced he'd been set up. But to my horror and anger, Gold decided not to fight the case. He said to me:

"What chance do I have in Nashville, a Northeastern Jew, now living in Israel? The minimum mandatory sentence in this case is a dozen years. I'm sixty years old. I can't do that time."

In October 1984, he entered a conditional plea admitting that he had fondled the private sexual parts of a ten-year-old girl in a Nashville, Tennessee, hotel room. He did so with the promise that he would seek counseling for a year, after which time the charges would be dismissed, and that was exactly what happened. But the damage was done. Gold, disbarred, disgraced, returned to Israel a broken man. I will go to my grave believing that he was not guilty.

I went on to investigate the nursing home scandals for Governor Hugh Carey before serving for two years as fire commissioner for Ed Koch. At home that first evening after being appointed the special state prosecutor for Howard Beach, my experience was one of the first things Pat brought up as she and I discussed the task ahead of me. She reminded me that every tough assignment I had taken on had resulted in some sort of triumph. More important, she told me, those successes were victories, in a way, of small groups of dedicated people over injustice. You can legislate against inequality, but laws don't enforce themselves. People enforce laws, just as people break laws. The Incident at Howard Beach was proof enough of that.

11

STRATEGY

When I went with Pam Hayes to pick up the records from
Santucci's office, I was hoping to avoid an acrimonious transfer.
He was waiting for us at a shiny conference table, with his assist-
ants fanned out on either side of him like all the king's men.

Santucci wore a conservative gray suit and a sheepish expression. At the other end of the table was the young, frail-looking
assistant district attorney named Brad Wolk. Wolk looked sick
(and in fact he was several months away from being admitted to
a hospital with a collapsed lung). Pam and I sat down, excited.
We were about to hear the first definitive account from law
enforcement officials of the incident at Howard Beach.

I pulled up a chair across from Lasak, Santucci's homicide
chief, and Pamela began writing in a notepad. The sturdy Lasak,
built like a Russian blacksmith, exchanged a brief, hard glance
with me and then began in the blunt speaking style that, along
with his penetrating dark eyes and habitual cock of his head,
reminded me of TV's Detective Columbo.

"That night, these four guys, Sandiford, Griffith, Grimes, and
Sylvester, they left Brooklyn and rode out to Queens. The purpose of their trip isn't very clear. It might have been to cop
drugs—"

Pam angrily interrupted him. "Just why do you say that?"

I nudged her and said, "Let him continue, Pam."

Lasak glared and went on. He told us about the car trouble, the search for the subway, the confrontation at the pizza parlor, Sandiford's being beaten as he ran down Shore Parkway, following Griffith through the hole in the fence.

"Sandiford said he saw some of the white kids get in cars, drive by him in a left-to-right direction, and begin to chase Griffith," Lasak reported. "A moment later he heard a noise, a 'boom,' and assumed that Michael Griffith was hit. And here's where we have a problem."

He stopped for one second and looked me in the eye.

"The trouble is," said Lasak, "there's no way a car can get on the highway traveling in the direction Sandiford claims."

"So what's the significance of that?" I asked.

"Well, later on, after Sandiford had identified Griffith's body on the parkway, he was placed in a radio car next to Dominick Blum, the driver who hit Griffith. Blum left the scene but came back with his father. Sandiford spotted Blum, and later, in the station house, claimed he was one of the mob. But it doesn't fit. Blum is a court officer with no connection to the white kids or their neighborhood. And even if he had been part of the gang that night, it would have been impossible for him to get on the parkway just at the right time to run Griffith down."

Pam and I peppered Santucci's staff with questions, and when I felt we understood their version of the case, I finally asked about something that had been bothering me from the beginning.

"Why did Sandiford refuse to cooperate with the investigation?"

There was a pause.

"He didn't refuse," replied Lasak, who, I assumed, was speaking for Santucci. "He was very cooperative until he hired that creep lawyer Maddox."

I could sense Pam stiffen. Alton Maddox may be an angry man, but Pam still admired him. I knew about Lasak's station-house confrontation with the attorney. Pam hadn't been there to see Maddox jabbing his finger into Lasak's chest. I squeezed her hand under the table and asked Santucci for the written file.

As we turned to leave, the district attorney pulled me aside and spoke to me in a casual tone. "You should speak with the DA in Boston," Santucci said. "His name is Newman Flanagan, and he had a similar case awhile back. He called me and said he could help."

I thanked everyone at the table and left.

Once we were back in the car, I called Catherine and asked her to get the phone number of District Attorney Flanagan and hook me up. Then I called Helman Brook, my appellate chief, with a preliminary report. "It looks like a bitch," I told him. "I'm not sure we have anything other than assault on Sandiford and Griffith. There doesn't seem to be any evidence that the white kids continued to chase Griffith after he got through the fence. And the DA's people doubt that the cars Sandiford described seeing have any connection to Griffith's death."

Brook told me the A-Team was ready to meet upon my return.

Pam stared at me in the backseat. She had been silent since we left. Finally she exploded. "You know, Joe, Santucci's people strike me as just a bunch of damned turkeys. They just don't seem to care."

I remained silent. *Oh, they had cared,* I thought, *perhaps more about racial public relations than actually solving the crime. But they cared. The case, however, was no longer theirs. Now I was the one who had been assigned to care.*

And I had become more clear about the assignments I would give to the A-Team. Walking out of Santucci's office, I decided that if and when the Howard Beach case got to court, Ed Boyar would be lead trial counsel. The idea of having Jim Kohler run the office in my stead and then step into the Howard Beach courtroom at the final moment just didn't sit right. Boyar would be on top of the case from the beginning, and he was a damn fine trial attorney. Richard Mangum would be Boyar's "second-seat" —backup to the lead counsel who acts as a backboard off which to bounce ideas. Mangum would also be responsible for cross-examining certain witnesses, arguing motions, and offering legal suggestions on site.

Before I met with the A-Team I sought out Al Pica, whose ability to calm and soothe skittish witnesses was legend. My chief investigator had picked out a staff of assistants to work on Howard Beach with names that reflected the pluralism of the city: Duffy, Smith, Pagani, Rodriquez. And there were two in particular I knew I would need: One was Gene McPherson, a black former Internal Affairs detective whose son Don was currently starring at quarterback for Syracuse University and is now a quarterback for the NFL's Philadelphia Eagles. Gene was the counterpart to Dennis Hawkins as a collector of detail; no document was ever overlooked by his computerlike mind. And the other was Terry Hayes, a tough, former uniformed police officer, the quintessential "Irish cop on the beat." A man with an easy charm, Hayes was quick to react to emergencies and would be a perfect liaison with the NYPD, which was sure to look askance at our investigation. After all, we were the second-guessers.

I invited Pica's investigators into the meeting with the A-Team and told the entire group what I had learned at Santucci's office, which, in truth, wasn't much.

"The story is too sketchy," I said, "and until we speak to the surviving victims, Sandiford and Grimes, I don't know where we're going on this. the key seems to be what happened to Michael Griffith after he got through that hole in the fence at the corner of 85th Street and Shore Parkway."

Catherine came to the door: District Attorney Flanagan was holding.

"I've got two of my assistants, John Kiernan and Jim Kelly, on extensions," Newman Flanagan said. "John tried the case I'd like you to know about. Jim was in on the appeal."

"Thanks, Newman," I said. "What can you tell me that's going to help dig me out of a deep hole?"

"Well, what we had sounds like a match to the situation you have down there," Flanagan began. "White gang, black guy chased to his death. We got the conviction, manslaughter. Proved proximate cause. And we got upheld on appeal. I think you'll find it interesting."

The back of my neck tingled. I loved his sense of understatement. The law is fairly clear that when a person sets into motion a set of circumstances, and it can be reasonably foreseen that those circumstances will result in injury or death, then that person is the proximate cause of that injury or death. That person, therefore, is criminally liable. Thus, the giant legal question hovering over the Howard Beach case was: Did the assailants who chased Michael Griffith through the hole in the fence foresee that he would run out onto the Belt Parkway and be killed? Were they the proximate cause of his death?

When Flanagan and his people were finished giving me a rough outline of their investigation and prosecution, my heart pounding a little with each successive detail, I asked if I could send some of my people up to meet with him.

"Sure, Joe. When?"

"Today," I told him. "I've got to move fast. The racial tension down here is about to bubble over."

Flanagan said he understood. It was now nearly noon, and I told him I'd try to have my people make the 1:30 shuttle. He asked me who I would be sending, and I put him on hold and walked back to the conference room. I made a quick decision that Flanagan's case would be a question of law, rather than investigation, for us. It could set a legal precedent, and on a more personal note it was precisely the excuse I needed to keep my unbearably cautious appellate experts off my back. By the time we really got rolling on Howard Beach my legal experts' devil's advocacy would be welcome. But at this stage in the investigation I wanted them out of my hair for a day or two. So I decided to send Brook, Hoffman, and Greenberg up north. I asked them into my office and they listened to my end of the conversation with Flanagan.

"Newman, I'm sending my appeals guys, Helman Brook, Hillel Hoffman, and Matt Greenberg."

Flanagan's burst of laughter nearly shattered my eardrum. "Hey, guys," I heard him yell to his assistants. "We've got Kiernan, Kelly, McGuire, and Maloney up here, and Hynes is sending us three guys named Izzy, Looie, and Moe."

My heart quickened for a moment as I heard that South Boston accent, the same flat-a sound I had heard in the Eastover Library three weeks before. But this time it belonged to someone who was already a friend.

After I hung up I turned to my three bemused "superbrains."

A shorthand sketch of Boston's "Savin Hill" murder was all they needed.

When I finished, Hilly Hoffman was the first to speak. "That's exactly what's missing," he said with a wry smile. "As if we don't have enough problems with this case, here you go sending the three of us to the land of Irish antisemites."

Brook, Hoffman, and I grinned at each other, but Greenberg missed the joke. "No, Boston's okay," he said earnestly. "I worked there for two years." Now Hoffman, Brook, and I broke up.

Off they went to LaGuardia Airport. I returned to the conference room and told Al Pica that I wanted to meet with the Queens chief of detectives, his assistants, and the detectives who caught the case.

"When, Chief?"

"Today."

Every decision I made would have to demonstrate my sense of urgency. I've learned over the years that when the person in charge feels and acts with a sense of crisis, the staff immediately gets the message that this project is special. Then I said what had been on my mind since the Santucci meeting:

"We've got to figure out a way to break one of those little tough guys, the heroes with the bats. Marty, Dennis, Richard, you three reread every Five and report filed. I want you to get a feel for every one of those kids, and their parents. Ed, you and Pam go over all the press reports again, and if we have any television newsclips, take a look at them. We've got to find out which of these kids will be the most vulnerable to an approach by us."

The team dispatched, I took a call from Larry Kurlander. Considering the number of reporters who were tying up my line—my secretaries had quickly become practiced at the art of the "No comment"—I was surprised he got through. Kurlander sounded pleased to hear that a meeting with Sandiford and Grimes had been set up for Thursday. I told him I had just come from Santucci's office. Then I filled him in on Flanagan's case and the proximate-cause angle, telling him I had three people on the way to Boston now.

"Larry, I said, "this is not going to be easy."

"What do you mean, Joe?" Kurlander veritably boomed into the phone. "I got the case on proximate cause, I had it when I was district attorney in Rochester. Didn't Santucci tell you about Kibbe? It went all the way to the Supreme Court, and we won it. Take a deep breath, Joe, you may be able to solve a homicide."

I wasn't convinced. Kurlander attempted to convince me, just as he had been trying to convince Santucci over the past several weeks. He gave me the outline of the Kibbe case:

On a cold December 30th in 1970, a man named George Stafford had been drinking in a tavern in Rochester, New York. By 8:30 P.M. he was so inebriated that the bartender refused to serve him. Stafford flashed a large roll of hundred-dollar bills and mumbled that he needed a ride home. Barry Warren Kibbe and Roy Krall, both residents of Rochester, took one glance at Stafford's bankroll and agreed to supply the transportation. The three men walked to another bar, where Stafford was again refused service. Yet at a third tavern money talked, and the three each consumed several drinks. Then they left in Kibbe's automobile, ostensibly to drive Stafford to his home in nearby Canandaigua. But once they were in the car, with Krall driving, Kibbe demanded Stafford's money. Stafford refused at first but gave up his cash after Kibbe slapped him in the face several times.

Then Kibbe forced Stafford to remove his trousers and shoes to prove that he had handed over all his cash. Finally, Stafford, stripped of his coat, shoeless, and with his trousers pulled down around his ankles, was thrown from the car. It was approximately 9:30 P.M., the temperature was near zero, and a howling north wind was whipping previously fallen snow onto the highway, obscuring the shoulder from the roadway.

At about 10:00 P.M. a college student named Michael Blake was driving his pickup truck northbound when he saw Stafford staggering through the beams of his headlights. Stafford was too drunk, Blake's reactions were too late, the truck struck and killed Stafford.

Krall and Kibbe were each indicted for murder and robbery, charged by the grand jury with that section of the New York State Penal Law which holds someone guilty of murder caused "under circumstances evincing a depraved indifference to human life . . . recklessly engaging in conduct which creates a grave risk of death to another person and thereby causes the death of another person."

At trial, both were found guilty as charged.

Their appeal presented an interesting question: both for the state's highest appellate tribunal, the New York Court of Appeals, and for me, assuming that we could uncover enough facts in our investigation to make a parallel case with The Incident at Howard Beach. On appeal, attorneys for Krall and Kibbe contended that whatever the defendants' actions did to cause the death of George Stafford, the actions of Michael Blake, the pickup truck driver, constituted an "intervening cause" which should absolve them of homicide.

As Kurlander spoke, it dawned on me that anyone facing a homicide indictment in the Howard Beach case would of course charge that Dominick Blum operated his vehicle in such a manner as to present an intervening cause of Michael Griffith's death.

But then Kurlander explained how the Court of Appeals had rejected the intervening-cause defense, ruling in part that "Kibbe and Krall left a helplessly intoxicated man . . . in circumstances from which he could not extradite himself and whose condition was such that he could not protect himself from the elements. . . . There can be little doubt but that Stafford would have frozen to death in his state of undress had he remained on the shoulder of the road."

The "only alternative" left to Stafford, the court ruled, "was the highway, which in his condition, for one reason or another, clearly foreboded the probability of his death. We do not think it may be said that any supervening wrongful act occurred to relieve the defendants from directly foreseeable consequences of their actions."

"In other words," I said to Kurlander, "if circumstances had existed for Blake to stop before hitting Stafford, Krall and Kibbe would have walked on the murder charges."

"That's right," he replied. "The Court of Appeals has set a standard of proof which says, basically, that in order for you to get guilty verdicts on any possible Howard Beach defendants, you're going to have to prove that they knew they were chasing Michael Griffith to certain death, and that Dominick Blum did not have sufficient time to react when and if he saw Griffith on the Belt Parkway."

"Are you kidding me?" I said to Kurlander. "This is help? How the hell do I prove that?"

"I have faith in you, Joe," was all Kurlander said before ringing off.

As I pondered Kurlander's Kibbe case, Al Pica interrupted to inform me that Chief of Queens Detectives Joseph Borelli and his staff had arrived.

"Get them some coffee, would you Al, and tell them I'll see them in about twenty minutes." First I wanted to tell my trial lawyers about Kibbe while it was still fresh in my mind.

Trial attorneys, myself included, look at the "world" of a criminal case from a very different perspective than do appeals lawyers. The words of *Dragnet*'s Joe Friday could be our credo: "Just the facts" are all we want. But appeals attorneys take the facts that we uncover and test them against legal precedents. "What test will the Court of Appeals demand?" is a refrain I've heard all too often from Brook, Hoffman, or Greenberg. Without their guidance, however, we'd be in a constant state of uncertainty.

Hershey, Boyar, Hawkins, Mangum, and Hayes—the trial lawyers—listened intently as I described the Kibbe ruling. Before long we had reached a consensus. The actions of Krall and Kibbe were brutally obvious. When they threw poor Stafford, drunk and disoriented, out of their car that terrible evening, they should have been aware of the possibility of his death. What we needed to do now was determine how the acts of the white mob in Howard Beach compared, if at all. I told them to think it through carefully and then I went out to deal with the police.

Deputy Chief Inspector Joseph Borelli, who had been the chief of Queens detectives for several years, is the epitome of what a New York City detective is supposed to be, both in rank and ability. A tall, trim man with thinning brown hair, he carries himself with a patrician air. And his piercing, dark eyes highlight a mind given to penetrating analysis. But when Borelli and I met less than a year before, on a case involving Mob boss John Gotti, our introduction was anything but cordial.

12

CHIEF BORELLI

In 1984 John Gotti was still only a lieutenant in the Gambino Family. And one day, he and an accomplice were accused of slapping around and robbing a thirty-seven-year-old refrigerator mechanic named Romual Piecyk. The man had just cashed his paycheck and was driving home on an early autumn evening when he was hemmed in on a narrow sidestreet by a double-parked car. He honked his horn twice, got out of his car, and was approached by two burly men. One of them shouted, "What the fuck is with you?" slapped Piecyk several times across the face, and reached into his shirt pocket and lifted several hundred dollars in cash. The other ordered the mechanic back into his car, "or else we'll kill you."

While this was happening, the illegally parked car was moved, and as Piecyk drove away he watched his assailants walk into a diner. He stopped several blocks away, called the police, and two officers from the 104th Precinct responded. Piecyk took the officers to the diner and pointed out the two men who had roughed him up and stolen his money. The two were arrested.

Several weeks later a Queens County grand jury indicted John Gotti and a Gambino Family associate named Frank Colletta on second-degree robbery and second-degree assault charges. Apparently, not many people within the law-enforcement establishment thought much of the prosecution's case, but this was the State's first case against Gotti in years. The day after the indictment was handed down, Piecyk read the newspapers, and though he was not mentioned by name, for the first time realized just whom he had fingered. He was understandably frightened out of his wits.

Detectives and the Queens District Attorney's Office assured Piecyk that his name would be kept out of the newspapers until the trial. And in any event, they told him, it was likely Gotti would plea to a lesser charge and the refrigerator repairman would probably never have to testify against the crime boss.

The Piecyk case was still pending in December 1985 when Gambino Family Director Paul "Big Paulie" Castellano failed to respond adequately to a corporate takeover attempt. He and a bodyguard were "retired" by a torrent of automatic weapons fire on a sidewalk outside a Manhattan steakhouse. Gotti succeeded Castellano as Boss of Bosses, and the newspapers were filled with unofficial reports that his had not been a passive coronation. In a profile of Gotti in the *New York Post* that hinted at his involvement in the Castellano rubout, it was reported that Gotti was also under indictment in Queens for robbery and assault, and that the victim had been one Romual Piecyk, who was scheduled to be the State's star witness. This was the first time Piecyk's name had been made public.

Piecyk's hands shook as he read the newspaper. The story also related how, several years earlier, one of Gotti's Howard Beach neighbors had accidentally run over and killed Gotti's ten-year-old son while backing out of his driveway. The neighbor apologized profusely to the disconsolate mobster, and no charges were ever filed. But the last time the man was seen, he was being dragged out of a Queens diner, beaten with a baseball bat, and thrown into a dark blue van.

As Piecyk was reading this horrible anecdote, his telephone rang. Nearly jumping out of his chair, he answered with a trembling voice. No response. Moments later the phone rang again.

"Hello?"

"Hello, scumbag," a voice said.

The line went dead.

By now Piecyk had drifted across the line from fright to total panic. He called Santucci's office but was told that both the detectives handling his case and the assistant district attorney assigned to him were out of the office. He hung up and the telephone rang again. This time he refused to answer. Instead, he ran to the bathroom and threw up. When the key turned in his front door, Piecyk grabbed a kitchen knife and hurled himself toward the vestibule. His startled wife dropped her bag of groceries. The telephone rang unanswered all night. Piecyk barricaded his front door.

Detectives arrived the next morning and plugged an answering machine into Piecyk's phone. They did not offer him police protection. The machine recorded obscene suggestions for the rest of the week. Fearful that he would lose his job, Piecyk finally left his fortress and returned to work. There were no more incidents over the next several weeks, and a daily phone call from the District Attorney's Office seemed to have a calming effect.

Then one day the refrigerator repairman was called to a job in an Italian restaurant in Ozone Park, Queens. Two men, who looked remarkably like Gotti and Colletta, stood in the darkened corner of the dining room. One made a slashing motion with his finger, sliding it across his neck. Piecyk grew pale, dropped his tools, and ran from the restaurant. Upon reaching home, he called his contact in the Queens DA's office.

"I'm finished," he said. "I'm not testifying."

Romual Piecyk then hung up, sat down, and addressed four letters, one each to Governor Mario M. Cuomo, Mayor Edward I. Koch, Police Commissioner Benjamin Ward, and District Attorney John Santucci. Each letter detailed the reasons why he feared for his life. Weeks passed, and Piecyk received no replies. Piecyk was convinced that John Gotti was one powerful mobster.

As the trial approached, Piecyk still refused to testify. He was arrested as a material witness and stuck in a Queens motel, in "protective custody." The ultimate insult, he felt: the victim of a crime incarcerated, while the alleged perpetrator, the Boss of Bosses of the New York underworld, walked the streets free on bail. If his house arrest hadn't further reaffirmed Piecyk's decision not to testify, a phone call to the motel in which he was sequestered surely did. The detective who answered the phone handed the receiver to an assistant district attorney, who in turn handed it to Piecyk. "Here," said the ADA, "it's for you."

"Mr. Piecyk," said the voice on the other end of the line. "My name is Bruce Cutler, and I'm the attorney for John Gotti . . ."

Piecyk, incredulous, threw the phone back at the ADA.

"What are you guys trying to do?" he shouted.

Moments later the assistant district attorney was apologizing to his star witness, explaining that Cutler merely wanted to know if Piecyk had retained a lawyer.

"How did he get this number?" asked a terrified Piecyk.

The ADA merely shrugged, and the prosecution's case against John Gotti and Frank Colletta went down the tubes in a motel near Kennedy Airport. Piecyk had to be restrained by handcuffs as he shouted over and over, "I want a lawyer now!"

A few days later, on the witness stand in the Queens County Supreme Court, Piecyk insisted he could not identify his assailants. Gotti and Colletta were sitting in the courtroom, twenty feet from Piecyk, but he refused to meet their eyes when asked if his attackers were in the courtroom. Piecyk trembled. Gotti smiled. The judge had no alternative but to grant the defendants' motion to dismiss the case.

The week after the dismissal, I received a phone call from Ronald Goldstock, head of the State's Organized Crime Task Force. He asked me if I was familiar with the "Gotti business" in Queens.

"Just from the papers," I told him.

"Well, Joe, one of our informants claims the Gotti case was fixed. He says he doesn't know who did it, but that it's all over town that Gotti engineered the dismissal, somehow getting to the complaining witness and scaring him into forgetting everything."

I asked Ed Boyar to look into the Piecyk-Gotti case, with Joe Piccione as his investigative assistant. In our office, Piccione is called "The Great Persuader." Within several days, Joe's patience paid off, and Romual Piecyk was sitting across the table in my office. He was a tough talker with hands the size of anvils, not the type one would expect to be easily intimidated. Yet he wore the dazed look of some lonely Silesian shepherd who had met a marauding party of Huns and somehow lived to tell about it.

Piecyk didn't know who I was, nor why my office wanted to speak to him, but he did give a hesitant account of the assault and his subsequent fear for his life. When he came to the part about the four letters detailing his terror, I gave a small start. When he finished, he asked me what I wanted.

"We'd like you to cooperate with our office," I told him.

"Would that mean testifying against Gotti?" he asked.

"It might." I tried to be honest.

"Take me home," Piecyk demanded as he bolted from his chair. To him I was just another law-enforcement drone, asking him to risk his life for nothing. I couldn't really blame the guy.

We took Romual Piecyk home, then began tracing his letters. Santucci's office claimed Piecyk's letter was never received. Cuomo's office said they had passed theirs on to Larry Kurlander, who had in turn forwarded it to Goldstock. Goldstock recalled shipping his copy to the NYPD's Organized Crime Control Bureau, or the OCCB. I told Al Pica that I wanted to interview the commanding officer of the OCCB immediately.

The following morning Assistant Chief Inspector Raymond Jones and an aide were waiting for me when I walked into my office. Jones, a tall, broad man with a direct, gruff approach, got right to the point. "Why have I been summoned to the State's anticorruption office?" he demanded.

I explained, and as I had expected, Jones knew nothing about the Piecyk letters. He turned to his assistant, Inspector Brian Lavan, for an explanation.

"Oh, yes sir," said Lavan, "I know about the letter. In fact, we received the copies sent to Governor Cuomo, the mayor, and the police commissioner."

Jones appeared surprised as he snarled to his subordinate, "Well, what did you do with them?"

A film of perspiration materialized on Lavan's upper lip. He stretched up to his full height of five feet, ten inches and tried to suck in a somewhat hefty stomach. Despite this stab at an officious bearing, a crimson tide rose in his cheeks.

"I put them in an envelope and sent them to Chief of Detectives Colangelo's office," Lavan told his boss.

"Why?" I inquired. It was my turn to be direct.

"Well, sir," stammered Lavan. "It was not an organized-crime case, so I thought it belonged in the Chief of Detectives' Office."

I glanced at Chief Jones and noticed that the crimson tide was infectious. His cheeks glowed like hot coals.

"Let me try and follow this," I said. "OCCB receives a letter, three letters in fact, from a robbery victim who admits that he's terrified of testifying against John Gotti. And you sent them to the chief of detectives, you sent them to Robert Colangelo's office, because the case didn't involve an organized crime, per se?"

"Yes, sir."

"Didn't the fact that this case involved Gotti, head of the Gambino Family, even remotely interest OCCB?"

Lavan corrected me. "He wasn't the boss then, Castellano was," he said.

"Inspector," I shouted, "are you saying that OCCB didn't know that Gotti was next in line to the throne?"

Lavan turned sullen. "I'm not sure."

I ended the meeting.

Next I determined from a very precise detective sergeant in Chief Colangelo's office that the three letters had been "routed" to the Queens Borough Detective Command, Joe Borelli's domain. Apparently, no one thought the missives were important enough to bother the chief of detectives of New York City. I was in a black mood when I called Borelli and asked him to visit 2 Rector Street.

"Can I ask what this is about before seeing you?" he asked.

"No," I replied in anger. By this time I was beginning to believe that the entire command structure of the New York City Police Department was corrupt, stupid, or a combination thereof. That afternoon an unhappy and wary Chief Borelli was seated in my office. When I finished relating the Piecyk affair, he shook his head wearily.

"It's the first I've heard of this."

I believed him, and I told him so. Having never met the man, I had assumed Borelli was as incompetent as the rest of the police with whom I had been dealing. Thus, I had been harsh over the phone. It was an uncalled-for assumption.

"You've been unfair to me," Borelli said. "I'll check into this right away and call you later." He stood, a tad too erect, and walked out the door. He was right. I owed him an apology.

Several hours later Chief Borelli's voice came over my phone: "Mr. Hynes, I found the screw-up." He proceeded to explain how an envelope containing the Piecyk letters had been misplaced by a civilian employee who subsequently went on vacation. As the explanation continued, I felt like a teacher being told that the dog ate the homework.

Later, I asked Ed Boyar, only semifacetiously: "Is it possible that John Gotti is using an intricate web of contacts within the various divisions of the Police Department to craftily arrange for the Piecyk papers to disappear in a civilian clerk's in basket? And we wonder why civilians won't cooperate with us."

The Piecyk case died a silent death, and I hadn't spoken to Borelli since.

Now I walked out of my office to meet him again.

"Mr. Hynes, what can we do for you?" The voice was Borelli's, all right, but the words were flat and weary. The chief, flanked by Detectives John Hammond and Frank Paulson, sat on one side of my conference table. The A-Team sat on the other. I took a chair at the head.

"Chief, what can you tell me about that night in Howard Beach?"

Perhaps because of our last encounter, Borelli seemed to have been extremely well briefed, and it soon became obvious that he was on top of what few facts were known about the attack. That, however, was the problem: Borelli was not privy to any more information than Santucci and his people. He and his detectives repeated Lasak's argument that not only was Blum an unlikely member of the white gang but that it would have been nearly impossible for him to time any collision with a fleeing Michael

Griffith. They were very convincing. Yet one thing still bothered me.

"How come," I asked, "Sandiford is so sure he saw the cars go past him left to right and chase Griffith onto the Belt Parkway eastbound? He's really adamant about that."

The detectives shrugged their shoulders. They had no answer.

"Chief," I said, "I don't think we have any alternative but to turn one of the kids. Only one of them can tell us what really happened. Even with Sandiford cooperating, it may be that he was so disoriented from the beatings that his recollection is seriously flawed."

There was no need to add that a faulty memory would kill us on the witness stand.

"What do you suggest?" asked Borelli.

"I want you to team your detectives with my staff of investigators, pair them off to work together. Then I want each team to go to the home of every kid and tell the parents that my office has taken over the case. Tell the parents that if they want to help their child, they should have their attorney contact me before it's too late."

I needed to establish an immediate working relationship between Borelli's people and mine. There was bound to be an initial unease between working cops and anticorruption investigators, and I wanted it out of the way as soon as possible.

"Chief, when can we start?" I was anxious. His answer was welcome.

"Now."

I walked the detectives toward the door and was nearly bowled over by a beaming Rose Pastore. "It's Helman from Boston," she told me. "He's got good news."

My three appellate attorneys had not been overjoyed when I informed them that they were flying north. They even tried to get me to postpone the meeting for twenty-four hours because, as Matt Greenberg told me later, Brook and Hoffman were afraid to fly and were hoping to take the train the following morning. But, safe at Logan Airport, they were met by one of Flanagan's investigators, Richie Demeo, who told them he had been instructed to look for "three little Jewish guys getting off the Eastern shuttle." Hilly Hoffman, kidding Demeo about

being Flanagan's token Italian, apologized for not sporting yar-
mulkes.

Demeo took them to the Suffolk County District Attorney's
Office, where John Kiernan, Flanagan's chief assistant, began to
outline the incident that had occurred in the Savin Hill neighborhood of Dorchester, Massachusetts, a community that bears
a certain similarity to Howard Beach: both are mostly white,
self-enclosed, with defined boundaries such as highways, bays,
and train tracks. The terrain of each had spelled death for a black
man at the hands of a white mob.

At 12:30 A.M., on March 13, 1982, a young black man named
William Atchison and his white friend named William Grady
were walking along Savin Hill Avenue when a carload of five
whites passed them and one shouted, "Hey, nigger, we're going
to kill you." Grady yelled back that Atchison was his friend.
Someone responded, "Then we'll kill you too," and the car made
a U-turn and started chasing the two men along the avenue as
its occupants hurled racial epithets and threats. Atchison and
Grady ran about four hundred feet to a nearby Massachusetts
Bay Transportation Authority (MBTA) train station and then
three hundred thirty feet more down the stairs to the platform.
The pursuers left the car and stood at a chain-link fence surrounding the station, heaving rocks and bottles down at the
platform.

Then two of the whites, William Joyce and Francis Xavier
Devin, scaled the fence and ran toward Atchison and Grady.
Grady ran back up the stairs and was knocked unconscious by
the other three assailants. Atchison leaped down onto the tracks
and began running. Neither Joyce nor Devin followed him.
Seven minutes and 1750 feet later, William Atchison was struck
and killed by an MBTA train traveling with its lights off.

During their trial and subsequent appeal, Kiernan explained,
the defense maintained that some other circumstance, an intervening cause, bore the blame for Atchison's death: the MBTA
for operating the train without lights; or the victim himself, who
had acted irrationally. But Flanagan and Kiernan managed a
manslaughter conviction for Joyce and Devin and it was upheld
on appeal.

When I took Helman Brook's call, I expected to hear the soft

Alabama twang that never reaches high C, the voice with which this low-key appellate expert had argued many a legal point. Yet Helman was more vibrant than I'd ever heard him before.

"They've got the carbon copy to our case, Joe. They got a conviction and they were upheld by their appellate courts."

After he gave me the rundown of the Savin Hill case, I asked if he was familiar with the Kibbe case.

"Sure, Joe. Matt, Hilly, and I were throwing that one around in the office this morning before you kicked us up here," he answered. (I should have known these guys would be way ahead of me.) "But this case in Boston sounds a hell of a lot better for us than Kibbe."

"Besides," said Matt Greenberg, who had been listening on an extension, "the Massachusetts Appeals Court, which upheld the manslaughter convictions against the two white kids, gives us strong language of support if we develop a homicide case. It found that their actions in chasing Atchison were the proximate cause of his death, even though the chase stopped almost six hundred yards before, when the black guy jumped onto the railroad tracks. But he didn't know they had stopped chasing him. He was still running out of fear."

I summoned all of my eloquence and let out a long, low "Wow!"

Then another thought struck me. "So in Howard Beach we might be dealing with nearly a dozen killers."

"That's right, Joe," said Greenberg.

"Just one more thing, Joe," Hellman broke in. "John Kiernan, the guy who prosecuted Devin and Joyce—well, he told us that since the convictions the white court officers have stopped talking to him. He says it got pretty rough during the trial, and stayed that way for a while afterward."

"What's so surprising about that?" I wondered out loud. "Since the Federal Court ordered public school desegregation in Boston, the city's been a firestorm of interracial chaos."

"So you don't think we'll have a problem?" asked Brook, putting a little more drawl into his voice for my benefit.

"In New York? No way," I replied. To this day I look back on that conversation and remain amazed by my naiveté. The court officers assigned to the Howard Beach trial were exceptional, but too many white people—many more than I ever expected—believed and carry that belief to this day that the special-prosecution approach to the case was a politically motivated overreaction.

The following morning I reflected that in the two days since Governor Cuomo had assigned me the Howard Beach case, we had made a lot of progress. My conference room was established as the War Room for the investigative phase of the case. A large flow chart stood on an easel against the back wall. The A-Team filed past it all morning, sitting amid empty coffee containers, crushed soda cans, and half-eaten deli sandwiches, discussing the implications of Savin Hill.

But as the day wore on, our outlook became grimmer. Al Pica called to inform us that his investigators, working with Borelli's detectives, were getting no cooperation from the families of the Howard Beach attackers.

Meanwhile, Ed Koch had come down publicly, and heavily, against my appointment as special prosecutor, saying: "It should have been handled in the regular process, with John Santucci taking the matter before a grand jury." He was careful not to mention me by name. I supposed that he had finally read yesterday's edition of the *New York Post,* his favorite newspaper and his staunchest supporter, whose editorial board had attacked Cuomo for caving into black community pressure.

Worse, that morning C. Vernon Mason was quoted in *New York Newsday* as saying that the Howard Beach victims would not cooperate with my office unless I also agreed to prosecute the driver of the car that struck Michael Griffith: "A good-faith investigation includes the arrest of everybody involved, including Dominick Blum."

Damn, I thought, *I am dealing not only with a panderer but with a guy who doesn't know the law.* For if Dominick Blum had known that he hit and killed a human being, then the laws of "intervening cause" would apply. If Mason had a whit of legal sense, he would have realized that a prosecution of Blum would negate the proximate-cause charges against the white gang, and every one of them would be let off the hook.

I felt like blurting this out to several of the reporters who called for my reaction. Instead, I seethed inside and took the high road. "I'm confident that at the conclusion of the investigative phase everyone will be satisfied that we did a fair and professional job," I told them. "I'm not saying everybody is going to be happy," I added. "But that's not my job. I'm a lawyer. I present facts." And all the while, I was thinking: *Read between those lines, Vernon!*

The next crucial step was our meeting with Sandiford and Grimes. We all agreed that they could be our last hope. And as the hour approached, I grew increasingly apprehensive. In fact, I had Rose Pastore call Mason's office several times to make sure we were still set. At 4:00 P.M. her voice squawked through the intercom: "It's confirmed." I felt more relief than I let show.

Thirty minutes later Pam Hayes, Marty Hershey, Ed Boyar, Dennis Hawkins, Richard Mangum, and I piled into two state cars for the ten-minute ride to Mason's office. Our strategy was to try to break Grimes and Sandiford into two separate interviews, with three attorneys for each victim.

"If," I warned the group, "Mason and Maddox want to participate in the questioning, and they probably will, I want everyone to remain cool. They are both criminal lawyers, after all, and they may be of some help. Besides, if we don't win their confidence today, it's all over."

Plus, I thought to myself, *they might have something positive to contribute*—despite my loss of esteem for Mason's legal acumen after his glib talk about indicting Blum. *Yeah,* I hoped: *They might have something positive in them.*

13

SANDIFORD SPEAKS

As I entered the lobby of 401 Broadway, the lower Manhattan building that housed Mason's eleventh-floor suite, I went over our ground rules one final time with Hershey, Boyar, Mangum, Hayes, and Hawkins.

We would take no notes, because we didn't want to generate any more discovery material. Any statement made by a witness and taken down in note form (or tape or videotape) automatically becomes discovery material, which has to be turned over to defense counsels. Both Grimes and Sandiford had previously given statements to investigators, as well as to the press, and both would, we hoped, soon be testifying before a grand jury. If anything said today contradicted those previous statements (a distinct possibility, given some of the wilder pronouncements following the attack), our case might be irreparably damaged.

As the elevator carried us silently upward, a palpable kinetic energy passed among us. No one had to say a word. We were about to hear our first eyewitness account of The Incident at Howard Beach, and everyone's senses were tingling in anticipation.

Suddenly Dominick Blum loomed large in my mind. I worried that the demand for his arrest would detonate the interview. I decided that if it came up, I'd stall for time. It was all I could do. But then what would Maddox and Mason do?

The elevator doors opened and we found ourselves in Mason's narrow waiting room, ten minutes early. His receptionist took our names and asked us to be seated. I stood, looking at the many pictures of Mason and leading political lights on the walls—the de rigueur decoration for an attorney's waiting room, the better to impress and, if need be, soothe prospective clients. Mason's unique touch included photographs of civil rights demonstrations from the early 1960s to the present, with framed posters of Malcolm X and snapshots of Martin Luther King, Jr., leading marches. I think I saw Dennis Hawkins, our resident radical, searching for himself among the white faces in some of the crowd shots.

The outer offices were also a collector's gallery of African artifacts—shields, baskets, ewers, and indigenous African art. Given my feelings about my own Irish heritage, I was quite taken with these reminders of a strong and proud tradition.

The dichotomous nature of C. Vernon Mason's civil rights commitment has, on occasion, left me bewildered. He had often railed at the Tammany Hall deals that he believed kept blacks from political power. Yet he once announced the candidacy of a black woman, Adelaide Sanford, for New York City schools chancellor while she was out of the country and unaware that the post was vacant. Reached for comment several days later in Kenya, Sanford described herself as "shocked" at her nomination.

That was the public C. Vernon Mason, the attorney who found "the linchpin of a racist power structure" in the New York City criminal justice system and who intermittently called for the resignation of Governor Cuomo, Mayor Koch, and a string of other political luminaries too lengthy to list.

The private C. Vernon Mason, whom I had met socially on several occasions, was soft-spoken to the point of shyness. He was patient and insightful, and would occasionally interject a salient point in a conversation in a smoky Arkansas drawl tempered by the tones of Columbia University Law School. With his horn-rimmed glasses and portly mien, Mason does not cut an imposing figure until he has an audience, a cause, and a bullhorn or microphone, at which point he becomes a Jeremiah. I wasn't sure which Vernon Mason we'd meet on this day.

In a few minutes, Mason's secretary ushered us down a narrow hallway with offices on either side. Maddox walked into the corridor to greet us, dressed in a starched white shirt and a dark-gray three-piece suit. I assumed he had just returned from court. Maddox's lopsided grin did nothing to blunt the piercing, angry eyes he threw on me like a searchlight. He looked younger than his forty-one years. Four of us received a curt nod, but Pam Hayes was greeted warmly.

Maddox's most sincere hello, however, was reserved for Ed Boyar, against whom he had tried several cases while Ed was an assistant district attorney in Brooklyn. In fact, Boyar had drawn Maddox in one of the civil rights attorney's first New York cases nearly a decade before. During the proceedings, Maddox was bollixing an attempt at impeaching a witness— demonstrating that the witness has given conflicting statements to the grand jury. When the judge called a recess so Maddox could compose himself, Boyar showed him the proper way to impeach a witness.

"You're in here trying a case against me and yet you're helping me? What are you doing this for?" Maddox had asked Boyar.

"We'll be doing business in the future," the ADA replied, "and I want you at least to get off on the right track here."

From that point on the two had a "friendly enemies" rapport, and Alton Maddox seemed to perceive Boyar's presence in our entourage this afternoon as an assurance that we were utterly serious.

I was leery of Maddox. I felt like that apocryphal old cop who heard about a new drug called marijuana: "I don't know much about that stuff, but it sure keeps bad company." I knew about the alleged assault on the court officers, of course. And I didn't admire his statement to the *Amsterdam News* before Judge Bianchi's open hearing on Lester, Ladone, and Kern: "There is certainly an official policy in this city never to convict a white person for killing a black person." I was forced to wonder if the attorney wasn't uttering a self-fulfilling prophecy. Richard Emery, a former attorney for the American Civil Liberties Union, went out of his way to warn me about Maddox before our meeting that day: "His methods are sabotage and the pursuit of racial division," Emery had told me. And this was from a lawyer who fought on the same side as Maddox in several civil rights cases.

"He's very big on charges and very short on proof," Emery added. "That's a technique we all learned to despise during the McCarthy period. Personally, I'll never work with the guy again." That fairly well constituted a complete condemnation.

But Maddox also had his defenders, who pointed out that the attorney's contentious antics constituted a sensible reaction to a racist criminal justice system. In fact, Maddox was proud of declaring the white race responsible for "creating" him and his tactics. "You can't give us an education and then ask us to be stupid," he was quoted as saying in several articles I'd researched. "If you don't want me to have a brain, you should have never let me go to your schools."

Detractors accused Maddox of being anti-white, a reverse racist. Yet his defenders saw only a sensitive man with a keen feel for injustice, a man who fought white racism by any means possible. He had grown up in Georgia during the tumultuous 1950s and 1960s, the son of a Baptist preacher, in a small community of the black Southern elite. His mother kept him away from white people, he said, so he would never have to feel subservient. In December 1967, when he was a senior at Howard University, Maddox was arrested for disorderly conduct and resisting arrest when he refused to move his car from an emergency parking zone. In the affidavit he filed appealing his conviction, Maddox said he explained to an inquiring police officer that he was waiting to pick up his aunt and take her to the hospital to visit her sick husband, and that he would move the car if someone needed to park in the space. The policeman pointed to the no-parking sign and said, "Boy, can't you read?" After the officer threatened to strike him, he agreed to move the car, but it was too late, for the officer then ordered him out of his car, once again employing the pejorative "boy," and Maddox was beaten and arrested. He spent five days in the hospital. Almost certainly, he carried the memory of that encounter to the courtrooms of New York.

Maddox had played a major role in two very visible recent trials. The first was the trial of the Transit Police officers accused of murdering the black grafitti artist Michael Stewart. Maddox's obstructionist techniques were such that Manhattan Supreme Court justice Jeffrey Atlas accused the attorney of doing nothing more than preventing the prosecution from making its case. And Maddox was supposedly on the prosecution's side, representing more than a dozen of the witnesses, as well as the Stewart family. Yet he and his colleagues, including Mason, became the major focus of the trial. The real difficulty was that none of the witnesses could identify the individual transit officers who arrested Stewart, nor had any of the witnesses seen the struggle between Stewart and the police.

Prosecuting the case, Manhattan District Attorney Robert Morgenthau's office developed a unique theory of liability which held the police responsible for failing to prevent harm to someone in custody. In the milieu of civil rights law, this places a tremendous burden on the Police Department, a burden I happen to agree with. Stewart's family and supporters really couldn't have asked for a craftier legal strategy, given the evidence. If Maddox had been truly concerned about bringing the perpetrators to justice, he'd have stepped aside and allowed the DA to do his job. Instead, he chose to hinder the proceedings, providing what the lead defense counsel called "valuable ammunition" for the transit officers. He was accused of tampering with grand jury testimony, coaching witnesses, and in general putting a stranglehold on the case. After the officers were acquitted, Stewart's family hired new counsel.

But the trial that shocked the city, and made Maddox's name a synonym for infamy in ethical circles, involved a white fashion model, Marla Hanson, who had been razor-slashed and horribly disfigured by two black men, Steven Bowman and Darren Norman, who had been hired by Hanson's jilted lover. Maddox handled Bowman's defense. (Earlier, Hanson's spurned suitor and former landlord had been convicted of first-degree assault for hiring the men.) During bitter cross-examination, Maddox referred to Hanson in a sneering way as the "little girl out of Texas with all the racial hang-ups," and at his lowest ebb, asked her to define the most vile word I know for a part of the female anatomy, a word which his client had accused her of being.

Remembering that outrageous trial, I wondered what term Alton Maddox might someday ask me to define.

Then C. Vernon Mason strode into the anteroom of his suite of offices. He greeted Boyar with the same exuberance as Maddox, and was a bit friendlier to me. Clad in an avuncular gray cardigan sweater, sagging and unbuttoned, he appeared to be the soul of relaxed serenity as he walked directly over to shake my hand. I made the appropriate introductions.

"Mr. Hynes," he said, "my client Timmy Grimes and his parents are in my office." Mason cocked his head over his shoulder. "As you know, Mr. Sandiford is represented by Mr. Maddox, and," he said, pointing, "he's over in that corner office. How do you want to handle this?"

I told him that I'd like Boyar, Hershey, and Hayes to interview Grimes, while Mangum, Hawkins, and I spoke with Sandiford. I had made the assignations at random, although I was careful to make sure that my trial team of Boyar and Mangum each interviewed a separate witness. We were led into Mason's empty library, and a few moments later Sandiford arrived through another door, Maddox trailing behind him.

Sandiford, dressed in a sportcoat with his shirt open at the collar, greeted us politely and sat down at the conference table. What I noticed first about him was his imposing bearing. He might have been one of the proud, lion-killing Masai warriors whose photographs were hanging outside on Mason's walls. Second, I was drawn to his eyes—doleful and sad, these eyes did not seem to belong to the tall, dignified man seated before us.

After quickly introducing Mangum and Hawkins, I attempted to relax Sandiford with some informal small talk. This is standard procedure for a prosecuting attorney at a first meeting with a prospective witness. People who face the possibility of testifying in court are extremely apprehensive, and they easily become hostile or, worse, clam up completely. The key is to put the witness at ease.

But small talk wasn't necessary with Cedric Sandiford. He was a different kind of witness. None of the usual polite strategy applied. For one thing, he was in pleasant surroundings. He knew these law offices, and his attorney was sitting beside him. But, more important, he told us he was outraged by what had happened to him in Howard Beach. The weeks of silence following the incident had unnerved him. He was desperate, he said, to tell someone in authority, someone who could do something about it, exactly what had happened to his stepson, exactly what had happened to him.

I had had clients like this once before. Nearly two decades ago I had defended two Brooklyn police officers accused of attempted murder. They couldn't wait to tell me their story, either. They turned out to be innocent.

Sandiford got right to the point: he remembered the 9:00 P.M. news broadcast interrupting the blare of the reggae music on Sylvester's car radio as the foursome cruised westbound on the Belt Parkway. And then he told his story, the tale of how they'd come to the New Park Pizzeria. ". . . and when we walked out there they were waiting for us. They surrounded us and one lashed me with the bat. I screamed and ran off, and that's when all hell broke loose."

The pained look on Sandiford's face told us he was actually reliving that horrible night, and the words, which I recall nearly verbatim, came out in an excited staccato. The running skirmish down Shore Parkway had lasted perhaps twenty minutes, and when it concluded, Sandiford said he and his stepson were driven to the fence at the corner of 85th Street. The words kept flowing. ". . . And I played like I was dead. Then some of them jumped into their cars and drove past me onto the highway."

Sandiford's eyes were shining now, and it was at this moment that I realized that he was going to be a terrific witness. He was filled with righteous indignation, and I was sure that if I could channel that emotion correctly, the man would give a splendid account of himself in front of a jury.

"In which direction did you see the cars drive?" I interrupted.

"From left to right," answered Sandiford. That, we had been told, was impossible. I stifled the urge to contradict him. Richard Mangum couldn't.

"Are you sure?" Mangum demanded, his voice a touch too strident. I punched his knee under the table. Maddox glared.

"Where did the cars go then?" I jumped in quickly.

"I saw them on the parkway a minute later," Sandiford said. "And then I heard a 'boom.' "

He stopped, choked up. Tears were streaming down his cheeks. I touched his arm, and he put his head down on the table.

"I understand, Cedric," I said. "It must have been terrible."

A sarcastic sneer creased Maddox's face. I answered with a look of my own, whose meaning, I admit, was quite clear: "Fuck you, Alton!"

A few minutes passed. The room remained quiet. Sandiford regained his composure and was able to continue.

After he followed Michael through the hole in the fence, "I was running, man, running down that highway for my life. I was bleeding. I was hurt. I was throwing those construction cones behind me. I was crazed with fear. After a while a policeman drove up, and I thought, 'Oh, thank you Lord, I'm saved.' I thanked the police officer who got out, I almost fell into his arms. And then I told him that I had been attacked by some white guys with sticks and bats, and I thought that they had killed my stepson Michael."

Here Sandiford paused for a moment, and a slight snarl formed at one corner of his mouth. "But then the cop said, 'Get against the car and spread 'em.' He searched me, ripped off my coat. Then he started asking me about some crimes committed down the road. He started treating me like a criminal. I wanted to know what the hell was going on."

I know the rules of the NYPD. I realize that police officers are instructed to search any man or woman they put into a patrol car. But as Sandiford described his indignity, I could not help imagining the treatment a white man would receive under similar circumstances.

As he continued his story, speaking haltingly as he described watching Michael Griffith's life ooze out across the highway, for the first time I began to understand why the police investigation had gone nowhere, why Santucci's prosecution had failed so miserably, why Alton Maddox was sitting here in this room with us. New York City, the criminal justice system, the *Establishment,* none of them had responded to a black man who believed his stepson had been the victim of a lynching. This man sitting before me had been beaten nearly to death by a white wolf pack. And instead of being treated with some modicum of sensitivity, he had been shunted aside by the legal system, mocked, literally accused.

"At the police station I was kept alone in a room for an hour," Sandiford continued. "I asked to call my fiancée, Jean, Michael's mother. They wouldn't let me use the phone at first. Finally I was allowed to get through to her. And just after I told her Michael was dead, while I was still talking to her, trying to calm her down, trying to console her, some cop grabbed the phone away from me. Said my time was up."

I wasn't just embarrassed; I was sick to my stomach. Dennis Hawkins lowered his head. Richard Mangum's ebony face had turned an ashen gray, matching the whiskers in his beard.

Alton Maddox continued to glare, and I asked him if he had anything to add. He shook his head no. Richard and Dennis began going over some of the finer points of Sandiford's narrative as I left and walked into Mason's office, where Grimes sat with his parents. The skinny teenager was sprawled over a leather chair. He was about five-eleven, wearing a white shirt with an old charcoal-gray suit. He also wore a silly-looking grin, not quite appropriate for one so young; it was like the smirk of a middle-aged drunk. His parents were small, wizened people— shriveled, I supposed, by the ravages of ghetto life. They say we live in an age that cries for a Dickens, but I wonder if a Hogarth might not better fill the bill. I have yet to see the television picture that can capture the hopelessness of the abject poor portrayed in the English artist's "Gin Lane," out of which these people seemed to have stepped.

To be sure, Grimes's mother was very pleasant. She acted a little frightened and bewildered, but she was trying hard to please. His father was another story. Each time Timothy would attempt to describe what he remembered, his father would interject with comments designed to hurt. "If I had been there, this never would have happened," he said at one point. And "I would have given them theirs, I wouldn't have run." Timothy coiled up within himself a little further with each remark.

As Hershey and Hayes finished up with Grimes, Ed Boyar

joined me in a corner of the room. "Pretty good, boss," he whispered. "Grimes can describe the confrontation outside the pizza parlor, where the white guys had the bats. And it sure as hell sounds like an assault to me. He doesn't have much to say about what happened after that. He says he jumped over a wall in the parking lot next to the pizza joint and began running north along Cross Bay Boulevard, toward the Belt Parkway. Someone threw a flashlight or a stick, and it bounced off his shoulder, and then one of his pursuers fell down, and he was able to get away."

"If memory serves from reading the Fives, that would be Bollander, wouldn't it?" I asked Ed. "The kid who had recently had hip surgery?"

"You got it, boss," Boyar answered. "Looks like it's all comin' together."

Through years of working together, I have come slowly and stubbornly to realize that Ed Boyar, despite his espousal of a political theory to the right of a Russian tsar, is an eternal optimist. So it was hardly a surprise to me later that Marty Hershey did not quite agree with Boyar's perception of the Grimes interview.

"Once again, Ed's being a Pollyanna," Hershey grumped when I relayed Boyar's analysis. "Grimes remembers what happened outside the pizzeria all right, but he says he has no recall of the initial confrontation, and that doesn't help us at all."

Hawkins, who had spent part of the interview questioning Grimes, was even more disturbed by our potential witness. Grimes was in shock, was Dennis's opinion, having difficulty focusing on exactly what was going on. Grimes was currently seeing a psychiatrist, Mason had explained, because he was having trouble "remembering things." I pondered the courtroom consequences of a prosecution witness with a self-avowed memory problem.

All in all, however, it had been a productive two hours. Interestingly, neither Mason nor Maddox said a word during the interviews. More interestingly, the subject of Dominick Blum's arrest was never broached.

Before leaving, I told the attorneys that we'd like to see the victims again, soon. I wanted them to accompany us to Howard

Beach. After an exchange of glances, Mason and Maddox agreed, and asked if they could come with their clients.

"Fine," I told them. "Why don't the two of you meet me at my office Sunday, and then we'll all pick up Timothy and Cedric in Brooklyn on the way out there. Say about eight A.M.?"

For once, I wanted to slow things down. I needed time. Time to visit Howard Beach myself. Time, I hoped, to break down one of the white kids, to gather information that might further spur the recall of Sandiford and Grimes. I had less than three days.

As we left Mason's office, the six of us felt such a shared sense of exhilaration that we decided to walk the fifteen blocks back to 2 Rector Street. It was a bitterly cold night, the wind off the river tunneling through the canyons of the financial district. A few of the lawyers on my staff, all seasoned and sober representatives of the Special State Prosecutor's Office, were almost skipping down the sidewalk. Part of this was the sense of relief at finally having actually met the Howard Beach victims, and we knew that would soon wear off. We still had to solve the jigsaw puzzle, but at least now they were letting us play with all the pieces.

14

"GOING NOWHERE"

Alas, the complexity of that puzzle soon tempered our emotions. Back in the office, the appellate team was overanxious for a report. Brook, Greenberg, and Hoffman had spent the day pulling apart files from Santucci, Fives from the police, reports from Highway Patrol, and statements from the defendants. Already a file cabinet was overflowing in our Howard Beach War Room. The files were all a mess, many unsigned or incomplete, and collating all the evidence by names, by dates, by category, by witness, and by participation was a painstaking task. My appellate staff's initial burst of giddiness upon our return did not hide the bags under their eyes as they took their customary seats along the western length of the conference-room table and began quizzing us, nonstop.

Simultaneously, those who had interviewed Grimes were eagerly and noisily exchanging notes with those who had spoken to Sandiford. The A-Team, Kohler, Nadel, and several investigators were all talking over each other. Hawkins turned to me with a quizzical look.

"Joe, I know you think I'm always quick with the psychological theories, but I got the sense that Grimes has been traumatized by the whole experience," said Hawkins, a former teacher of emotionally handicapped children. "It's terrible what that father's putting his kid through. He's creating more guilt. So how's this for a theory? What if Timmy Grimes knows more about what happened that night? What if Timmy Grimes saw Michael Griffith get killed but is blocking it out because of this huge sense of guilt?

"Here's a guy who left his two friends there," Hawkins continued amid the din. "He knows all the terrible things that subsequently happened. Of course he's going to have problems talking about it. Is it possible that he ran back down onto the highway and watched Sandiford being beaten? Is it possible that he was the black man all those 911 callers saw on the Belt Parkway? Is it possible Timmy saw Michael get hit?"

I told him that that might be too much to ask. Everyone agreed, however, that what Timmy Grimes had given us so far really didn't amount to much. At one point someone even called him a worthless witness, and Pam Hayes exploded.

"Of *course* he's a worthless witness!" she shouted in a sarcastic tone. "I mean, he's only a textbook case. Start with being the baby of eleven kids. Throw in the lead paint he probably ate when he was a baby. Then the foster homes."

The conference room grew deathly silent as Pam's voice trembled.

"The end result has got to be *him,* Timmy Grimes. What do you think he's going to turn out to be: *George Bush?* This conversation is ridiculous."

We were all tired. By the time we decided to call it a night, the mood had turned decidedly glum.

All the way home, I thought about what I'd heard that day. Sandiford had painted a horrible picture of normalcy turned upside down, of a young group of partygoers transformed suddenly into a murderous mob. I couldn't lose the picture of the huge black man, down on his knees, grabbing the bat from little Jon Lester's hands and pleading, first with his eyes, then with his words: "My God, please stop. Don't hit me again. I've got a son at home just like you. Please don't hit me."

Sandiford's description nearly brought to life the image of Lester wrenching the baseball bat out of the black man's grip and smashing him across the forehead with it. How could San-

diford *not* be able to identify the boy who did this to him? Yet
he'd been unable to pick Lester out of mug shots he'd been
shown by the detectives. I hoped things might be different if
they came face to face in court.

And what of the rest of the mob? Sandiford was adamant about
not seeing any faces—save one. Yes, he had said, he was "fairly
sure" he would recognize Dominick Blum.

Wonderful, I thought. *The only face my principal witness can
recall is that of a man whom the evidence points to as being
innocent. And if in fact Blum did intentionally manage to run
down Michael Griffith, there's the defense's "intervening cause"
and there goes my case.*

And then there was Grimes, who seemed out of it all, unable
to provide anything more than an unconnected sketch of what
he thought had happened; Grimes, who had trouble remembering things and who already had been involved in two scrapes
with the law since that terrible night.

At home that Thursday evening, I heard from both Chief
Borelli and Al Pica, reporting that none of the original twelve
defendants seemed interested in talking. Their men were going
to begin canvassing teenagers who had not left the Schorr party.
The news was a fitting cap to the day.

"This case is going nowhere," I told Pat over a midnight steak
and vodka martinis. "I've got absolutely nothing that I can
prove." By the end of our meal, Pat had set the new worrying-
isn't-going-to-change-anything record in our twenty-five-year
marriage. *Somehow,* I thought, *things have got to get better
tomorrow.*

At eight o'clock Friday morning, the A-Team, minus Brook,
Hoffman, Greenberg, and Nadel, set out for Howard Beach in
two cars. Leading the way, and carrying Mangum and Hawkins
along with me, my driver cruised through the Brooklyn-Battery
Tunnel, the tube connecting lower Manhattan to Kings County.
It was a sparkling, clear January day, and as we picked up the
eastbound Belt Parkway, the waters of New York Harbor glis-
tened.

Forty-five minutes after we left Manhattan, Tom Mulvihill

drove our car onto Exit 17-S, Cross Bay Boulevard, and I realized I must have been through Howard Beach every time Pat and I ventured from our summer cottage in nearby Breezy Point and drove to Vincent's Clam Bar on Cross Bay Boulevard. This was an Italian restaurant that serves calamari and shrimp in the hottest sauce north of Juarez and, yes, had strung "fairy lights" across its façade the night that the three black men had found it "too ritzy" to enter. As we pulled into the town's business district, I didn't know that I would not be going back to Vincent's soon without a police escort.

At Cross Bay Boulevard and 157th Avenue we saw the building shown endlessly on television for nearly a month: the New Park Pizzeria had become, improbably, the city's newest tourist attraction. Passengers, black and white, on their way to and from nearby Kennedy Airport were ordering cabdrivers to pause at the pizza parlor, and irate residents of Howard Beach were up in arms. Most felt, justifiably, that the community as a whole had been unfairly tarred because of the actions of a few punk kids.

Aware of this hostility, the city had ordered a police cruiser and two uniformed officers to sit prominently in the parking lot adjacent to the pizzeria to guard this new landmark. Staring at the intersection, I paused for a moment, attempting to visualize the confrontation that night in December.

Next we drove north one block to 156th Avenue, or Shore Parkway, and made a left. We crawled along the intersecting streets, past 90th, 89th, 88th, 87th, 86th, and finally 85th. This is where the two black men had run the gauntlet. We got out of the cars to inspect the chain-link fence dividing Shore Parkway from the Belt Parkway at 85th Street. The repair job had been seamless, and we had to look closely to find where the rip had actually been. As I examined the fresh links, I became angry for a moment. The repairs had obviously been made on the orders of some Queens County bureaucrat, as if the new links in the fence would also blot out the memory of the ugliness that had occurred that night.

"Mr. Hynes," yelled Tom Mulvihill, breaking my reverie, "call on the car phone."

It was big news.

Rose Pastore informed me that the logjam had broken: James Gucciardo, representing his nephew Tommy, and an attorney named Rick Librett, representing Robert Riley, had both called the office.

"Also," Rose added, "Chief Borelli called. He may have some good news."

I never asked how she divined these things. Tom took me to a pay phone, and Rose connected me to the law offices of James Gucciardo.

"Joe," he began, and I was somewhat surprised at his informality, "I was a detective in Brooklyn when you worked for the Legal Aid Society. Listen, my nephew is in the Howard Beach jam, but he'd like to help. Can I see you?"

"How about this afternoon?" I asked him.

"No," he replied, "I can't. I have a court appearance. Can we do it Monday?"

"Monday? Are you kidding? Monday will be too late."

This is known as the prosecuting attorney's version of "the train is leaving the station." Prosecutors learn early in their careers that to cut a deal with a suspect you have to convey a sense of urgency. That is, a prospective defendant had better be willing to cooperate now, otherwise it will be too late.

"Jim," I told Gucciardo, returning the informality, "I intend to start presenting evidence to a grand jury no later than the end of next week. If your nephew wants in, he had better be in my office no later than tomorrow afternoon. By the way, who's representing him in the case?"

"I am," Gucciardo said.

"Are you sure it's smart to repesent your own flesh and blood?" I asked him.

"That's my decision, Joe. Can I come in around two o'clock?"

I said that would be fine and asked if he was bringing his nephew.

"We'll see," said Gucciardo, who hesitated before adding, "Joe, I want a walk for my kid on this. No charges."

"Well, I doubt if we can do that," I answered. "But let's see what we can work out."

Librett, Riley's attorney, wasn't in, so I had Rose patch me in

to Chief Borelli, who informed me that Billy Bollander's father
had gotten in touch with one of his detectives and wanted to talk
to me tomorrow.

"Tomorrow!" I shouted into the phone. "How come everyone
thinks we have all the time in the world with this thing?"

Borelli was nonplussed. "I don't know, Mr. Hynes, but we
have the old man and we have the kid, and the earliest the father
can see you is three P.M. tomorrow."

"Okay," was all I could say.

On the drive back to Manhattan, I filled in Hawkins and Mangum. We were making progress, and that was exciting, but we
still didn't know what kind of information we'd get from the
kids. Back at the office, Keating called and talked me into a lunch
date with the Irish Mafia. I told him I'd be there as soon as I
reached Riley's attorney, Librett. Rose got him on the phone
around noon.

"Mr. Hynes, my name is Rick Librett, I represent Robert
Riley, and your detectives went to his house."

Oh boy, I thought. *Here comes the standard defense attorney's
complaint about Gestapo tactics.*

"Yes," I told him in an icy tone, "that was at my direction."

"Oh, I'm not complaining," Librett shot back good-naturedly,
stunning me a little. "I'm a former assistant DA from Nassau
County, so I know the drill. Can I come and see you?"

"Certainly," I said and asked him if he could make it that
afternoon.

"No, I can't make it today," he replied. "And since Monday's
the Martin Luther King Birthday holiday, how about Tuesday
morning?"

By Tuesday, I told him, I'd probably have an agreement with
another of the gang members, and I didn't intend to cut a deal
with more than one. We settled on Sunday morning at eleven.
I told him to bring his client and made a mental note to push
back by a few hours the on-site inspection with Sandiford,
Grimes, and their attorneys.

At lunch, Tierney, Keating, Russert, Nadel, and I were joined
by an old friend, the attorney Harvey Louie Greenberg, whom

we refer to as the Irish Mafia's "personal counsel." Among my friends, and with some assistance from a bottle of Pinot Grigio wine, I began to relax for the first time since my appointment as special prosecutor.

Harvey Louie Greenberg is that ultimate practitioner of the law, adept equally in the wells of civil and criminal courts, skilled at trial as well as appellate work. Between his private practice and various government assignments—for Greenberg was often temporarily drafted by government agencies—he managed to dispense free legal advice to a bevy of public officials, me included. His expertise and versatility were just what I needed.

I told the Irish Mafia what I had on the case so far, certain that my remarks would go no further than the table, and when I concluded, I expected the cynical Keating to speak first. Of course, he did. "Maybe," he said after a thoughtful pause, "you can get Mario to supersede you." I had to admit it wasn't a bad line.

When the laughter abated, Harvey Louie Greenberg asked the question I have since grown to detest: "Joe, what were those guys doing in Howard Beach anyway?"

I lashed back at him. "What the fuck difference does that make, Harvey?"

"All the difference, Joe, if you develop a case. And so far, from what I've heard, I don't hold much hope of that. But if you do develop a case, you better be prepared to prove what they were doing there. Because any lawyer who defends those kids will be shouting that question over and over again."

He was absolutely right. I had been a prosecutor so long that I had forgotten the first maxim of the defense attorney: "When you don't have the law on your side, argue the facts. If you don't have the facts, argue the law. And if you don't have either, shout prosecutorial misconduct." Given the nature of contemporary law enforcement, with its reliance on moles and informers, I could add a fourth tenet to that legal saw: "And if charges of prosecutorial misconduct don't work, attack the character of the prosecution witnesses." In my case, that meant Sandiford and Grimes.

I suddenly envisioned a defense attorney, blood in his eye, carving up Grimes like filet mignon.

Then I excused myself and went to the phone. I dialed, and Boyar answered.

"Ed," I said, "just what were those guys doing in Howard Beach?"

I had to keep myself from laughing.

"You know, boss—the car broke down. They were walking. What are you talking about?"

"Can we prove that their car broke down?" I said. "Why did they walk back to Howard Beach instead of going to the Cross Bay Boulevard Bridge, where they got the water from the toll booth collectors? And what about Blum's car?" I added. The question just popped into my head. "Did the police go over it thoroughly?"

Boyar said he'd get back to me. When he did, his answer was disheartening. The police had merely given Blum's smashed automobile a quick inspection before releasing it to Blum's father. Dennis Quirk, the president of the Court Officers' Union, Blum's union, had the car now. It was in his garage.

I called Quirk to find out what the hell he was doing with the car. He said he was holding it for "evidence," and added that I was free to come and pick it up.

"Dammit, Ed, who was running this shoddy investigation?" I muttered when I got Boyar back on the line. He was, naturally, at a loss for words. Then I returned to Harvey Louie Greenberg's theme. "And what about the sixty-four-thousand-dollar question, the one we're sure to hear every day at trial: Just what were those guys doing in that neighborhood?"

"Boss," said Boyar, clearly frustrated, "this is the United *States.* They didn't need a passport."

He was, of course, right.

15

CUTTING DEALS

The story still had too many holes. For example, we couldn't lay out who drove with whom when the teens left Schorr's party for the New Park Pizzeria. Lester said he was with Farina, but Farina recalled being with Ladone. Ladone remembered seeing Pirone on a corner that Pirone swore he was never on. And so it went. The suspects' statements were a jumble of inconsistencies and memory failure (convenient or otherwise). Details were impossible to pin down. Eyewitnesses were offering conflicting accounts. And the labyrinthine diagrams of the chase down Shore Parkway were driving me crazy with frustration.

I turned in early Friday evening, only to be awakened by a late call from Boyar. He sounded frantic.

"I drove out to Howard Beach on my way home from work, boss," he said. "And I found a back way onto the highway from 85th Street. It's just like Cedric said."

We agreed to meet at the New Park Pizzeria at eight the next morning. A few minutes later the phone rang again. "Charles-call-me-Joe Hynes" was Richard Mangum's pet phone introduction, "we've got some good news."

"I know, Richard, Boyar just called. He found the secret route to the Belt Parkway."

I sensed a fleeting hesitation at the other end of the line. Then three words thudded from Mangum's mouth: "So did I."

He was clearly disappointed that Boyar had reached me first. I realized immediately what had happened. My two assistants, independently perplexed by the certainty with which Cedric Sandiford delivered his story, had each traveled to Howard Beach and made the separate discovery. I suppose it was that kind of initiative that made my office different.

I called Borelli at home and asked him to meet us at Howard Beach at 8:45 the next morning. I asked him to bring Lasak. I didn't tell him why.

In the morning, Boyar and Mangum were waiting, both smiling and excited-looking, when I pulled up at the pizzeria. They hopped in and we retraced the route we had taken yesterday. When we reached the corner of 85th Street and Shore Parkway, the spot where Sandiford had been beaten to the ground, Boyar told me to continue around a bend where Shore Parkway bears left. We passed the curve, the Howard Beach Jewish Community Center, St. Helen's Catholic Church, and as we approached 157th Avenue, both my passengers shouted, "Take a right."

I inched west along 157th Avenue, a vacant lot on my right, until I was again directed by another stereo shout: "Take another right. Here."

A cut in the curb, large enough for a cement mixer to squeeze through, led to a dirt road, which snaked ahead for several hundred yards through a moldy construction site before climbing a small hillock. An unimpeded path to the shoulder of the east-bound Belt Parkway ran down the other side of the knoll. From our vantage point, it was evident that a person standing at the corner of 85th Street and Shore Parkway would have an unrestricted sightline to a car entering the highway. Traveling left to right.

Just as Sandiford had said.

"So Michael crawls through the hole, and the gang jumps into their cars, and a few seconds later Cedric, who's still lying on the grass on the other side of the fence, sees the cars chasing Michael east," said Mangum. "Michael spots his pursuers, tries to cross over to put the divider between him and them, and gets hit. Makes sense."

The three of us drove back in silence along the frozen ruts of the muddy path; their freshness and depth left no doubt that the shortcut was well traveled by the residents of Howard Beach.

When we reached 85th Street and Shore Parkway, I turned the car around and Richard pulled out his stopwatch. Gunning the engine, I raced along the dirt road onto the Belt: forty-two seconds.

It took six seconds longer the second time we ran the course. Perhaps the weight of Borelli and Lasak in my backseat accounted for the extra time.

The chief of Queens detectives was clearly embarrassed. Two investigative attorneys unfamiliar with Howard Beach had discovered a rather obvious back route onto the highway that his detectives, who patrolled the area, had told him didn't exist. Borelli and Lasak had to be wondering what kind of investigators they had working under them. I was too polite to ask.

After our dramatic demonstration—for we had just trundled Lasak and Borelli into my car without telling them what we had discovered—Borelli invited us back to his office to meet with the detective who said he was bringing in William Bollander and his father later that afternoon. After a short debriefing, the man sauntered back to his squad room and Boyar and Mangum left the station house looking for coffee. Borelli and I were alone for the first time since the Piecyk case. This time he appeared more relaxed.

"Joe," I asked him softly, "why did Sandiford feel you guys jobbed him that night? Just what the hell happened?"

Borelli returned my gaze carefully before responding. I think he suspected that I still held him responsible for bungling Romual Piecyk's complaint. He sized me up from behind his desk and finally answered, in anger and frustration. The gut reactions of a "cop's cop" gushed forth nonstop.

"I'm not entirely sure if one thing in particular set Sandiford off," he told me. "The lieutenant from the Accident Investigation Squad could have been a lot more sensitive. And I've been unable to find out who it was who thought it was a good idea to keep Sandiford sitting in a patrol car for several hours with Griffith's body lying in full view. And if I ever lay my hands on the asshole who interrupted Sandiford's telephone call to Michael's mother, I will personally ride his ass out the door."

There was no stopping him now. He went on to argue that his "guys," meaning the Queens Detective Division, had been handicapped from the moment they came onto the case.

"We didn't have anything to do with it. The uniforms screwed this case up, and it's a goddamn shame," the chief continued. "Review all the statements taken from those little mutts after the attack, and you'll find that if you do ever make a case, my guys have given you most of your ammunition."

Furthermore, he offered, his office was taking uncalled-for heat from the brass, the press, the public, everyone, because Ladone, Lester, and Kern had "walked free."

With the possible exception of Detective Fiorillo's illegal interrogation of Lester, Borelli's investigators had in fact done a superb job at the station house. And most of the interviews taken were to be deemed admissible evidence after judicial review. Yet I still felt that Borelli's claim lacked substance, that somehow the entire Queens criminal justice system was at fault for the snafus.

"Let me tell you what I have to deal with here in Queens," Borelli said, pointing to the newspaper sitting on his desk. The lead story in *New York Newsday* was the first extended interview with Santucci, who defended his decision to withdraw from the case: "I had no doubt that what I did was the right course," the DA was quoted as saying. "This is the first criminal case I gave up. If I didn't give it up, and if all the charges were thrown out by the grand jury, they would have said my own ego was to blame." (I couldn't help wondering where Santucci's ego had been the morning of December 21.) It went on like that. And then Borelli explained what happened from his point of view.

"After I was filled in about the attack and its racial significance, I got down to the One-Oh-Six and called Lasak in Santucci's office and filled him in. I told him 'The mayor is coming, the police commissioner is coming, the brass is descending upon us.' 'Don't worry, Chief,' he told me. 'I'll take care of it right away.'

"And how does the DA's office take care of it?" Borelli asked.

"By sending a fucking kid with less than two years on the job. That's how."

He was finished, wrung out, and we both stared sullenly at the floor. Boyar and Mangum coincidentally appeared with containers of coffee, and the four of us began to discuss the wild card in this game: Dominick Blum. He was a forlorn character, his life seemingly shattered along with his windshield that night in Howard Beach. He was denounced almost daily by Mason and Maddox, and thus he was being hounded by the press. The Blum family home in Brooklyn was under a twenty-four-hour police guard. As a man caught between the law and the community, Blum spent the majority of his time ducking reporters and paparazzi. He told Quirk, his union leader, that he felt "like he was alone in the world."

Was it really possible that his girlfriend had slept through the crash? That was what he claimed. And no witnesses as yet had reporting seeing Blum stop, make his determination that it was an animal or tire he hit, and leave. I had assigned Marty Hershey and Boyar to the Blum angle of the investigation, and so far the hapless court officer appeared clean.

"I can't believe this," Blum confided to another friend, who was also a reporter. "I haven't been in Howard Beach since I was a little kid. I don't know these people. Do you think I'd want to hang out with sixteen-year-olds? There were a million people who could have been driving past that spot on the Belt Parkway at that particular time, and any one of them could have hit Michael Griffith."

Borelli was inclined to agree with Blum's defense.

"But Sandiford puts Blum at the pizza parlor, and he has him running down the street with the gang," I reminded the chief. "And so far, everything Sandiford's said—everything that everyone else finds implausible—has panned out."

I arched my eyebrows. There was no need to remind him again of this morning's discovery of the path to the Belt Parkway.

"I still have serious doubts," said Borelli. "He's twenty-three, too old for that crowd. We can put him at the play at Brooklyn College earlier in the evening. And when he hit Griffith, he was in the westbound lane. So even if, as Sandiford claims, Blum was part of the gang, and used that dirt path to get onto the highway"—and here Borelli returned the gesture and arched his brow—"he'd still be going eastbound. Left-to-right, Joe, which means he'd have to get off at Cross Bay Boulevard, make a left on the overpass, and drive back down onto the highway westbound in order to run the kid down.

"Now I deal in probabilities," the chief concluded, "and though anything is possible, I just don't think it's probable that Dominick Blum intentionally killed Michael Griffith. And you can tell Mason and Maddox I said so."

I was impressed with the analysis. And by the time he was through, none of us had much doubt about his conclusion. Nevertheless, the law of "intervening cause" was to prove so important to our case that I later hired an accident re-creation specialist who independently established Blum's innocence. If Blum *had* run down Griffith intentionally, that would have broken the death-link between the black man and the white gang.

By 1:00 P.M. we were back in the War Room, my two Sherlock Holmeses taking a powerful ribbing from the deskbound appellate crew for their amazing powers of deduction. Mangum, a certified ham, was particularly taken by their good-natured jibes, especially as he had admitted to me privately that he had been frightened out of his wits driving the dark roads of Howard Beach the night before. I was glad he was getting the attention. Then an investigator interrupted to inform me that James Gucciardo was outside.

I recognized Jim Gucciardo immediately from my Legal Aid days and introduced him to Marty Hershey and Doug LeVien. The four of us walked into my office and Gucciardo mentioned that we had been on opposite sides of a few criminal cases, but I had no recollection of any. (Apparently he, too, had learned his small-talk lesson well in law school.)

I asked if he had reconsidered representing his nephew Thomas. No, he said, the family couldn't afford another lawyer. "This thing has really gotten out of control," he added. "Tommy is a good student, a hardworking kid."

Apparently, when he walked his nephew out of the 106th Precinct on December 22, Jim Gucciardo had no idea that young Tommy's friends would spend the rest of the day giving each other up. William Bollander had sworn to investigators that his buddy Tommy Gucciardo bragged of wielding a tree limb against Cedric Sandiford "like Conan the Barbarian." That statement had yet to be made public.

I straightened Gucciardo in his seat by warning him that I was taking this attack very seriously and would probably file homicide charges against several of the teens.

"Against Tommy?" he asked, obviously shocked.

"Jim, I don't know how it's going to develop. But if I can prove one or more of these kids chased Michael Griffith into the path of Dominick Blum's car, I'm going to the grand jury and asking for murder."

Gucciardo's shock turned to rage, and he bolted from his chair. "I think you're nuts!"

"Calm down, Jim."

This was exactly what I had been concerned about; it is axiomatic in the legal profession that lawyers do not represent flesh and blood. Gucciardo sat silently, composing himself for a moment or two before asking me exactly what I wanted.

"I want the kid to tell us everything."

"What does he get? Does he walk with no charges?"

"No. He has to plead guilty to a felony."

He was out of his chair again. "Forget it, Joe. He's not going to be a felon."

"Jim, your nephew was involved in a night of horror." I stood up to face him, a touch of rage in my voice now. "One man's dead. Another was beaten senseless. He's not going to walk away clean."

Livid, Gucciardo stomped to the door, turned, and snarled, "I'll call you tomorrow."

"Don't let it go beyond tomorrow, Jim. It may be too late."

He smiled ironically. I guessed he'd used that phrase more than once during his years on the force. But I wanted him to understand that I was serious.

"This is no bullshit game," I added sincerely. "I'm making a deal with only one kid."

*

I walked him into the waiting room, where, sitting forlornly on the couch beside Borelli's detective, were a small man and a lanky, blond teenager, his left arm in a cast. Billy Bollander had recently undergone an operation to transplant bone from his hip to his wrist. His brown canvas cap and vacant grin brought to mind nothing so much as a picture I had once seen of Hitler's brown-shirted youth corps.

I ushered the Bollanders and the detective into my office, hoping the sight of the trio, so obvious in their intentions, would spur Gucciardo into cutting a deal.

"Let them see each other, Joe," Pam Hayes had urged me earlier that day. "Let every one of those little gangsters know that their pals are scurrying like rats."

I explained to Bill Bollander, Sr., that I intended to start presenting evidence to the grand jury within a week, and that I was looking for someone to cooperate.

"I'm not going to go into much detail, because that's something for me to work out with your lawyer," I told the father. "Someone eventually has to represent your son. I cannot deal with you."

Mr. Bollander nodded for me to go on. I glanced at his son, who was wearing a smug, unconcerned expression.

"I want Billy to tell me exactly what happened that night. Who was present and who did what."

"And then what?" the father asked. "Will he have to testify?"

"Yes, he will."

"Billy," he commanded, and the kid leaped from his chair as if shot from a silo, "go outside."

I looked more closely at Mr. Bollander as Billy shut the door behind him. He was really just a tired old man, chain-smoking cigarettes, his clothing in need of repair. The deep lines etched into his face made him appear much older than I guessed he was, and as he adjusted his rimless bifocals the light caught a drop of moisture in the corner of his eye. He leaned slowly forward, looking me square in the eye. Then, in a flat, even tone, he uttered a statement I'll never forget: "Mr. Hynes, I can't let my boy testify. You gotta understand, Mr. Hynes"—he paused here to choose the right words—"not everyone in Howard Beach is

God-fearin'. I don't want to come home from work one day and find a slab of cement where my house used to be."

So, I thought, someone had finally reached the nub of the problem. If not exactly Murder Incorporated, the tiny village of Howard Beach was certainly more than a speck on the Organized Crime Control Bureau's map. John Gotti's presence alone would guarantee that. And Gotti had neighbors in the same business. I'd heard that Mob people were going door to door, collecting money for a Howard Beach defense fund. In addition, my own sources told me that at least one member of the gang had family connections to the Cosa Nostra: Michael Pirone's father, Vito, was alleged to be a small-time bookmaker and hood, with an extensive criminal record. He was known to associate with, if not work for, one Frederico "Fritzy" Giovanelli, a mid-level Genovese Family underboss and loanshark. When Fritzy was accused of killing a cop, Vito Pirone offered to put up his house as collateral to make Giovanelli's bail.

I thought about all that as the Bollanders left my office. Could I seriously hope that anyone in Howard Beach would be willing to break the code of *omertà*—to "turn"?

Scare tactics certainly hadn't worked with former detective James Gucciardo. He called at 4:30 that afternoon, informing me that he couldn't let his nephew plead to any charge. I told him that I still thought it was a mistake that he was representing kin and mentioned that I'd seen him in court.

The classic prosecutorial tool is the "turn," an attempt to use a guilty party to testify against others who are equally guilty. This almost always revolves around a deal, in which the "singer" provides evidence in exchange for a lighter sentence. The benefits of this technique are fairly obvious, but its morality is fiercely debated. To me turning someone is morally neutral, although not something I like to do.

As I drove home that night, I pondered the problem of trying to turn a resident of John Gotti's backyard. Then, exhausted, I gave up. My head hit the pillow at 9:00 P.M. I was out cold by 9:01. I tossed and turned all night, and by five o'clock, my head full of worries, I was up brewing coffee. By six I had showered, shaved, and gathered up Sunday's three daily papers. I had been special prosecutor for five days, and I still had no clear picture of what had happened at Howard Beach.

Murray Kempton's column in *New York Newsday* brought me brief solace: "It is a blessed relief to know that all official inquiry into the dreadful pre-Christmas festivities that ended with the death of Michael Griffith in Howard Beach will be henceforth the sole province of Special State Prosecutor Charles J. Hynes," he wrote in his inimitable style. "Hynes is the best of remedies for the noisy incoherence into which the matter had been writhing before his appointment."

I couldn't help feeling flattered. Then I had to laugh, as Kempton wrote, "No question from us of the professionally curious class ever draws from Hynes a reply beyond the minimum that social pleasantry requires." Little did he know that as he was praising me for plugging the prosecutorial leaks, I had virtually nothing to leak. At this moment, I hardly knew anything more about the Howard Beach case than the journalists covering the story.

But other writers, perhaps taking their cue from the mayor, saw my appointment as a bow to strong-arm pressure from the community's black radicals. For all of Kempton's praise of my quiescence, I began to fear charges of "whitewash" from the black community if I didn't have someone arrested in a hurry.

16

THE TURN DANCE

As I arrived at my office on Sunday morning, I spotted a small group of people standing at the elevator banks in the otherwise empty lobby. There was a tall, solidly built man in his late forties, a tiny, sad-looking woman, and two broad-shouldered young men. This was the Riley family. And I could feel everything begin to shift.

Their eyes never met mine as I walked through the small lobby and entered the elevator. Obviously, they were waiting for Librett, the lawyer, before coming up to see me. When the doors closed, the Rileys were all staring hard at the floor.

Upstairs, most of the A-Team had already arrived, and the War Room, with a haggard platoon of lawyers and investigators lounging about, looked like an army bivouac. I told them who was in the lobby and then started to deal with the delicate question of who was going to be at the meeting with Librett and the Rileys.

Everyone wanted in on what we believed would be a major breakthrough. Arbitrarily, I selected Boyar and Mangum, my trial team, and Helman Brook, my appellate expert. At the last moment, Dennis Hawkins made a strong pitch to be included, "Hey, Joe, I know these kids' statements better than anybody else around here. I've been reading this stuff backward and forward. If he's going to tell you something that's not true, I'll be able to pick it up." How could I refuse? Hawkins was in too.

I was surprised that no one else complained about being left out, and I took it as an indication of collective self-confidence. Then we were told that Librett had arrived. The "turn dance," as the street cops call it, was about to begin.

I asked an investigator to escort the Riley family to a temporary grand jury room on the floor above us while Librett and his private investigator, a grizzled former NYPD detective sergeant named Al Simonella, entered my office. A former assistant district attorney, Librett was not unfamiliar with the turn. We shook hands all around.

"Bobby Riley doesn't know a hell of a lot," said Librett, a large man with dark ringlets of hair that grazed his shoulders. "But he can place some of the kids who were involved in the attack at the scene."

He paused to measure my reaction, and I obliged with none.

"But I want a promise of a complete bath, Joe," he continued. "No prosecution. He walks."

Brook, Hoffman, and Greenberg had collated enough statements for me to realize that Bobby Riley was more than just an observer in the Howard Beach attack. And they had told me so in no uncertain terms. Matching up every report they could lay their hands on, the three had concluded that Riley was most likely a ringleader. This wasn't yet evidence that would stand up in court, of course. And I had told my staff that it wasn't my style to cut a deal based on someone's gut feeling. That, I suppose, accounted for the shocked faces of my staff when I replied to Librett.

"Your client's not telling you the truth," I said to the defense attorney. "I understand, because I've been on your side. There's really nothing you can do about that. But let me tell you, he's lying to you."

"I grilled him tough, Joe, I grilled him hard," he protested. "I believe him."

"That's because you don't have what we have," I answered, and paused.

"Tell Bobby Riley and his parents," I said, "that the next time they hear from me will be when you tell them to appear in Queens County Supreme Court to answer an indictment charging him with intentional murder."

The room was suddenly still. I felt very far out on a limb. Librett finally stirred and got up from his seat. I was sure he was going to gather his clients and walk out of the building.

"All right, Joe," he said, "give me some time with them."

With that, the attorney walked out the door of my office, trailed by his private investigator, escorted by Dennis Hawkins.

As soon as the door closed behind them, Helman asked incredulously, "Joe, perhaps you wouldn't mind telling us the basis for that threat?"

"Helman," I replied evenly, "one of these creeps is going to break, and we may end up with a half-dozen murder indictments. Chances are it'll be this guy. And the sooner the better. I was just trying to move things along a little bit."

When Hawkins returned, a broad smile was only partly concealed by his six-inch cigar.

"Let me get this straight, Joe," he chided me. "You never cut a deal based on someone's gut feeling?

"And there's one more thing, Joe," Hawkins added. "I can't tell about Librett, but his investigator sure thinks you're full of shit."

"Why do you say that?"

"Because as I led him to the elevator he was whistling the melody to 'Fairy tales, can come true, it can happen to you. . . .'"

We all laughed. Except Richard Mangum, who argued that Librett was probably singing the same tune upstairs to the Riley family, and that we were fast running out of potential witnesses.

"Maybe," I told Richard, "but his first obligation is to his client. So before he takes the chance that we're bluffing, he'll lay everything out for the kid and his parents. I've been there, Richard. And even if Librett's sure we don't have the evidence yet, I'm betting he's not going to gamble with that kid's life. He has to know from his experience as a prosecutor that, with so many defendants involved, somebody's going to break."

After an hour, Librett called down from upstairs. He needed another twenty minutes with the Rileys, he said, "but we're making progress." My heart skipped a beat. Forty-five minutes later, the attorney returned, this time alone.

"He's got it all, Joe, the whole story. What will you do on a plea?"

In Librett's absence we had debated just that question. It did not sit well with any of us that we would be bargaining with one of the alleged killers of Michael Griffith. But Helman Brook had best summed things up when he said, "Riley may be a scumbag, but he's *our* scumbag."

Librett was aware that murder two was the strongest indictment allowed in this case. In New York, first-degree murder charges are brought only when the defendant is accused of killing a police officer. I told him, "Riley will be indicted along with however many others for murder in the second degree. But he'll plead guilty to assault in the second degree." Assault two is a serious felony, punishable by up to four years in jail.

"Will you recommend no jail time if he's completely truthful?" asked Librett, who I believe already knew the answer.

"No, Rick. I'll leave that up to the judge. But I do promise to personally appear at sentencing and lay out the extent of his cooperation."

"Will you recommend Youthful Offender?" he pressed, a criminal status that in New York State results in the sealing of the defendant's criminal record, which is in most cases public record.

"No, but I won't oppose you if you ask the judge to grant Riley Youthful Offender treatment," I answered.

Librett left the room, promising to return promptly with a decision. I was impressed with the way he handled the negotiation.

"Okay, we got a deal," he said ten minutes later. "I'll bring the kid in tomorrow."

"What?" we all shouted. One of the first rules of the turn is never to let anyone sleep on the deal. Too many things can go wrong. We wanted Riley in this room, answering our questions *now*.

"Joe, please, trust me," pleaded Librett. "This is a very close family. See the other kid in there? Joe Riley, Jr.? He's a New York City cop. They understand how this works, they want to do it, and they understand the consequences. But they want to talk it out. I promise, they'll be here tomorrow. Please don't make another deal."

"Rick, I hope you're right," I told him. "I can't promise anything, but I won't bullshit you. I'm not expecting anybody else today."

He said Robert Riley would be in my office on Monday. When the Rileys and Librett left, Boyar turned to me and smiled. "Just like a frigging soap opera, huh, boss?"

Two hours later we were with Maddox and Mason and Sandiford and Grimes, traveling in an undercover surveillance van toward the backroads of Howard Beach. The van was leading a flotilla of seven or eight automobiles, packed with the A-Team and a brace of my investigators. I even let my appellate lawyers out of the office. They had been locked up in the War Room so long that I was hoping that a field trip into fresh air and sunlight would knock the pallor off their faces.

Grimes had brought along his girlfriend, Cheryl Sandiford, Cedric's niece, who was rather overt in her affection for Timothy, hugging and kissing him all the way to Howard Beach. This made Mason, a church deacon, noticeably uncomfortable, and I felt a certain embarrassment myself. While Pam Hayes fought motion sickness in the back of the cramped, windowless van, and Grimes and his girlfriend wrestled in a corner, Sandiford, Mason, and I discussed everything from the church to the civil rights movement, the attorney invoking the Scriptures several times. I recall one citation being particularly apt: "One witness is not enough to convict" (Deuteronomy 19:15). And Mason also told me that he knew blacks who had threatened to visit Howard Beach with guns to exact their own form of revenge, but he had advised them against such intemperate action. Yet Mason struck me more as the type to allow others to debate the use of violence while he acted as moderator, confident that someone else would make the case for law and order.

Bundled up against the bitter January cold, we must have been quite a sight when we reached the New Park Pizzeria, where Hilly Hoffman and several of my investigators went in to buy slices. Nearly twenty people walked and drove the routes down which both Timothy and Cedric had fled. At one point

Richard Mangum looked up and noticed several white men in a car trailing us. My investigators more or less surrounded them and found out that they were merely curious Queens detectives working on a separate case.

It had been three weeks since Cedric had been at the scene. As we walked down Shore Parkway, stopping before homes and driveways where he had been beaten, he appeared to be in a trance. In front of Theresa Fisher's sister's home, a passing white motorist shouted at Maddox: "Fuck you." Maddox stared stoically and made no response. Grimes was no help at all; he sat sullenly in the van with his girlfriend, waiting for it to be over. So we concentrated on Sandiford's re-creation, all of us eventually finding ourselves on the other side of that chain-link fence, walking eastbound on the shoulder of the Belt Parkway.

While we were there, three cars made their way onto the Belt Parkway via the dirt road. Boyar and Mangum beamed as we headed back to our cars. Then, walking in small groups next to the parkway, LeVien, Mason, and I took up the rear, with Sandiford just ahead of us, flanked by Maddox and Mangum. Suddenly, as if taken with some suicidal urge, Sandiford furiously burst out onto the highway.

Dodging cars, he made it to the divider, close to the point where his stepson's body had lain. Then he started to cry.

As the rest of us stood stunned on the side of the road, LeVien sprinted out after Sandiford. Holding the black man gently by the shoulders, he straddled the narrow concrete divider, still splotched with the dried blood of Michael Griffith. Mason and Maddox watched in mute horror as horns blew, tires squealed, and speeding cars swerved to avoid the pair.

LeVien later said he wasn't sure exactly what to do next, other than move Sandiford to safety. And the two stood stone solid, clutching each other, until Sandiford composed himself.

Then Dennis Hawkins, apparently unable to contain his anxiety, waited for a small break in the Sunday traffic and ran out to the divider. It was just at that moment that LeVien persuaded Sandiford to dash back to the shoulder. Now Hawkins was left standing out in the middle of the highway, watching cars zip by. He was there for several embarrassing minutes.

Sandiford later told Richard Mangum he felt as if something had drawn him to make his near-suicidal dash. "I just wanted to see if it was possible to get across and get back," he said sadly. "Sometimes I think I should have died myself that night."

On the drive back, everyone was subdued. At one point Maddox inquired, "When do you go to the grand jury?" I felt it was none of his damn business, yet I tried not to look annoyed. I don't think I was successful.

"Maybe two weeks," I answered tersely.

Maddox didn't respond. He didn't have to. The glance he exchanged with Mason said it all: "More bullshit from whitey."

17

A KILLER SPEAKS

"He never went through the hole in the fence."

"What?"

"The dead guy, Griffith, he never went through the hole in the fence," said Robert Riley in a low, even monotone. "He was dead before they even went after the tall black guy, Sandiford. We chased Griffith up 90th Street. Onto the Belt. We watched him get hit, fly into the air. It was gruesome."

I was speechless. This was on Monday morning, January 19, 1987, a day set aside in New York State to honor the memory of Dr. Martin Luther King, Jr. A month had passed since The Incident at Howard Beach. And here was this slouching bear of a kid, six feet tall and 190 pounds and looking like nothing so much as the old cartoon character Baby Huey, informing us that our entire investigation had been based on erroneous information.

If Michael Griffith had indeed been killed long before Cedric Sandiford reached the hole in the fence at 85th Street and Shore Parkway, then we had been looking in all the wrong directions.

Riley's soft blue eyes avoided every other pair in the room. He sat in the leather chair, next to his lawyer, in the center of my office and stared at the floor, intoning his story as Boyar, Mangum, Hawkins, Brook, and I listened. Tight auburn curls framed a long, cold face overflowing at the jowls (we were soon to find out) from too much beer. He looked like a typical "dopey" nineteen-year-old. His story was anything but dopey. It was chilling.

I wondered if Riley realized how serious his position was. I was certain that neither he nor any of the youths in the white mob had any notion of the meaning of proximate cause. Did Riley have any idea that he had committed a murder?

When he had first walked into my office, I repeated the ground rules of our interview. Riley said he understood that if I felt he was telling us the truth, I would agree to a plea bargain, knocking the homicide charge down to felonious assault. He knew there was a good possibility that he would still do jail time. Yes, he added, he knew he would have to testify against his friends. Rick Librett, seated next to his client throughout the interview, had listened carefully before nodding his assent.

I was ceding a great deal to Bobby Riley in exchange for his cooperation. According to the law, he was a killer. But if we didn't have his cooperation and testimony, the dirty little secret of what had occurred in Howard Beach might be secure forever.

According to the old Irish saying, the wheel of fortune is oiled by whiskey. Who knows if the sober son of a corrections officer and the brother of a New York City patrolman would have followed Jon Lester into that night? But Bobby Riley confessed to gulping down more than two six-packs of beer, an admission that would surely send his pals' defense counsel into paroxysmal joy.

He had followed the two basic rules of being a defendant: never talk to the police if you're going to be indicted, and if you think it's going to be bad, get to the prosecutor's office quickly. Riley wasn't the first of those boys to respond to my request to come in and cut a deal. But Rick Librett was a former prosecutor who knew all about the art of the turn, and he was the first on my dance card.

I had begun the interview as I do all others, by attempting to relax the witness.

"Are you okay?" I asked when Riley first walked into my office.

"Yeah."

"Would you like a cup of coffee or a Coke?"

"Nah."

"Okay—then listen, Bobby, we're just here trying to figure out what went on. You know more than we do, so we need you. Why don't you start off by telling us what you did that day. Before Stevie Schorr's party. Tell us anything you can remember, and I know it was awhile ago, so take your time."

"Well, after I left my job—I'm a delivery boy at the drugstore—I went home and ate, and then I got ready for Stevie's party." At eight o'clock that night, Riley continued, he arrived at the Schorrs' kitchen door with a case of Budweiser, twenty-four twelve-ounce cans. Steven Schorr's mother directed him to the paneled rec room downstairs, where a few dozen kids were already milling about. Schorr's mother had left the kids alone for the rest of the night. "Happy Birthday" was sung (badly and off-key, as Riley recalled) and records were played and some of the kids danced. Around eleven, Cindy the Cop peeled off her clothes, and a bunch of teenaged boys and girls—ranging in age from thirteen to eighteen—watched with mixed curiosity, awe, and lust as she undulated, kicked off her shoes, slid down her blue trousers, and unbuttoned her tunic to reveal a black bikini bra and a matching G-string.

Riley was standing in a corner, drinking a beer, when suddenly Lester, DeSimone, and Bollander ran in excitedly from dropping off Claudia Calogero and began "yelling about niggers on the Boulevard."

"Fight, fight!" DeSimone shouted as he bounded down the basement steps.

"There's niggers in the pizza parlor, and we should go back and kill them," Riley recalled Jon Lester bellowing.

"Some niggers started with us at the pizza parlor and they're still there," added Bollander, the last of the trio to enter the Schorr home. And with that, Riley said, they ran back out the door and he, Scott Kern, Jason Ladone, Mike Pirone, Tommy Farina, James Povinelli, Tommy Gucciardo, Harry Buonocore, and Buonocore's girlfriend, Laura Castagna, followed.

"What happened next?" I asked.

"Well, we ran out the kitchen door and headed for our cars," he answered.

"No," Dennis Hawkins interjected. "After Lester told you that there was trouble on 'the Boulevard,' what happened after that?"

Riley stared at us with a dumb, blank expression. "Nothin'," he said.

"Nobody said anything?" pressed Hawkins. "Nobody asked what they did, or what they said, or what was the problem?"

Slowly, sheepishly, Riley shook his head no. Instead, he explained, he and Lester, and the ten others raced into three automobiles and, tires squealing, sped toward Cross Bay Boulevard to "get the fuckin' niggers."

With that, Riley stopped abruptly and blushed. He looked at Richard Mangum, the only black person in the room. "I'm sorry," he said softly.

"That's all right, son," Mangum answered impassively. "I've heard the word before."

Unlike Sandiford, I thought, this boy is going to make one terrible witness.

"We just wanted to frighten them," he said, his voice barely a whisper, the outlines of sweat under his white cotton shirt expanding. "I guess it got out of hand. We got out of the cars with a couple of baseball bats. Somebody had a tire iron, and somebody picked up a tree limb. One of them had a knife."

"In the New Park Pizzeria parking lot?" I asked. "That's where you saw one of the black men with a knife?"

"Yeah, he flashed it. It was the one that I read in the paper called Grimes."

Hawkins and I exchanged a look as Dennis made a note on a legal pad.

"Only one knife?"

"Yeah, just one. One that I saw. Some of the kids said two of them had knives, but I only saw one."

"Who had a bat at this point?" asked Richard Mangum.

"Scott Kern. He took it out of my car and he was slammin' it on the ground, tryin' to threaten them."

"And that's when they started running?" Mangum followed up.

"They took off when I grabbed the bat from Scotty and got ready to swing it at them. They ran behind the tile store across the street."

"What happened to the cars?" asked Ed Boyar.

"I left mine in the parking lot. Gucciardo drove one of them. He made a left off Cross Bay Boulevard onto Shore Parkway. That's where I jumped in."

"Okay," said Richard, "now you're in the car and you're chasing the black guys . . ."

"Not chasing them, really," said Riley, "just keeping up. And it wasn't both of them. They came out onto Shore Parkway from behind the stores on Cross Bay Boulevard. They ran down Shore Parkway for a block. Then they split up."

"Show us," I said, glancing toward the map of Howard Beach on my wall.

Riley looked at Rick Librett momentarily, then lumbered across the room to the chart. "Here," he said, pointing to the narrow, one-block section of 90th Street between Shore Parkway and the berm of the Belt Parkway. "The bigger guy goes straight down Shore Parkway, I didn't see where he went after that. And the other cuts up 90th, running toward the Belt."

Boyar and Hawkins exchanged dubious looks.

"And what did you do?" asked Mangum.

"We followed him up to the Belt, right to the metal barrier. That was as far as the car could go. Then we got out and chased a little on foot, yelling at him."

"Who followed Griffith?" I asked.

"Everybody, I think."

In the heat of battle, Robert Riley was unsure of each of his friends' movements. Yet by piecing together his recollection with what we had already gleaned from witnesses and the statements of the gang, we had our first road map of the attack in Howard Beach.

Billy Bollander had chased Grimes up Cross Bay Boulevard, Riley said. But Bollander's hip went out during the run, and as Grimes ran north over the Belt Parkway overpass, Harry Buonocore came to Bollander's aid. James Povinelli eventually joined them.

Griffith and Sandiford ran down a back alley behind a Tile-O-Rama store, chased by Riley, Kern, Lester, Jason Ladone, and Michael Pirone. Where the alley emptied into Shore Parkway, Tommy Gucciardo, driving John Saggese's red Oldsmobile, was waiting for them. Saggese, too drunk to drive, was in the car.

Riley described how, out of breath, alcohol pumping through his veins, he got into the car with Saggese and Gucciardo. Kern, Lester, Ladone, and Pirone continued running down Shore Parkway, following Griffith when he made his right turn onto 90th Street. The Oldsmobile containing Riley, Saggese, and Gucciardo was close behind. On 90th Street, the car overtook the running pursuers. Michael Griffith, up ahead, was fleeing for his life.

Hawkins broke into Riley's narrative: "We have a witness who swears Michael Griffith ran through a hole in the fence between 85th and 86th streets."

"No way," said Riley, still standing beside the map. "We chased him onto the highway right here at 90th Street."

"You still had the bat?" asked Mangum.

"No, Lester grabbed it from me. He was one of the kids on foot."

"Wait a minute, Robert," said Helman Brook, a touch of sarcasm edging into his voice. "Are you trying to tell us that Jon Lester, this scrawny little kid, came up and took the bat out of your hands?"

Riley shifted on his feet. He outweighed Lester by a good fifty pounds and apparently was more embarrassed about letting that runt grab the bat from him than he was about killing a man. But he nodded. "Yes. We were struggling for it, pulling it back and forth, and he got it. I told you, I was drinking."

"And where was Griffith at this point?" asked Boyar.

"Halfway across the Belt. We were at the guardrail at the top of 90th Street, screaming at him."

"Screaming what?" Mangum asked softly.

"I'd rather not say it," Riley answered.

"You'd better fucking say it," boomed Mangum. The room became deathly silent.

"We were . . . you know . . . we said . . ."

Brook looked sharply at Librett, who turned to his client.

"Say it, Bobby," demanded the defense attorney. "Say the words."

"We were screaming, 'Nigger, you ain't gettin' away. We're gonna fuckin' kill you. You better run, you black prick.'"

War whoops and lances, I thought sadly as the roomful of attorneys allowed Riley's vivid picture to sink in. *Those black guys must have felt like they wandered into Indian Territory.*

"Did you have the bats and the tire irons then?" I asked.

"Yeah," Riley answered. "We were waving them over our heads. Shouting loud and waving the bats."

"Did you see anyone else on 90th Street?" I asked.

"Like who?"

"Like the people in the houses," I continued. "Did anyone come to their stoop? Did any porch lights come on?"

"I didn't notice," Riley replied. "But there were Christmas lights on." And here he paused, the terrible irony finally striking him. "Every house had Christmas lights."

I fought the anger inside me. There had not been one telephone call to 911 from the residents of 90th Street. The two-hundred-foot-long stretch of the street between the Shore and Belt parkways was quiet, tree-lined, and had neatly groomed, two-story houses, many with fences. In essence, it formed a tunnel from which Michael Griffith had no other escape but the Belt Parkway.

"What happened next?" Boyar demanded.

"The black guy jumped over the divider and got hit by a car going the other way," Riley replied with a small shiver. "It sounded like a thud or a loud thump. His body went flying through the air. Ten or twelve feet up."

Riley stopped and glanced at each one of us in turn. No one responded.

"And I got back in the car with Michael Pirone," he continued, "and Michael, he was crying. Then I got sick."

"Did anyone go after Griffith, out onto the parkway?" asked Hawkins.

"No."

"Did he ever look back?"

"No."

Dennis had established that Michael Griffith had not known the chase had ended. I knew Boston's Savin Hill case was running through his mind.

Riley concluded, saying he and Pirone had seen enough. The others, he added, "turned to go get the other one. They ran back down 90th Street and turned right onto Shore Parkway."

All of Riley's answers had been delivered in a flat monotone that revealed no emotion. But this last was too much for any of us.

Brook spoke up. "Do you mean," he asked, "that after they saw Griffith's body fly through the air they immediately turned around and headed back down 90th Street to get the other one?"

"Yeah," Riley said quietly.

The remainder of this night of brutality fell into place. We knew from the Fives that Tommy Farina, who had been lagging behind the main group, was the first to spot Sandiford after Griffith was killed. The tall man was ducking in and out of driveways and front lawns along Shore Parkway. After warning him to leave the neighborhood, Farina watched passively as Lester and the others caught up to Sandiford and began beating him. Farina was picked up by Sal DeSimone on Shore Parkway, and the two drove away. When Riley returned to his car on Cross Bay Boulevard, he said Laura Castagna was still sitting in it. She had, in fact, kept his radio and makeup light on while the engine was off and his battery was dead. Some of his friends helped push him home.

By the time Robert Riley was finished talking with us, we had accounted for the whereabouts of all twelve white youths during the attack in Howard Beach.

Matt Greenberg, perhaps the most cautious attorney on my staff, raised the tough questions first.

"Who says Riley's version is the truth? And if it is, what those kids did certainly was awful. But can we prove they committed a crime? Where's the corroboration? We need corroboration to take to a grand jury if we expect to get any kind of indictments."

It was Tuesday, January 20, moments past 8:00 A.M., and the A-Team was sprawled about the War Room digesting Riley's statements from the previous day. We now believed that we might have the complete story of the Howard Beach attack. Riley's astonishing revelations had shifted the action to 90th Street. He had filled in many of our blanks. His story made more than a little sense. But Greenberg was right: there were still questions to be asked.

We had all wondered, if Griffith had indeed crawled through the hole in the fence as Sandiford said, why his body was discovered back closer to the site of the original attack. Why hadn't he run the other way, toward Brooklyn? We were pretty sure that all three black men knew that Brooklyn was in the other direction. Riley provided the answer. But if Riley's story was true, then why was Griffith's body discovered so far from where 90th Street met the Belt Parkway? Riley had said he had been hit directly in front of the screaming gang.

Mangum's and Boyar's detective work in finding the dirt path meant nothing anymore. But the existence of the dirt path did cast initial doubts on Riley's version of events.

"I've got big problems with Riley's story," said Pam Hayes, the first to answer Greenberg. "It doesn't connect with anything we've put together so far. Number one, why would Sandiford lie about the hole in the fence? Number two, why weren't there any 911 calls from 90th Street, if that's where all the commotion was? And number three, how does Griffith's body get all the way—what was it, about a block and a half?—from 90th Street to where he was ultimately found?"

"I'm working on getting an accident simulation together at a test track," said Mangum. "That could shed some light on your last question."

Boyar looked at Mangum in surprise. "You think Riley's telling the truth?" he asked.

"Yeah—I bought most of it."

"This is the kid with the bat, Richard," Hayes interjected. "This is the kid who led the chase. He came in here for one reason: to cover up his own role."

"If Riley's telling the truth," I interrupted in a futile attempt to forestall the impending donnybrook, "then Michael Griffith died at least four or five minutes before Sandiford was beaten. That means those punks watched him die and *then* turned to get Sandiford. Now half the goddamn city believes Griffith's death was a tragic accident, that he merely panicked during a street fight. Does Riley's version sound like a street fight to anybody here? Where's our evidence to establish that time sequence?"

"The timing of the 911 calls ought to tell us something," said Mangum.

Pam Hayes, not giving up, said, "Joe, the secret entrance to the Belt that Ed and Richard discovered proves that Sandiford was telling the truth."

Dennis Hawkins was shuffling through his research.

"Okay," he said, "we've got two motorists calling 911 about a body in the fast lane of the Belt. The first call came in at 12:56 A.M., and then another one at 12:58. But six minutes before that, at 12:52, we have the call from Theresa Fisher, the eyewitness who was visiting her sister. She's telling the police that a bunch of white kids are beating a black guy in front of her house."

"And that was *six minutes earlier*," said Boyar, who exchanged a look of triumph with Hayes. "So then Sandiford got beaten first, just like he said."

"And Robert Riley," added Hayes, "is selling us a bill of goods."

"Maybe," I said. "But what if it took the motorists several minutes to pull off the parkway and make their calls? I want a legal strategy here, people. I want to know where we go based on Robert Riley's story."

As Greenberg had pointed out earlier, even if Riley's story were true, legal problems loomed. For one, Cedric Sandiford's credibility as a witness was even more impugned now. His story directly contradicted Riley's version of the attack. Sandiford insisted he saw Michael Griffith crawl through a hole in the fence five blocks from where his stepson had actually run out onto the highway.

"So what do we do about Cedric?" asked Hawkins.

"I'm going to treat him like the victim of a crime who's been severely assaulted," I answered. "It was a terrible night. He'd been hit in the head with a baseball bat. We're going to tell a grand jury that he knows only some of what happened, not everything. And we don't have to tell him about Riley's version for now."

But I realized our problems didn't end with Sandiford. There was some doubt that a grand jury (and later a trial jury) would believe the word of Riley, a witness who admitted to leading the charge against "the niggers." It was precisely for this aspect of criminal justice that the legal tenets of corroboration were established. Webster's defines corroboration as "confirmation by additional proof." The New York State Code of Criminal Procedure puts it in a legal context, stating that no one can be convicted of a criminal offense based upon the uncorroborated testimony of an accomplice. Riley was an accomplice. His testimony was uncorroborated. So we were still not all the way home.

In the Savin Hill case there were other witnesses. We had no other witnesses to Michael Griffith's final moments. And in the Kibbe case Krall and Kibbe had admitted to throwing their victim onto the highway. None of our defendants admitted to forcing Griffith out onto the road. Thus, from the moment Riley walked out of our office, the A-Team had been consumed in a search—so far, futile—to corroborate his story.

I sent Borelli's detectives and Al Pica's investigators out to conduct an intense canvass of the houses along 90th Street. No one, of course, had bothered to look for witnesses there before. The street had never been mentioned. But the canvass produced nothing. To a person, the residents explained what sound sleepers they were. Riley had said that nearly every boy in the chase was shouting on that narrow, quiet street. Nonetheless, "I didn't hear a thing" was clearly the general refrain of Howard Beach.

Our only alternative was to concentrate on the statements each of the gang members had made to police. Except for Gucciardo, who refused to speak to investigators, each youth acknowledged the confrontation in front of the pizzeria and the running dogfight down Shore Parkway. In varying detail, most of them discussed the beating Sandiford received.

But there was no mention of 90th Street. It was as if it had never happened.

The Howard Beach youths had all hired defense attorneys, and they were already leaking what was to be their basic line for the next nine months. That is, the attack had been merely a quaint, old-fashioned rumble run amok, a blameless tragedy, à la *West Side Story*.

"This was nothing more than a street fight between two groups," Pirone's attorney, Stephen Murphy, told a reporter the day after Riley appeared in our office. "One side happened to be black, one happened to be white. Sure, the whites ganged up on the tall black guy. I don't condone that, but I understand what happens in the heat of the battle."

The elfin Murphy, an Irish bantam cock who lives up to his nickname, "The Screamer of Queens Boulevard," during even the most casual of conversations, then proceeded to raise a swollen, disfigured right hand. He balled it into a fist. "Broke every knuckle in street fights when I was a kid. I know what it's like. As for Howard Beach, it's just a shame one of the black guys panicked and ran out into the street. Nobody wanted to kill him."

We knew better. With revulsion, and more than a little wonder, I contemplated the numbing image of the gang chasing Michael Griffith to his blood-spattered death, and a split second later turning to "go get the other one." That was not the behavior of decent human beings. It was, I told Larry Kurlander over the phone, the actions of feral beasts. For once the governor's criminal justice coordinator was rendered speechless.

That night, the sight of Griffith's body flying through the air had been too much for Pirone, who became nauseated and wept. Even the besotted Riley, who up until that point had been in the vanguard of the attack, was finally overcome with disgust.

But there were no such reactions from Lester or Ladone or Kern. How many more took direct part? Riley hadn't been sure. He couldn't account for the precise actions of all eleven of his friends that evening. Yet someone had hoisted that tire iron and tree limb. Someone had shouldered that baseball bat. Someone had gone for more blood.

By Tuesday evening we were discussing what to present to the grand jury. The most serious charges we could request a grand jury to return were second-degree murder and first-degree manslaughter. The murder charge required us to prove "a depraved indifference to human life." Manslaughter required proof of "recklessness." For example, if someone is wildly spraying a crowded street with machine-gun bullets, that person is exhibiting a wanton and callous indifference to life and should be prosecuted for murder. Whereas someone driving an automobile at a great rate of speed down that same crowded street is only demonstrating a reckless attitude toward human life. The distinction is a fine one.

By Wednesday, with the debate in the War Room now raging into its second full day, minus a short time-out for sleep, my trial lawyers clamored for a murder indictment. My appellate experts hounded them for evidence. They were firing verbal darts back and forth. I said nothing.

The appellate intellectuals were willing to concede that Riley *might* have provided enough evidence to warrant manslaughter charges, although Greenberg was proving intransigent. But a murder charge, they argued, was out of the question.

"Murder in the second degree is not a charge made lightly, nor has it been successfully prosecuted very many times in the State of New York," said Helman Brook, with Hoffman and Greenberg nodding in agreement.

Richard Mangum argued that the gang's motives were certainly depraved, citing their decision to turn and hunt down Sandiford after watching Griffith die.

"Look at their relentlessness," Mangum said. "They were out to kill this guy. If they had caught him they would have beaten his brains out. Instead, Dominick Blum inadvertently did the job for them. Then they turned on Cedric."

"Wonderful," replied Helman sarcastically. "That about nails down assault charges on Sandiford. Now where's your homicide corroboration for Griffith?"

My appellate crew sat on one side of the conference table, stoic and pessimistic amid their law books and legal pads. My trial guys fidgeted at each other, anxious and frustrated. Mike Nadel, who combined an appellate lawyer's legal thought-processes with a trial lawyer's practical judgment, floated between the two groups. The lines of demarcation, however, were not always drawn so clearly.

Street cops have a saying: "Ask two lawyers a question, you get four answers. Ask four lawyers a question, you get four thousand answers." I suppose it means we all have egos. Ten such legal egos encircled my conference-room table, irreverently debating strategy. I was put in mind of Babel.

Once, as Hilly Hoffman—whom Pam Hayes dubbed "Mr. Detail Personified" for his appellate nit-picking—was explaining for perhaps the one thousandth time precisely what kind of corroboration we needed, Marty Hershey interrupted him harshly.

"Fine, Hilly, fine. We already know what it is. We just don't know where the *hell* it is. Now instead of telling us what we need, why don't you help us *find* it. Got it?"

Tempers were raw. Even my lead Howard Beach trial attorneys went at each others' throats. At one point Mangum stood and berated the entire room, although I believe his outburst was really directed at the fates.

"Dammit, those little racists said they were at New Park Pizza!" he roared. "They said they chased Cedric and Michael. They said they beat up Cedric. Why isn't their failure to mention 90th Street a kind of inverted corroboration?"

He continued, less heatedly: "We can use their motives—racial violence—to supply the reasonable inference that omitting 90th Street is an admission of guilt."

"Bullshit!" shouted Ed Boyar. "We can't use that, because that's not the law."

Helman Brook was up out of his seat, pacing the left side of the room. I noticed Pam Hayes's eyes well up, no doubt in frustration. I'd like to think that the members of my staff are all equally sensitive to the plights of other human beings. But I knew that Riley's story, told just the day before, was searing a touch deeper into Mangum, into Hayes, into Gene McPherson and my other black investigators. It could, after all, have happened to them.

As if reading my thoughts, mild-mannered Hilly Hoffman jumped back into the fray. "What kind of fucking madness is this?" he shouted. "How does Queens County in 1986 suddenly become Philadelphia, Mississippi?"

"This shit could happen anywhere, even in Harlem," growled Boyar, who had made the point before.

It was nearly 6:30 P.M. Wednesday. I had heard enough. Angry at what I saw as a wasted day exploring the whys and wherefores of arcane theories, I felt it was time to make my position quite clear. I raised my voice:

"Let's get it straight, people. This is not a seminar in social justice. This fucking case is plain and simply about a homicide and a very serious assault. We've got an accomplice named Bobby Riley and we all know he's telling the truth. But the law requires that we *prove it.*"

I spat out those last two words in the unlikely event that someone was missing my point.

"I don't want creative corroboration," I went on. "I want sufficient legal evidence. Now somewhere in this fucking case there is a large dose of corroboration, and the nine of you are going to find it. And I don't want to hear anymore bullshit social commentaries. If any of you don't understand that, take off. This is a murder case and an assault case, people, nothing else."

The room remained quiet for several seconds. Then Dennis Hawkins spoke. "Joe, we've been at this for seven days without a break," he said. "Why don't we knock off for tonight and start fresh tomorrow morning."

"Bullshit!" I shouted. "No time off. We're almost there, and we're not quitting tonight until we analyze every statement and come to a conclusion."

In fact, we were not almost there; we were almost nowhere. But I wasn't going to let up.

"If we decide there's no corroboration, we can all take a week off, because all we have is an assault case," I continued, walking toward the door. "And an assault case can be tried by any first-year law student . . . or even one of you guys. I'll be back in an hour."

I slammed the door behind me, well aware that when I returned, the A-Team would be close to a resolution. They would either discover the corroboration or not. Corroboration, unlike horseshoes and hand grenades, is never *almost* there.

Down in the lobby of 2 Rector, I saw the last of our building's stockbrokers, bond traders, and investment bankers scurrying through the revolving doors. *The whole world is going home,* I thought.

Well, I was going to a bar.

Outside, in the slick, wet January evening, the spire of Trinity Church towered over the snow-covered tomb of Alexander Hamilton. I walked north on Broadway. Find Harvey Louie Greenberg, I thought. If he doesn't have an answer, at least he'll say something that sounds like an answer. Greenberg is not one to keep his mouth shut for long. Plus he'll buy me a beer.

I stopped at the first pay phone and dialed, anticipating the dulcet tones of Camille Pinzone, known to the Irish Mafia as "the Fabulous Camille, loyal personal secretary and office manager." Instead, I heard a recording. Greenberg's office was closed.

A dark downtown joint named Moe's was Greenberg's current watering hole, so I turned now with a purpose and headed back south. When I walked into Moe's, the place was nearly empty. Feeling sorry for myself, I wondered why I had ever gotten into government business in the first place. The bartender, much too chatty for my mood, said he hadn't seen Harvey all day. Two bars and two Heinekens later, Greenberg was still missing in action, and I was left to sort out my problem alone.

Dammit, think like a trial lawyer, I told myself over and over. *Contrary to what editorial writers and defense attorneys think, the law isn't an ass. The corroboration is going to be there. They committed the crime, it has to be. There was a reason these little creeps hadn't mentioned 90th Street when they gave their statements.*

It was nearly 9:30 P.M. when I gave up on Harvey Louie Greenberg and began the solitary trek back to 2 Rector. Had I known that for the next year I would be accompanied by bodyguards wherever I went, I might have savored that solo jaunt just a little more.

An air of jubilance greeted me when I pushed open the door of the War Room.

"We broke up into groups and reviewed each of the kids' statements," Helman Brook said deliberately, as if addressing an appellate tribunal, for he knew I was mad and he was treading very lightly. "Our friend Dennis here provided the breakthrough. He found it in Scott Kern's statement. Kern told Detective Mandel that, as he was running down the street, he noticed that Bobby Riley had a bat in his hand. Kern said he saw Riley hand it to Jon Lester, and they both continued chasing Griffith and Sandiford."

"So?" I said obtusely. Helman eyed me as if I were deaf.

"So, Riley told us that the bat was snatched from him by Lester as they were running down 90th Street, Joe. There would be no reason for Riley to lie to us about that. And he certainly would have told us if Lester had grabbed the bat somewhere else. The laws of corroboration require only that there be some evidence that tends to connect the person with the commission of a crime. And Kern's statement tends to corroborate Riley's."

Hawkins interrupted Brook: "The reason that little bum was able to see the bat go from Riley to Lester is that he was on 90th Street chasing Griffith. And that, Joe, is bingo for us and curtains for Kern."

"And Lester hangs himself with his admission to Brad Wolk that he 'chased the little black guy with a baseball bat,' " said Brook. "He puts himself in possession of that baseball bat, and Riley says that possession took place on 90th Street."

"And finally," Helman said, smiling for the first time, "Ladone's statement should have jumped off the page at us. He said he saw Michael's body fly into the air. Now, he told us he saw this from 85th Street, where Cedric was beaten. But we know that's impossible. They didn't go after Cedric until after Michael was hit. They all stayed away from 90th Street in their statements, but these three at least said just enough to put them in the soup."

My mind was already jumping ahead. *Only three? We can prosecute only three of them?*

"What about Pirone?" I asked. "Riley said he was there, chasing Griffith up 90th Street."

"A bit more difficult," Helman replied. "We can go on the theory that he's lying. He said he couldn't run because of that car accident he had a few years back. But when he returned to the Schorr party, he told his girlfriend his legs were hurting. The police have that in their Fives, she told them Pirone was sitting in the Schorrs' backyard rubbing his knees. It was an innocuous statement, but it might help us convince the grand jury. She also said Lester told her that night not to worry, because Pirone had nothing to do with it. That 'it' is Griffith's death. At least that's how we'll play it."

Legal tenets such as proximate cause and corroboration apply, technically, to both grand juries and trial juries. But any prosecutor worth his or her salt knows that you use the legal aspects of a case to secure indictments in the grand jury, and that the trial jury is a whole different ball game. All our exercise so far had been centered on bringing back indictments from the grand jury. Trial jurors sit there presumably weighing evidence, but in actuality they are studying the character of the witnesses, and they miss very little. If my staff could find me the legal means to secure indictments and bring me into court, I'd lay those laws before the judge as my reason for being there and then paint that jury a picture of horror they'd never forget. And it looked like the A-Team was close.

"Do you think that's enough?" I wondered aloud. Hilly Hoffman, his voice brimming with confidence, answered quickly.

"Joe, it's thin stuff. But I think if we get the indictments it will certainly survive a motion to dismiss"—the prosecution's worst nightmare—"and after that it's up to the jury."

"It's the best we've got, Joe," Matt Greenberg added softly.

At least my appellate people were all in agreement. "Then let's get on it," I said. "What about a grand jury?"

When Dennis Hawkins casually mentioned that a grand jury was already in waiting, I was surprised, because—despite my bluffs to Jim Gucciardo and Rick Librett—I had yet to even think about the technical aspects of summoning a grand jury. In New York City, each borough's district attorney convenes a grand jury for a month at a time. It had been my plan to request from Santucci an additional grand jury that would serve for that regular month-long period but would be special for Howard Beach. It was an out-of-the-ordinary request, but I had done it once or twice before. However, I had never mentioned this strategy to Hawkins, whom I was now staring at with a dumb look on my face.

"Well, Joe," Hawkins said, "you knew we were going to have at least an assault charge anyway. So I had one of the regularly selected grand juries set aside out in Queens. It's convening out in the old Jamaica Courthouse, where we can keep Bobby Riley away from prying eyes. It's ours full time. I called Santucci and he arranged it personally."

Ed Boyar asked me when I wanted to present to the grand jury. Before I could answer with my typical "tomorrow," Mike Nadel was out of his chair and in my face. After my volcanic explosion when the staff asked for a break several hours before, he wanted to be sure that we had all our facts straight. Nadel had my number.

"Wait, Joe, for once. Can we please go home tonight and think about this, and then plan our strategy after we think it through?"

Everyone waited for my eruption. This time I fooled them. "Sure," I said. "Meeting adjourned."

Within five minutes the special state prosecutor's staff was engaged in a raging snowball fight outside on Rector Street.

18

"THE ANSWER IS NO"

During the drive home, Doug LeVien turned uncommonly serious. The street cop was worried that our star witness would back out of his pact.

"Boss, get Riley into that grand jury room right away," he said. "Without him you got zilch."

"What's the rush?" I asked.

"John Gotti's not the only wise guy in Howard Beach," he said, and added one of the verities of a New York City detective: *There are no secrets in this life.*

The origin of the phrase is unknown, but its meaning is clear to anyone who has ever worn a badge. The translation in this case: "Somehow, someway, someone is going to blow your investigation by getting to Robert Riley before he walks into that grand jury room, and your case will be a memory."

LeVien, my organized-crime expert, had spent several months with his family in the Federal Witness Protection Program, hiding from the people he had investigated. He knew the Mob's ways and he was issuing a warning. I decided then and there to schedule Riley as my first grand-jury witness, early next week. I expected it to take that long to work out a written plea-bargain agreement with Rick Librett, prepare Riley for testimony, and explain fully to Riley that he would be testifying without immunity. Under New York State law, a witness who testifies before a grand jury automatically receives complete immunity for whatever he says and whatever he did. Under our agreement, Riley would waive that right.

The next morning I assigned each member of the A-Team a set of potential witnesses, with instructions to break down their statements and recommend charges to bring against each of the twelve gang members. We spent the remainder of the week tracking down our potential witnesses and completing our paperwork.

We spoke to the the Toscanos and to Theresa Fisher and made arrangements for the medical examiner to take the stand and describe Michael Griffith's cause of death. We summoned several of the defendants' parents who had made statements to the press and police. Hawkins and Hershey interviewed most of the teenagers who had attended the Schorr party but had not taken part in the attack. We decided to bring some of them to the stand in order to "set the scene."

That Friday, January 23, Riley signed his cooperation agreement. The following night we had him out cruising Howard Beach in our observation van. Beginning at the pizzeria, Riley filled in the blanks of Sandiford's story—up to 90th Street. When we reached the spot where the youths had watched Michael Griffith die, Riley became very upset, lowered his head, and cried into his sleeve. *Now,* I thought, *we are ready to go to the grand jury.*

According to New York State law, the prosecutor is the legal adviser to the grand jury. Grand jury proceedings are similar to a trial in that the jury of twenty-three citizens determines the facts of a case based on the testimony it hears. But whereas in a trial the judge charges the jury—advises it what law to apply to the facts before returning with a verdict—in a grand jury, it is the prosecutor who charges the citizens, asking them to return with an indictment.

A trial jury can vote guilty or not guilty. A grand jury can vote an indictment with various counts, or crimes, or it can vote "no-true-bill," finding the evidence insufficient to establish a crime. A defense attorney is allowed into the grand jury room only when a client waives personal immunity. Thus, in our case, Rick

Librett would be the only outsider present, to help Riley. Maddox, for instance, could not accompany Sandiford in to testify, but I planned to ask him to show up at the courthouse anyway, to help keep Cedric calm.

I also decided that Riley and Grimes were to be prepared and brought into the grand jury by Boyar, my lead trial attorney. He had spent the most time interviewing both. Sandiford would be handled by Hawkins, with whom he had developed a friendship. I also elected to make Dennis part of the trial team, perhaps handling press. For both Dennis and Boyar, the grand jury presentations would be a good warmup for the trial. I wanted them in shape if we ever got to court. Over the next several days I sat in on discussions with all three. Something seemed out of synch, however, and Helman Brook was the first to bring it into the open.

"Sandiford likes Dennis well enough," he told me, "but he respects you. For Godsakes, he's hugged you every time he's seen you since the second time you met. It should be you that takes him into the grand jury room. I know he'll feel more comfortable."

Helman's drawled emphasis on the first word "grand" reminded me of Gregory Peck as Southern lawyer Atticus Finch in *To Kill a Mockingbird.* I felt a little sheepish, as if I were refuting Finch himself, when I shook my head at Brook's idea.

"No, Helman. I did that stuff my entire career. And that's why I am where I am now, able to hire good people to do it for me. I'm in charge of the whole operation, but it's the guys like Ed and Richard and Dennis who are used to going to court. Trial lawyering is a young man's game, Helman, and you and I have had our day."

I said this as a joke, attempting to get him to drop his serious scowl. My ploy didn't work.

"Joe," he said softly, "if you want this to go smoothly, you had better do it. I'm not kidding."

"Helman, the answer is no."

19

GRAND JURY

Six days later, I was pacing before the grand jury. "What is your full name, sir?" I said.

"Cedric Horesford Sandiford, sir."

Helman Brook had been right. The night I told him no, I went home and changed my mind. The rapport I enjoyed with Cedric was simply too great to ignore. If I didn't have Sandiford present the facts of the attack to a jury of his peers, he might have been hurt, or angry, and I couldn't risk that. In addition, I felt I knew him well enough to put him at ease and help him over any rough spots. A friendly lawyer never hurts.

Our strategy was proceeding according to plan. Riley went first (as LeVien had advised). Ed Boyar walked him through his narrative, which was virtually the same as the story he told in my office. Then Timmy Grimes took the stand, and the only new evidence he presented was that he had zigzagged through traffic several times across the Belt Parkway during his running escape.

We had all been surprised at Boyar's minor success at getting through to Grimes, who still "didn't know nothin'," and was at first a difficult witness. When Boyar, for example, attempted to lead him through his escape route with the aid of an aerial map of the neighborhood, Timothy just couldn't relate to it. Ed set the exhibit aside and went on with an oral examination. Grimes wasn't trying to conceal anything, he was just a bit slow on the uptake.

The medical examiner was next, and then Theresa Fisher, whose courage I truly admired. She had been harassed by threatening calls, and since she was not under police protection, it would have been easy for her to "forget" the entire ordeal. But she faced her fellow citizens, and under Pam Hayes's questioning, described Sandiford's beating for the grand jurors with the same sense of urgency she had used with the 911 operator.

Each witness painted a little more of the picture of the night of December 19 and the early-morning hours of December 20, 1986, and then it was time for Sandiford to administer the coup de grace. He was the one man (we hoped) who could pull it all together.

Earlier in the week I had called Justice Phillip La Gana in Brooklyn to ask him for a favor. "Philly," to those of us who had worked with him the Brooklyn DA's Office, was presiding over a homicide trial involving a white Catholic priest who had been shot to death by a young black man. Alton Maddox was defending the young man, and it was his contention that his client had been picked up by the priest to perform sodomy. When a struggle ensued over payment, Maddox argued, a gun discharged and the priest was killed.

I told La Gana that I needed Maddox for an afternoon, because I was putting Cedric Sandiford, his client, before the grand jury. It would be useful to have Maddox present on the ride out to Queens, to help steady Sandiford. I also felt he deserved to be in the courthouse, even though he would not be allowed in the grand jury room. At first La Gana was difficult.

"I'm trying a murder case here, Joe, and you want me to interrupt it for you?" he asked, teasing me. "Are you telling me that my case isn't as important as yours?"

"Don't give me that bullshit, Philly!" I yelled into the receiver. "You know what Howard Beach means to the city. Things are about to explode around here, and I just want one afternoon."

"All right," he said, "you can have him, but don't come to my court before twelve-thirty in the afternoon. Maddox has to work until one."

I entered Part 16 of the Brooklyn Supreme Court just past noon. Maddox was cross-examining the detective who led the

investigation into the priest's death. I was surprised. Absent was
the raver who inspired crowds. In his place stood an accomplished trial lawyer, carefully conducting an obviously well-
planned cross-examination.

Standing in the shadows of the courtroom, I was struck by the
discovery that Maddox had what trial lawyers call "courtroom
presence." It's a kind of legal charisma, demonstrated most often
in the use of voice modulation and the physical manner with
which a lawyer strides through the "well" of the courtroom.
Inside the gate that divides judge, jury, defendant, and attorneys
from the public, Alton Maddox became Perry Mason, delivering
his lines and choreographing his movements like an actor doing
Shakespeare.

"Your Honor, may I have just a moment to review the documents?"

"You may, Mr. Maddox," replied Justice La Gana.

"Thank you, Your Honor, I believe I'm ready to proceed."

No, I realized, not Shakespeare, but *L.A. Law.* It was exactly
what jurors in the age of television have come to expect. Too
many jurors have a preconception of how attorneys should look
and act. Maddox had every move down pat, in contrast to his
opponent, an assistant district attorney who slouched at his table
looking aloof, projecting a demeanor that had to be abhorrent
to jurors. Not once did the ADA rise from his seat to make an
objection. (Several weeks later, when the defendant was acquitted because some of the jurors cited insufficient evidence, I
thought of the ADA's lackadaisical posture.)

"Ready for the grand jury?" I asked Maddox when La Gana's
trial was adjourned, and in a flash the surly scowl was back in
place, pasted on his face.

"The question is," he said to me, "are you ready?"

Now, standing before my own jury, with Maddox outside in
the hall, I was the one worried about my comportment. At first,
my staff was angered by the mere handful of black faces among
the predominantly white panel of grand jurors. Minorities make
up nearly a quarter of Queens County, and some of the A-Team
didn't feel that our grand jury was truly *representative.* But

Sandiford strode into the courtroom room with such purpose that, without uttering a word, he projected an attitude of righteousness that would impress jurors of any color. He was a dignified and proud *victim*. Gently, carefully, I began to draw hard answers from him.

"Mr. Sandiford, I direct your attention to the evening of December 19, 1986. Do you remember where you were at about nine o'clock that evening?"

"Yes, sir."

"Where were you?"

Slowly, carefully, I walked Cedric Sandiford through that horrible night. Grand juries were convened, by law, in secret, and the ornate and little-used Jamaica Courthouse was far from the sniffing snouts of the Queens Borough Hall newshounds, several of whom might have stumbled across one of our well-known witnesses had we convened, as was normal, in Queens Criminal Court. Sandiford was seated beneath the magnificent dome of the churchlike courtroom. And twenty-three citizens of Queens County, New York, sat on the oak benches, listening with rapt attention before they had to decide whether Sandiford's assailants would stand trial for murder.

"And what did you say to the white youths who argued with you in that crosswalk. Mr. Sandiford?"

"I said, 'Fuck you, you honky motherfucker.' Now I'm sorry for that language."

An intelligent prosecutor will lay out a litany of his witness's past "bad acts" in order to soften their effect in front of the jury. If I didn't present the facts of Sandiford's criminal record, or Grimes's criminal record, or the encapsulated bullet in Michael Griffith's body and the cocaine in his blood, a defense attorney could destroy our case with character assassination. It was my job to inform the grand jury that yes, Sandiford had used the word "honky" while yelling at Lester, but that was not a viable reason for chasing Griffith to his death.

So I was pleased that Sandiford looked directly at me and gave a thoughtful answer to each of my questions, including the use of the inelegant phrase "honky motherfucker." My first impression had been correct: he was making a tremendous witness.

And yet I was concerned. As grand jury proceedings are conducted in secret, Sandiford had no idea Riley had testified about 90th Street two days earlier. And he still believed he saw his stepson crawl through a hole in the fence near 85th Street *after* the mob had attacked him.

If and when this case came to trial, I would have enough problems with the erroneous description of the attack Sandiford had already given to the *Amsterdam News*. Defense counsel would be all over the inconsistencies and inaccuracies Cedric had told the newspapers. I preferred not to be forced to deal later with flaws in his grand jury testimony as well. So I limited the questions to what had happened to Sandiford himself.

That was probably enough. Vividly, Cedric described to the grand jurors his confrontation with the armed mob and the subsequent run for his life.

"Did the chase continue uninterrupted?" I asked. Sandiford seemed puzzled by the question. It was my first attempt to hint to him that something had happened that night of which he was not aware.

"I'm sorry, sir?"

"Did the mob ever stop chasing you?"

"Yes, it did," he answered, still looking perplexed.

"Did the chase ever begin again?"

"Yes, sir."

"How much time passed?"

"Maybe five, ten minutes," Sandiford said.

That was precisely the answer I needed. Those few minutes were the window of opportunity through which I could make the grand jurors understand what happened that night. Five to ten minutes to chase Michael Griffith up 90th Street, as Riley has testified, before returning for Sandiford.

"Then what happened?" I continued, and Sandiford recounted remarkably the horrible details: the baseball bat and the tree limbs and Theresa Fisher and the Toscanos' dogs. I led him through the narrative to the point where the highway patrol officers had taken him to view Griffith's smashed body.

"At that location was a body shown to you. Mr. Sandiford?"

"Yes, sir."

"Who was that person?"

"My stepson Michael," Cedric answered through tears. "He was dead."

"Thank you, Mr. Sandiford."

My car was like a tomb on the drive back to Maddox's law offices. As Tom Mulvihill gradually eased the Dodge onto Court Street in Brooklyn, Sandiford finally spoke.

"Are they gonna get away with this?" he said.

Maddox wore his smug look.

Before I answered, the three of us walked to the entrance of Maddox's building. At the elevator, I turned to face Sandiford.

"Cedric," I said, "what's been done to Michael is over. But I promise you, those kids are going to pay a price."

Sandiford thanked me, turned, and left. I wondered whether he believed me.

The next morning, two days before I was scheduled to deliver my closing arguments to the grand jury, a story in *New York Newsday* nearly shot down our case. Unlike trial juries, grand jurors are not directed to ignore anything in the media about the case on which they are sitting. *New York Newsday*'s exclusive, front-page narrative traced the events of that night in Howard Beach in vivid detail, detail obviously culled from access to police reports.

The leak bore the clumsy thumbprints of a classic Police Department operation. Someone had apparently decided that the detectives involved in the investigation were not receiving enough credit. That someone had also decided it was time to set the record straight. There was no mention of the department's crude treatment of Sandiford, nor of its investigative blunders.

It was a puff piece, a paean to the police, but there was nothing good about the story for us. Now, if indictments were voted by the grand jury, the defense's first motion to dismiss would be grounded in pre-indictment publicity. And the motion papers would be delivered with some deadly ammunition: the *New York Newsday* headline and story.

"Who leaked it?" asked Bob Keating during our pre-dawn jog.

"My pals the cops, who else?" I answered.

"That may be," Keating warned me, "but you'll share the

blame. There's not going to be a reporter in town who won't think you did it, and they'll all be mad at you for playing favorites. Furthermore, your grand jurors will all have seen it. You better speak to the A-Team fast. Get them to prepare something for the grand jurors, and you read it."

"No," I replied, "I'll have Boyar read it. I don't think it's wise for me to become more involved in the case than I have been. I'd prefer to direct the troops."

"Joe," Keating said very firmly, "get it out of your head that you're a bystander. This is your case to win or lose. It's that simple."

By 7:30 A.M. every radio newscast was headlining the *New York Newsday* story. A call from Helman Brook interrupted my shower.

"Joe, this *Newsday* thing is awful. You've got to say something to the grand jury. Hilly's already at the office, drafting a statement. Matt's on his way. I'll review it for you and have it ready by nine o'clock. That gives us two hours before the grand jury meets."

That morning, when I walked into the Jamaica courtroom that housed the panel, a hush fell over the room. I suppose the jurors could read the anger on my face. To make matters worse, several of the jurors held *New York Newsdays* on their laps. One sheepishly allowed his to slide to the floor. Hoffman had worded my statement to make it clear to any appellate judge who read it that, though the jurors may have been tainted by press reports, our office had taken immediate action.

"Mr. Foreman and ladies and gentlemen of the grand jury," I began, trying to control the wrath in my voice. "This morning one of the city's newspapers has written a story about the work of this grand jury. The story is highly speculative and it contains substantial inaccuracies. The newspaper account is being repeated by local radio stations. And I suppose by this evening it will be all over television. I also suspect that by tomorrow the other newspapers in town will also be carrying some portion of this story."

The grand jurors, sensing the seriousness of the situation, were giving me their complete attention.

"As your legal adviser in these proceedings, I want to repeat what I told you before this grand jury convened. During your deliberations, you are not"—and I emphasized the word "not" so forcefully that a frail old woman in the first row flinched in her seat—"to consider anything you have heard, seen or read about this case in the media. Nor should you from this point on watch, read, or hear anything about this case in the media. Leave the room if you must, tear out pieces of the newspaper, but, in the interests of justice, ignore reports about Howard Beach. Nor should you discuss these matters with members of your family or friends."

Now I looked directly at the *New York Newsday* readers on the panel. I wanted to finish with the sternest warning possible.

"To do otherwise would break your oath as grand jurors. Is that very clear?"

Their mumbled reply, recorded dryly by the court stenographer as a simple "yes," was delivered by only a few, who sounded like a chastened class of schoolchildren. I thanked them and left the room. Later that afternoon, Helman Brook stopped me in the hallways of 2 Rector.

"Joe," he said, "you've got to deliver the charge."

"Helman, I've already decided that I will."

At 10:00 A.M. on Thursday morning, February 5, I was once again standing before the Queens County grand jury, explaining to them how to check the boxes of the charge sheet for either "found" or "unfounded" charges. The charge sheet contained thirty-two separate criminal counts. There were no questions. The grand jury retired to deliberate at 11:25 A.M.

At noon the grand jury asked for lunch and at 1:15 another note was sent out asking where lunch was. The episode gave me new insight into the strange workings of the borough of Queens. The grand jury warden, the court clerk responsible for the nuts and bolts of the operation, informed me that the lunch order had been placed at the Pastrami King, a delicatessen on Queens Boulevard across the street from the Queens Criminal Court-house.

"But this is Jamaica," I stammered, flabbergasted. "Why the hell was lunch ordered from a place in Kew Gardens, two miles from here?"

The warden merely answered me with a knowing smile. In Queens, I found out, even grand jury lunches are a political contract.

My charge had been lengthy, so I wasn't expecting a quick resolution. I was right. The Howard Beach grand jury retired for the night without reaching a decision. No one on my staff, with its collective ten thousand grand jury presentations, could recall a panel deliberating overnight. It was simply unheard-of.

"Think of it, Joe," said Larry Kurlander, who called the next afternoon, ostensibly to lend moral support. "Not only will you break the record for deliberations by a grand jury but you're likely to get a no-true-bill in your 'Case of the Decade.' Seriously," he added, "what do you think is holding them up?"

It was obvious that the governor was concerned. I told Kurlander that I honestly didn't know, and I had no intention of speculating.

At 5:30 P.M., February 6, ten and one-half hours after deliberations began, the grand jury warden announced solemnly: "Mr. Hynes, the grand jury wishes to see you. They have acted."

As I entered the courtroom, one of the female black jurors was crying. *Damn,* I thought. *That doesn't bode well.* But then I saw the charge sheet lying on a lectern in the center of the room. I scanned the list.

We were in.

A no-true-bill had been returned on several of our requested charges, but in the main I was elated. Every member of the white mob had been indicted on some charges, ranging from second-degree murder to first-degree riot. Five of the twelve, not counting Riley, faced substantial penalties.

Lester, Kern, and Riley were indicted for murder in the second degree.

Lester, Kern, Ladone, Pirone, and Riley were indicted for manslaughter in the second degree.

Lester, Kern, Ladone, and Gucciardo were indicted for attempted murder in the second degree and assault in the first degree.

I felt like hugging every member of the panel.

We all hurried back to 2 Rector elated. Kurlander was the first to call with congratulations for my staff. They had worked twenty-four straight days and nights to get to this moment. And now the Howard Beach case had passed its first critical stage successfully. The mob had been indicted.

I had Dennis Hawkins prepare a press release. We would unseal the grand jury indictments at arraignments the following Tuesday, February 10. I told the A-Team to take the weekend off.

The next morning, Saturday, February 7, the headline in the *New York Post* read: NO MURDER CHARGES IN BEACH CASE. The story was attributed to "sources." I was driving to the trial advocacy class I teach at St. John's University when a nervous investigator rang me on the car phone.

"Joe, the governor called, personally," he nearly shrieked into the phone. "He's at the mansion. He said to call right away."

"Call him and tell him I'm on my way to St. John's, and I'll ring him in about ten minutes."

Which is what I did.

"Professor Hynes?" Mario Cuomo's voice was firm, with a hint of sternness. "Do you have a problem?"

"Governor, if you mean about the *Post*, I don't have a problem. They have a problem."

"Goodbye," replied Governor Mario Cuomo, and he hung up the phone.

The
Trial

20

JUDGE DEMAKOS

The indictments were formally filed on February 9, in the New York State Supreme Court in Queens County. The arraignment of the twelve teenagers (Laura Castagna was never charged) was held the following day in Part K-3 of the court, presided over by the Honorable Alfred E. Lerner, acting chief administrative Supreme Court judge. Lerner had replaced Judge Francis X. Smith, who was suspended pending his trial for bribery. Only in Queens . . .

K-3, a cavernous courtroom which would also serve as the site of the trial, could barely hold the more than two hundred fifty spectators and reporters who clamored for admission. Some fifty journalists covered the proceedings, with seven television stations sending live "feeds" of the pre- and post-court comments out over the air. As we entered the courthouse among a throng of chanting spectators, I felt as if I had indeed pulled back the flap of some surreal Big Top. I expected this kind of reception, but I had never really experienced it firsthand. Although we were all a bit overwhelmed by the media attention, I hoped that the experience would prove useful in toughening our troops to the spotlight. The three front benches were filled with columnists, reporters, and sketch artists as the court clerk opened the proceedings with the formal language of the system of justice.

"All rise. The Supreme Court for the State of New York in and for the County of Queens is in session."

Justice Lerner stood at the center of his bench, appropriately somber.

"All you who have business before this honorable court draw near," the clerk announced. "Give your attention, and you shall be heard. Please be seated."

Then the court stenographer recorded our "appearances," first our names and the state office we worked for, then the names of the defense attorneys and their clients. Gabriel Leone, a polar bear of an attorney representing Scott Kern, boomed his reply and abruptly added, "I'm ready for trial."

Judge Lerner looked annoyed. "Mr. Leone," he demanded, "please wait for the official arraignment."

I smiled and whispered to my seconds, "Welcome to Queens Boulevard, guys." We had officially entered another legal universe. The Queens County criminal justice system was a cosmos where corridor deals were the coin of the realm, where howls and shrieks were admired courtroom decorum, and where "the letter of the law" was open to several interpretations. As Ronald Rubinstein, the attorney for Jason Ladone, remarked in self-contragulatory fashion on the courthouse steps: "We're all from Queens Boulevard. That means we do our best work in a phone booth."

As an old Court Street hand, and a former Rackets Bureau chief, I felt right at home.

"Mr. Clerk," Judge Lerner said evenly, "call the arraignment calendar." The clerk complied, and K-3 became a silent canyon.

"Under indictment number 890/87," the court clerk bellowed, "the People of the State of New York versus Scott Kern."

Thus was born *People v. Kern*.

When the Howard Beach trial fades from public memory, it will still be cited in case studies, textbooks, and briefs until the end of time as *People v. Kern*. It will be so for two reasons: the severity of the charge and the order of the alphabet. In a multidefendant case with multiple charges, it is practice to call the most serious charge first. Kern, Lester, and Riley were charged with homicide. Alphabetically, Scott Kern went down in legal history.

From the holding pen (a small series of cells to the right and

behind Judge Lerner) strode little Scott Kern. There were perhaps one hundred thirty pounds of him, stretched thinly over a
five-foot, eight-inch frame. Kern wore a dapper sports jacket,
shirt, tie, and trousers that set off his chalky white face and
sandy, styled haircut that we used to call a ducktail when I was
a kid. He hardly presented the image of a killer.

Already, I saw that we faced a theatrical problem. For Kern
and his companions in mayhem—Lester, Ladone, Pirone, nearly
all except the hulking Riley—would be dwarfed by their chief
accuser, Cedric Sandiford. Kern seemed to shrink appreciably
and disappear into the shadows of his attorney, Leone.

The court clerk continued: "Mr. Kern, you have been indicted
under Number 890 of 1987 for the crimes of murder in the
second degree, the attempt to commit the crime of murder in
the second degree, assault in the first degree, and riot in the first
degree. How do you plead—"

"Not guilty, and I'm ready for trial," Leone shouted, flashing
a contented grin and drowning out the clerk's unfinished "guilty
or not guilty?"

Next the clerk inquired, "On the question of bail . . . ," and I
rose from my seat. I had decided several days earlier that I would
ask for six figures, a very high sum, because I was looking for the
maximum impact. I wanted everyone, from the public to the
defendants, to realize that I was taking this case very seriously,
and I wasn't going to make life easy for any of these punks. I gave
Judge Lerner a brief recitation of the facts of the case, conclud-
ing with an explanation of the heavy jail sentences that accompanied the charges if the accused were found guilty.

"And so, under all the circumstances," I told Lerner, "I respectfully ask Your Honor to set bail in the amount of one hundred thousand dollars."

The collective gasp from the spectator section then escalated
into a roar, and the Howard Beach trial had the first of its
many outbursts. Like a judge in a movie, Lerner warned that
in the event of another eruption he would be forced to clear
the court.

Gabe Leone obviously thought that this did not apply to him.
He called out: "Your Honor, this is *crazy*. Mr. Hynes has *no case*.

These young boys were merely defending themselves from un-savory characters who invaded their neighborhood."

I heard again the words of Harvey Louie Greenberg: "What were they doing there in the first place, Joe?" And I thought, *They're starting already.*

Before I could respond (or Leone could finish), Lerner inter-rupted, giving the newsmen their next day's headline: "This case is truly an American tragedy. If the evidence supports these charges, the jail sentence could be substantial. Bail is fixed at fifty thousand dollars."

A stunned silence fell over the courtroom.

The remainder of the arraignment was fairly routine. Bail was set at $50,000 for the homicide cases, $15,000 for the rest. When Robert Riley's case was called last, Rick Librett stepped forward. I moved into the well of the court and placed my arm on his shoulder and heard a slight rustle through the spectator section behind me.

"Let me handle this, Rick," I whispered, and he nodded as-sent.

"Your Honor," I began, "since January nineteenth of this year the defendant has been cooperating with my office. He has testi-fied before the grand jury which voted the indictment. Were it not for his help, many of these defendants might have gone unnoticed. I respectfully request that he be released into the custody of his attorney, Richard Librett, Esquire."

For the first time, most of the Howard Beach defendants and their families realized that Riley had turned. During our entire investigation he had gone about his life normally with his friends—school, parties, activities. Instantly, now that they knew what he was, shots of "Rat!" and "Turncoat!" bounced off the walls of K-3. Lerner jumped to his feet, and his voice sliced through the din. "The very next person to move or talk will be arrested." The courtroom fell silent again, Riley was re-leased into Librett's custody, and the arraignments were ad-journed.

As I was leading our team out of the building, a woman in her sixties pushed close to me and snarled, "Mr. Hynes, don't rail-road these kids." I didn't respond.

In the lobby of the courthouse there was a near riot of report-

ers and technicians. But it was finally over. Twenty-seven days
of incredible tension. I felt it was now up to my trial team of
Boyar, Mangum, Hawkins, and Hoffman to put together the
Howard Beach prosecution. For me, active participation in
Howard Beach was history.

Every six weeks or so I sit down to lunch with former New
York State attorney general Louis Lefkowitz and Judge John F.
Keenan, both good friends, both insightful people. Keenan and
I held various posts under Lefkowitz during his forty-year career
in New York State government, and we both looked forward to
these political seminars because of our Irish obsession with king-
craft.

Both men were in a position to give me an objective opinion
regarding the prospects of Howard Beach. In fact, it was my
respect for Lefkowitz's political acumen and Keenan's trial experience that would have a profound effect on me the afternoon
we met, a week after the arraignments.

"Who's trying the case, Joe?" Keenan asked as soon as I was
seated in the swanky Italian restaurant on Manhattan's Upper
East Side. I noticed he skipped the usual political amenities.

"I've got a terrific team," I told the two of them. "Ed Boyar
is my lead counsel, and he's got more than a dozen homicide
cases under his belt from his days with the Brooklyn DA. He's
a tremendous trial attorney. I've got a black lawyer named Richard Mangum second-seating him. Mangum's savvy, he knows
the streets, and he knows Queens. Used to work for Santucci out
there."

I didn't mention that Mangum had never tried a homicide
case before. Recently, Richard had taken to strutting through
the office and jokingly boasting that a murder trial was a prosecutor's easiest task. Just that morning he had pulled me aside for
one of his typical pep-rally lectures.

"Stars did the homicides when I was in Queens, Joe," said
Mangum, who *had* tried his fair share of drug, rape, and assault
cases. "I was never a star. But if you ask me, trying a homicide
is a walk in the park. You do two cases a year. You have all the
best investigators at your disposal. And you have the best evidence. Most of the time you got a dead body, for heaven's sake.
And sometimes you even have a confession. Usually there's some

pretty good witnesses, or the homicide charges wouldn't have even made it out of the grand jury. Finally, you have the emotional involvement of the jurors.

"That's what we got in Howard Beach, Joe," Richard continued. "Who can get emotional over a summation, or even an opening statement, if you're talking about some guy who broke a screen door and stole a color television and six hundred bucks? But you talk about our case, I think it's a snap."

I didn't quite see it that way, although I appreciated his enthusiasm.

I related Mangum's story to Keenan and Lefkowitz, and rounded out my rundown of the team with Hoffman as my appellate expert at court and Hawkins as media spokesman. Lefkowitz was remarkably impassive. Finally, Keenan looked up from his calamari and asked plaintively, "So where's the Irish guy?"

"Why is that so important, John?" I replied.

"Because, Joe, I know Queens. Why aren't *you* trying the case?"

"For one, because I'm not a homicide prosecutor, and for two, because I've got an office to run."

Then Lefkowitz spoke: "Joey, this case *is* your office. Cuomo probably should have abolished the Special Prosecutor's Office years ago. But you hired some people who gave it some juice. You have to try the case."

Later, back in my office, I relayed my luncheon conversation to Helman Brook.

"I have an idea," he said. "Why don't you just do what Rudy Giuliani did in the Friedman trial. You always said what he did was just like giving a couple of after-dinner speeches."

The most highly publicized United States Attorney in history and a narrow loser to Dinkins in the mayoral race, Rudolph Giuliani had recently portrayed himself as the lead counsel in the corruption trial of Bronx County political leader Stanley Friedman. Although Giuliani *did* actually cross-examine Friedman—who was charged with bribing officials of the New York City Parking Violations Bureau in exchange for exclusive, lucrative contracts—the U.S. Attorney had otherwise limited his

trial participation to the opening and closing statements, leaving
the rest of the case to his subordinates. Friedman was convicted.
  "By the way," Brook added. "Guess who our judge is."
  "Who?"
  "Tom Demakos."
  "So how do you read that, Helman? Good or bad?"
  "He's a tough guy. I think it's good . . . if *you* try the case."
  "Goodbye, Helman."

A trial judge is selected randomly by the New York State
Office of Court Administration. Yet if "the play's the thing" to
Shakespearean actors, then "the judge's the thing" to trial lawyers. The first words of an attorney scurrying into a courthouse
are, "Who's sitting?" In Thomas Anastasisos Demakos, I felt the
luck of the draw was to be ours.
  Tom Demakos, born in Manhattan in 1924 and raised in the
Bronx, worked for several years as a certified public accountant,
then graduated from New York University Law School in 1962
and began a seventeen-year prosecutorial career capped by his
appointment as chief assistant to the Queens County district
attorney. Known as a tough, yet fair, prosecutor and judge,
Demakos's trial reputation was enhanced by two cases he prosecuted.
  In the first, in the early 1970s, Demakos was assigned to prose-
cute a Queens housewife named Alice Crimmins, charged with
the murder of her five-year-old son and the manslaughter of her
four-year-old daughter. Demakos's adversary was a Queens
County legend from the criminal bar named Herb Lyons, whose
smooth and erudite style starkly contrasted with Demakos's
growling, pit-bull approach.
  Lyons subpoenaed the "peeping Tom" records of the NYPD
to determine if someone was skulking through Crimmins's
neighborhood the night that her children were allegedly ab-
ducted. Demakos was outraged. Lyons was questioning the in-
tegrity of his eyewitness, Sadie Ermonski, who testified that she
saw Alice Crimmins leading a small child from her apartment
with one hand and carrying what appeared to be a second—
wrapped in a blanket.

"If Mr. Lyons really wants to know what happened on that bloody night," stormed Demakos in a courtroom packed with reporters, "if he really wants to know who saw those two children being led to their deaths, tell him to turn to his right and ask that lady." And here he thrust his finger out, pointing at Crimmins.

This kind of righteous rage nearly caused a mistrial and blew the case for Demakos. Most damaging was when he mentioned in summation that Crimmins had failed to take the witness stand in her defense, which is, of course, a right guaranteed by the Fifth Amendment. "She doesn't even have enough courage to stand up and tell the world that she killed her children," he said to the jury, over Lyons's heated—and sustained—objections. Although Demakos got his conviction, I'm sure it would be reversed today on that statement alone. Times have changed, especially in the appellate courtroom. In fact, a lower court of appeals did overturn the conviction for a number of errors, but the New York State Court of Appeals overruled that decision and reinstated Crimmins's guilty verdict.

But it was the case Demakos prosecuted a year later that was to have a far greater effect on my life, and on the Howard Beach trial.

It took place in 1972. I had been the Rackets Bureau chief in Eugene Gold's office for nearly two years. The Queens district attorney, Thomas Mackel, recently indicted (and then convicted on charges that were dismissed years later) by Special Prosecutor Maurice Nadjari, had resigned, and I wanted the job. I devised a plan to lobby Governor Nelson A. Rockefeller, the first step of which required Gold's help and advice.

At first Gold found the idea absurd. "Joe," he said, "you could never get elected. The governor would appoint you as an interim, you'd fill in for a few months, and then you'd get killed in the primaries. It's a dumb idea."

But I persisted and finally persuaded Gold at least to run my name past Rockefeller's top adviser, Attorney General Louis Lefkowitz. When Lefkowitz went through with the formality and requested my résumé, Gold took it as a sign that there wasn't much interest in my application. Lefkowitz already knew

everybody he would be likely to hire, and he didn't know me.
But then, several weeks later, one Friday at noon, Gold excitedly
told me Lefkowitz had called with renewed interest in my application. The attorney general had asked around about me and
received good reports.

Twelve hours later, just past midnight on a quiet backstreet in
Queens, a young black teenager named Walter Glover confronted a white police officer named Thomas Shea, who was
investigating the report of a prowler. The cop fired point-blank,
claiming later that he saw a flash of metal in the youngster's
hand. Glover was pronounced dead on arrival at the hospital
emergency room; no weapons or metallic objects were recovered at the scene.

I spent that Saturday watching special television news reports
of the killing of Walter Glover as the city's black community
began to rumble and stir. "So here's the first crisis of the soon-to-
be-appointed district attorney," I nervously told my wife. I
made more than one telephone call to the Gold residence to
discuss possible approaches to the Glover investigation.

Early Sunday morning, it was Gold who called me. "Joe," he
said slowly, "the Queens thing may be dead."

"What do you mean, Gene? What Queens thing?"

"Louis Lefkowitz just called," he said. "Rockefeller wants to
appoint a new Queens DA early next week. But he doesn't think
you have the necessary name recognition. Joe, there's nothing
we can do about this."

All I could say was "Right," and it dropped from my mouth
like a stone. I turned to Pat, who saw the look on my face and
needed no further explanation.

The succeeding days could have been a primer for Howard
Beach. The term "special prosecutor" was not yet in vogue, but
if black politicians and community leaders didn't have the vocabulary down, they surely had the intent. They wanted a new
district attorney appointed and they wanted officer Shea investigated. Immediately. Under mounting pressure, Rockefeller
chose Michael F. Armstrong.

This man had the necessary name recognition. A burly Irish-
man, a graduate of Harvard Law School, Armstrong was an

assistant U.S. attorney in Manhattan. His initial notoriety was limited to the legal and law enforcement communities, stemming from his prosecutions for stock manipulation of financier Louis Wolfson, whose support payments to United States Supreme Court Justice Abe Fortas, though legal, created such an appearance of impropriety that President Lyndon B. Johnson's nominee for chief justice was forced to resign in disgrace. Armstrong put Wolfson in jail, and (although this case would pale beside contemporary insider-trading prosecutions) everyone with a legal degree admired and respected Michael Armstrong.

Next came the Knapp Commission hearings, when the tough, Irish-Catholic investigative lawyer began to probe a police department whose roster read like a Tipperary phonebook. He turned several corrupt detectives at the core of the police scandal, and their televised testimony produced daily front-page headlines. By the time the hearings concluded, Mike Armstrong was famous.

Now Rockefeller wanted him as Queens DA. Later, after Armstrong and I became friends, I realized how wise the choice had been. At the time, however, I was in a pet, and as a salve of sorts Gold created the position of first assistant district attorney for me, with a substantial hike in pay.

Months later a Queens grand jury found that Officer Shea did not act with justification in the shooting death of Walter Glover and indicted him for murder. Armstrong assigned the case to his best trial lawyer, Assistant District Attorney Thomas Demakos.

The trial judge assigned to the Shea case was a gruff old bear named George Balbach, himself a former attorney of such accomplishment that he, too, had achieved legendary status in the saloons of Queens Boulevard. Balbach liked to be in control of his courtroom. He and Demakos were bound to clash.

Demakos was looking forward to it. He didn't anticipate the obvious, but successful, strategy Shea's lawyers had devised.

Both prosecution and defense in any jury trial may make challenges "for cause" and "peremptory" challenges during the selection of the jury. Challenges for cause have to have a legal basis—if, for example, a potential juror knows one of the trial participants or has been the victim of a similar crime. A peremptory challenge requires no explanation, and it was this type that had traditionally been used, and misused, by prosecutors to exclude minorities. In the Glover trial, Officer Shea's lawyers turned the tables on the prosecution, using their peremptory challenges to knock every black and Hispanic off the jury so that Shea went to trial with twelve whites as his peers.

Demakos exploded, charging his adversaries with racism. But his outburst drew a reprimand from Balbach, and Shea was acquitted by the all-white jury.

At home that evening, I told Pat about my lunch with Keenan and Lefkowitz and my recollections of Thomas Demakos.

"Then it's clear to me that you should definitely try the Howard Beach case," she said quite simply.

"Why is that?" I asked.

"Because the judge, with his temper, sounds just like you."

I had been thinking along the same line, but not for the same reason. Lefkowitz was right. The Howard Beach case *was* my office. I had to try the case.

The following morning I handed out pre-trial assignments. Dennis Hawkins had proven effective dealing with the media during the 77th Precinct investigation and trials, and I gave him back that job, full-time. I told Hilly Hoffman that I wanted him as my "law person," backing up the trial team at the prosecutor's table.

"Joe, I think Matt deserves to be there," Hoffman said with typical unselfishness. Hilly looked on Matt Greenberg as almost a younger brother. "He's done most of the appellate research on the case, he knows the most about it in terms of legal technicalities, and I really don't need the press exposure."

Greenberg, a shy man, protested, but it wasn't a bad idea. He was, after all, a brilliant appeals lawyer. I acquiesced, and told Matt to draft a backup staff.

Then I turned to Boyar and Mangum, and, gulping for effect, named them my "second seats."

"I'll be the lead," I said to the group, "but only if I can limit my involvement to the opening and closing remarks, my two after-dinner speeches."

They smirked, just as Pat had done the evening before when I told her of my intentions. *Yeah, sure,* her look had said. *A guy like you won't be happy unless you're running the whole show.*

21

HUNTLEY HEARINGS

Things moved slowly for the next several months. Oddly, meetings with Keating and the Irish Mafia, my habitual solace, proved monotonously distressing. Only Harvey Louie Greenberg, who had recently been spending a lot of time with our group, believed that I should try the case. Keating, who had long since chosen court administration over trial work for himself, objected on purely pragmatic grounds: I hadn't successfully prosecuted a case in sixteen years, not since I was an assistant district attorney and put away two punks for murdering an Episcopal priest in Brooklyn Heights. As rackets chief, I was an investigator and an administrator, not a trial lawyer.

"And besides," Keating added, "what is there to gain? It's not like you're the only trial lawyer in the office. Maybe you could have been another Clarence Darrow if you hadn't stopped trying cases regularly, Joe. But face it, there's rust on your rust."

But to change my mind now, after I had committed myself to the A-Team, would have involved losing face, one thing I believe a leader can never do. Plus, I reasoned, just about every piece of advice Keating had given me concerning Howard Beach—from our very first conversation when he implored me to say no to Cuomo—had been comically wrong.

The staff devoted March and April to presentations at Huntley hearings—from the landmark decision, *People v. Huntley,* in which New York State's top court had held that "a defendant against whom a statement is to be used is entitled to a full hearing to see whether that statement was given freely and without coercion." We had to prove to Demakos's satisfaction that the Howard Beach teens had spoken to Borelli's detectives of their own free will.

During one marathon session in State Supreme Court, the eleven defense attorneys were invited to question the detective commanders who ran the unit the night the defendants were brought into the 106th Precinct. Lieutenants Sean Driscoll and Dan Kelly explained that the white teenagers had arrived at the precinct of their own volition and had never been questioned under duress. Demakos generally ruled in our favor, allowing a majority of the statements to stand.

In the give-and-take over which 911 emergency calls would be allowed to stand as evidence, the defense attorneys were battling hard to retain short-order cook John Laffey's original telephone call reporting "suspicious blacks" inside the New Park Pizzeria, which they felt cast the victims in a negative light. In exchange for that call—and assuming that we would simply want to corroborate Theresa Fisher's testimony about seeing Sandiford being beaten—they allowed us to include whichever 911 calls we could produce. Thus, we put into evidence a chart the A-Team had fashioned, showing the times of all the 911 calls received the night of The Incident. Defense counsel accepted it. What they didn't realize was that the chart, corroborating Riley's version of events, clearly proved that Griffith was already dead by the time Sandiford was attacked, and that their clients were the killers.

At one point it appeared that the trial would begin in May. Then a court date was set for early summer. But because of the sheer bulk of the pre-trial hearings, as well as the conflicting schedules of the defense attorneys, Demakos was forced to order several adjournments. That didn't bother me at all—I needed all the time I could get.

At a meeting shortly before Memorial Day, Demakos agreed to split the Howard Beach case into at least two separate trials. I felt that a trial of eleven defendants—for Riley was copping a plea—would prove too unwieldy, and I wanted to ensure that the most serious charges would not be lost in the wash. Our proposal did not meet with any serious objections from defense counsel, nine of whom (mostly those whose defendants were charged with lesser crimes such as riot) had already filed motions to sever their cases from the others. The primary trial, for it involved the most serious murder and manslaughter indictments against Kern, Lester, Ladone, and Pirone, was scheduled for early September. We used the extra time well.

Pica, LeVien, and the investigators spent most of their days re-interviewing key witnesses, including Theresa Fisher, who was receiving continual threats to her life and whom we placed under a sort of unofficial police protection.

Ed Boyar was put in charge of photographing the scene from every conceivable angle, and twice he went aloft in police helicopters for aerial shots. Videotapes were made of the escape routes of all three of the victims. We wanted to—we *needed* to—place our jury in Howard Beach on the night of the attack. We had to make them see that the close-fitting houses and fenced-in properties of the short block were really a tunnel and Michael Griffith's only means of escape was the Belt Parkway.

Mangum and Boyar flew out to Detroit to hire an accident-reconstruction expert to replicate Griffith's death. The re-creation took place on a warm Friday in March, in the parking lot of the Pontiac Silverdome football stadium.

"Wait'll you see this car smack the dummy," Mangum announced as he returned, waving a videotape of the accident reconstruction.

Griffith's body had never left any drag marks on the Belt Parkway. Nor had there been a marker, such as an empty shoe, to show exactly where he had been struck. How his body came to rest approximately one hundred twenty-five feet from where Riley had seen him hit remained a weak spot in our case. I never doubted that the defense would jump all over the discrepancy between Sandiford's testimony and Riley's. We had to prove beyond reasonable doubt that Riley was correct. He was, after all, the witness upon whom most of our corroborating evidence was based.

So it was with nervousness and great anticipation that the A-Team piled into the War Room to view Mangum's tape.

"Pow," said Richard, standing tantalizingly close to the office VCR, but refusing to press in the tape until he could summon up a full dramatic effect for us. "The collision sends the dummy, Michael's exact weight, one hundred seventy-five feet down the road. On a fly. Then we did it again a second time. Pow again. And that's right within range of where they found Griffith's body. And the test cars they used—the test cars had the same marks in the exact spot as Blum's. Wait until you see the videotape." We were indeed waiting anxiously. "With the car moving, and the dummy moving at the same speed, it gives the illusion of going straight up in the air. Like Riley says. They call it a 'throw distance,' and the expert is ready to testify for us."

By this time we were all ready to kill Mangum, who apparently wasn't big on suspense. By the time the tape got rolling, it was almost an anticlimax.

Lawyers may be great wordsmiths (or bullshitters, depending upon your point of view), but they are usually fairly poor scientists. It took several explanations before any of us could begin to grasp the physical concept of how Michael Griffith's body hurtled so far through the air. But it had certainly hurtled. And based on a relative degree of scientific certainty, we could now prove that in court.

At the conclusion of the Huntley hearings, I convened the trial team to hear everyone's impressions of Demakos.

"He's tough, boss, but he knows his business," said Boyar, and the others agreed. Yet, despite my faith in the staff, this was one "tough" judge I was going to have to check out myself. You can learn a lot about a judge by asking other trial lawyers. But, as I teach my students, there is no substitute for a firsthand look at the judge in action. (I also recommend watching a known adversary, but unfortunately, none of the Howard Beach defense attorneys had trials scheduled that summer.)

It was July, our family was spending the summer at Breezy Point, and as I tiptoed through the house in the pre-dawn blackness searching for a pair of jeans and a T-shirt, I decided that this

was as fine a day as any to make the aquaintance of Justice
Thomas A. Demakos. I took my usual 5:00 A.M. walk along the
shore, going after coffee and the four daily papers, and I bumped
into Joe Miller, a neighbor and friend from high school. After
serving as a sergeant in the NYPD, he had become a member
of my nursing home investigation team. When I met him that
morning, he was kicking out of a five-mile jog.

Miller issued his standard greeting—"What's up, old sock?"—
and I told him where I stood in the Howard Beach case.

On the quiet, oceanside street, Joe Miller leaned over con-
spiratorially and whispered, "C'mon now, Joe, tell the old sarge.
What were they really doing in Howard Beach?"

I'm sure I reddened, but Miller's infectious smile softened the
harsh words I wanted to spit out.

"You know," I said to him, "they might have been doing a lot
of things in that neighborhood, but that kid didn't deserve to
die."

"Maybe," Miller said, walking off. "But are you sure this wasn't
something that just got out of hand?"

Miller's nickname was "Archie," as in "Bunker." So his observations were far from startling. But I knew that, as a Queens
County resident and upstanding citizen, he wasn't alone in his
opinion; he was precisely the kind of guy I would find in my jury
pool.

That thought stayed with me during an uneasy drive out to
Queens County State Supreme Court.

When I entered K-3, Judge Demakos was on the bench, finishing up some routine calendar matters—a sentencing, a few
adjournments. He then began jury selection for a homicide case,
which was, alas, typical for our time: two rival drug lords had
decided that competition was not a healthy marketing factor,
and, with two blasts from a double-030 shotgun, one had re-
claimed his monopoly. The prosecutor was a young assistant
district attorney named Jim Quinn, one of Santucci's rising
young stars. Quinn would surely have been ordered to try the
Howard Beach case had the Queens DA retained jurisdiction.

Demakos ran a very tight ship during jury selection, permit-
ting only the most focused questions. Some judges allow lawyers

to ask about such plainly silly and irrelevant matters as personal tastes in food or clothing. And some lawyers adopt a strategy, as I do when I can get away with it, of posing questions that point up weaknesses in the opposition's case. As a prosecutor, Demakos had walked down that path, but as a judge, he, quite correctly, would have none of it. Each juror should be an empty vessel, hearing the strengths and shortcomings of a case for the first time during trial, not through cleverly framed hypothetical questions during jury selection.

I have always advocated finding the brightest possible group available for a jury through the use of creative questioning during jury selection—the voir dire, from the old French "to say the truth." I want to hear my questions answered with more than a grunted "yes" or "no."

For instance, three typical jury-selection questions: "Can you be fair? Will you listen to all the testimony before making up your mind? Do you today have an opinion about this case?" will inevitably produce the following responses: yes, yes, and no. And those answers tell me absolutely nothing. I do not feel I have to resort to queries about food or fashions in order to obtain a broader idea of the human beings who might serve on my jury. But I would like to know, for instance, what a prospective juror recalls having read about a certain case or just what kind of news stories in general a person usually reads.

However, I knew that in the Howard Beach trial that intelligent jurors, or even reasonably bright jurors, wouldn't be enough. The avalanche of pre-trial publicity would taint any jury pool to the extent that the regular voir dire process would be insufficient. So I commissioned an analysis to compare the news coverage of Howard Beach with that of another sensational case, the recently concluded trial of New York subway gunman Bernhard Goetz. The results floored me: there was more line coverage in the four city newspapers in the six months following the Howard Beach incident than there had been in the two and one-half years between Goetz's shooting rampage and his guilty verdict for weapons possession.

After I had been hanging around Demakos's courtroom for three days, the judge finally motioned me up to the side of his bench. "Can I help you with anything, Mr. Hynes?" he asked, and I told him I was just visiting.

"What exactly are you doing here?" he pressed. I asked him if he was a football fan.

"Well, yes, I am," he said.

"In that case, Your Honor, imagine that you're next week's opponent, and I'm the competition's head coach. I'm merely scouting the pre-game films."

His smile told me he understood, and he said he felt we were both in for "an interesting trial."

Three weeks later Jimmy Quinn had another murder conviction under his belt, and there was little I didn't know about the style and courtroom demeanor of Thomas Demakos, trial judge. Now my staff could anticipate the kind of evidentiary rulings he would be likely to make at our trial. Matt Greenberg and his appellate people would eventually produce thirty-six memoranda of law addressing every conceivable legal issue, and tailored to fit my descriptions of how Demakos would rule.

But more important, from studying Demakos's habits I had learned something that might really matter: when to shout out and when to shut up. We were, after all, still on Queens Boulevard.

22

THE QUEENS
BOULEVARD CREW

The summer moved rapidly and so did our pre-trial preparation. While the A-Team threw themselves into the Huntley hearings, trips to Michigan for the accident re-creation, and, in the case of the appellate lawyers, preparing memoranda of law, I spent considerable time prepping Cedric Sandiford and Timothy Grimes.

I returned to Howard Beach a number of times (always, on orders from Al Pica, surrounded by tough investigators who were ready to handle anyone that came near me). I walked the victims through their escape route. I probed for a mislaid fragment of memory that might advance our case. When we weren't at the scene, we were conducting mock cross-examinations in the moot court we set up at St. John's Law School. I wanted Cedric and Timothy to get the feel of being in a courtroom.

I felt that we had all the information that we needed—and all we were going to get—from Sandiford. He spent most of the summer watching the Irangate hearings on television, and he mentioned more than once that "I'm going to be ready for these guys, for the defense attorneys. I see in the papers what they're saying about me, how I'm supposed to be a bad guy looking for trouble in Howard Beach that night. But I've been studying Ollie North. He's got it down. I'm going to be ready."

As the law demands, we made all of our records available to the defense attorneys at a series of pre-trial meetings called discovery hearings. These were instituted to ensure that by the time a case gets to trial both sides were privy to the same information. "Surprise witnesses" are a figment of a screenwriter's imagination, and I remember the long faces Boyar and Mangum wore as they virtually lived at the Xerox machine, copying every Five, statement, and report we had gathered. At the same time, we received a list of witnesses the defense planned to call to the stand. It was insubstantial, which only confirmed my feelings that *their* case was going to be based on attacking *our* case.

Nothing really surprised us. Soon after handing over our documents, selected leaks involving the criminal records and past "bad acts" of the Howard Beach victims began appearing regularly in the newspapers. Reporters phoned for my reaction. I thought the leaking was cheap, even lowdown, but I bit my tongue and offered "No comment."

Sandiford and his assigned "baby-sitter," Doug LeVien, got along well. Somehow, Doug was familiar with several aspects of the Caribbean basin, and the two discussed the odd politics of the Cooperative Republic of Guyana, where East Indians outnumber native blacks, who nonetheless control the government. I once heard the surprising LeVien rating island soccer greats with the athletic Sandiford, and I even took part in a round-table discussion comparing the merits of certain Caribbean carnivals. We were all learning something about each other.

Gradually, we explained Riley's version of events to Sandiford. We told him him that our investigation led us to believe that Riley was telling the truth. At first, he found the news disturbing and embarrassing. But as time wore on he seemed to accept the fact that somehow, in some unexplainable way, he had gotten the story wrong.

Grimes, on the other hand, was a nightmare for us. He had found a job as a janitor, and continued under a psychiatrist's care. One doctor speculated to me that he was suffering from the effects of lead-paint poisoning . The most I could ever get out of him was grunting, grudging, monosyllabic answers to even the most basic questions. In many ways, this was still the same violent young man who had been imprisoned for armed robbery at the age of fifteen. For most of the time I knew him he carried a knife. I had more or less given him up as a lost cause. But I had to call him to the stand. I couldn't risk having defense counsel carve him up before *I* laid out his past for the jury.

Once, I gathered the entire A-Team around the conference table and asked Timothy to describe exactly what had happened when he stabbed Cheryl Sandiford days after the attack. Grimes said he had been "up" on crack for several days when he visited Cedric's niece, and after he finally fell asleep on her couch, her stirring in the room awakened him in a frenzy.

"I just grabbed the hunting knife, it was laying on the TV, and I slashed twice, bang, bang," he said, leaping out of his seat and banging his hand on the conference table with such ferocity that Matt Greenberg grew pale.

Wonderful. But this was also irrelevant to the case. Grimes might have just finished holding up twenty-three grocery stores or he might have just received the Nobel Peace Prize. Neither should have mattered in the context of Howard Beach. There, on that cold winter's night, he was attacked because he was black. But jurors were human. How could I convince them of the injustice of the Howard Beach attack after they'd watched him re-create the act of plunging a hunting knife into his girlfriend?

I wasn't sure. But an isolated incident one Sunday morning in Howard Beach convinced me that this racial hatred had to be exposed. I had returned to 90th Street alone to meet photographers from the Police Department's Crime Scene Unit because, even with Boyar's aerial shots and our videotape, I wanted everything we could get to make the jury understand the block's "tunnel effect" on Michael Griffith. As I stood waiting for the detectives, an old station wagon with a man, woman, and two small children backed out of a driveway and stopped directly in front of me. The man sprang from behind the wheel and shouted, "Hynes, you traitor, you're just no goddamn good."

"Why is that?" I asked, keeping my voice very calm.

"Because here it is Sunday, and you won't fucking leave us alone."

I cringed, looking at his children. "Do you live here?" I asked.

"Yeah!" he shouted, the veins rising in his neck.

"Did you hear anything that night?"

"No," he said, sneering, "but I can smell that kind—not to mention your kind—a mile away."

I could only shake my head and murmur, "I feel sorry for you, buddy," as I walked away.

"I don't want your fucking pity, pal," he replied, and his station wagon squealed away. I had no way of proving it, but I guessed he was heading for church.

Throughout the long process, I wondered if my trial team was savvy enough to overcome such deep-seated emotions. Our opponents were attorneys skilled at defending homicidal maniacs, truck hijackers, Colombian drug dealers. The special prosecutor's team, with our mundane government corruption cases, appeared, in comparison, to be playing in the minor leagues.

To prepare for a rapacious defense attorney one must think like a rapacious defense attorney. Unfortunately, of the entire A-Team, only Hershey, Hayes, and I had spent any time on the defense side of the bar, and Pam's experience was limited to the New Jersey Public Defender's Office, hardly a hotbed of cutthroat ambition. I decided that the time had come for the team to get a dose of the best-informed lawyer I knew: Harvey Louie Greenberg.

As a heavyweight orders a sparring partner to mirror the style of an upcoming foe, I brought Harvey in for a full-contact affair at a mock trial held at St. John's.

"Be your obstreperous self," I told him. "I want you to tear the case apart."

Ed Boyar opened the proceedings by explaining that my opening statement would be accompanied by an impressive and elaborate display of charts, maps, and aerial photographs of the scene of the attack.

"How?" asked Harvey.

"Pardon me?" asked Ed.

"How do you get all these wonderful things into the opening statement when they are not evidence?"

Some of the confident faces around the room went blank. I looked at Ed, then at Helman, Hilly, and Matt.

"Well?" I said.

Harvey broke the silence: "There is a federal statute that permits the introduction of exhibits for the *limited* purpose of assisting the jury to understand the opening statement. But there's no comparable statute in New York State. So how do you get them in?"

By that point my observations of Demakos told me he was such a practical guy that I was sure I could sell him on the charts to be displayed so the jury could follow my opening remarks, but, eager to set the tone, I let Harvey's objection stand.

And he went on to challenge my troops on every point, giving them a taste of the streetfighting legal code. This was more than a tour de force, it was a brutal warning. And with each challenge our strategy crystallized. The order of witnesses and exhibits was established, for instance, only after an uneasy dispute.

"What were *they*"—Harvey stared viciously at Pamela and Richard as he underscored the word "they"—"what were they doing in Howard Beach?"

"Sylvester's car broke down," responded Boyar, becoming testy.

"Yeah? And exactly how are you going to prove that?"

"Either Cedric or Timothy, or both for that matter," interjected Mangum, whose blood was also rising.

Harvey jumped from his seat, walked to the witness stand, and turned to face the A-Team. "Let me get this straight," he said derisively, pounding his fist on the stand. "With a dozen leaks planted in the newspapers, with your counterparts from Queens Boulevard implying all over the nightly news that your victims were in Howard Beach to peddle drugs, or to commit mayhem, or whatever, that's your *answer?*"

He was nearly shrieking. "You're going to have two stone junkies take the witness stand and explain that their car broke down in Howard Beach? Are you people nuts!"

The room was suddenly still. It was 1:30 P.M. and lunch had not yet arrived. Harvey offered to buy me a beer.

"We'll be back in a half-hour, someone call about lunch," I yelled over my shoulder at the nine irate and red-faced attorneys. On the way out, I imagined them sticking imaginary pins in an imaginary voodoo doll bearing an uncanny likeness to Harvey Louie Greenberg.

By the time we returned from lunch, the A-Team had figured out the obvious answers to Harvey's conundrum. Both the tow-truck driver who drove Sylvester to the garage and the mechanic who replaced his blown transmission would be called to testify that car trouble had indeed brought the victims into Howard Beach. Harvey smiled for the first time that day.

The order in which we would call our witnesses was thus designed to emphasize the strong points of our case and disguise the weak. Our most compelling testimony, undoubtedly from Theresa Fisher and Cedric Sandiford, would be used at the most strategic points of the trial. Fisher would testify early, her dramatic recollection of the beating serving to wake up the jury. Sandiford would be called closer to the end, a vivid reminder to each juror of how much was at stake.

In between, we planned to "hide" witnesses such as Dominick Blum and Robert Riley—despite the fact that they were the critical underpinnings of our homicide case. This would be done in the hope that the jury would forget the woeful image they each projected in their totally different ways.

By the end of Harvey's eight-hour session, I was fairly sure the staff knew just what it could expect. With that in mind, I put Ed Boyar in charge of Bobby Riley. The defense attorneys were going to be rough on Riley, and he was barely a step above Grimes on the eloquence scale. He was a nervous, sweaty kid, and I have seen the notion of giving up one's accomplices on the six o'clock news induce amnesia in less timid souls.

Prior to his grand jury testimony, while he ostensibly remained "just one of the guys," Riley had spent all his time with his friends and schoolmates, so as not to arouse suspicion. But when they were arrested on February 10, the little dirty dozen had huddled together in their holding pen, wondering if someone had turned State's evidence.

"We were locked up, the twelve of us, in the cell eating, and they had the news on TV," Michael Pirone would recall. "Riley was saying, 'Who's the rat? We're going to find out who the rat is. Wait'll I find that rat.' We were wondering ourselves. And then we went to get our indictments, and Riley went for his, but he never came back. Everybody wondered where he was. Finally we found out from Todd Greenberg, Billy Bollander's lawyer, exactly where Riley had gone. It was the last time I ever saw him."

Now Riley was an outcast, vilified in his hometown. He spent his days behind drawn curtains at home with his family, which had been placed under police protection. The *New York Post* ran a profile on him with the front-page headline: PORTRAIT OF THE LONELIEST TEEN IN HOWARD BEACH.

After Boyar had run through six or seven sessions with our star witness, I cautiously approached him, in hope of good news.

"Things are going just terrific with Riley, boss," was Boyar's sanguine reply. I wondered if he'd taken that big, dopey lug to Lourdes and miraculously transformed him into a credible witness.

"Do you think he's ready for Harvey?" I asked.

"Absolutely," said Ed.

Harvey Louie Greenberg had also volunteered to play the part of a defense attorney in a mock cross-examination of Riley. I wanted him to rip Riley to shreds. I was sure the defense was already practicing their own moves.

On a sunny Saturday in August, Boyar escorted Riley into the lower Manhattan law suite of Washor, Greenberg and Washor to see just how "terrific" Riley would be. Eight hours later, an exhausted Ed Boyar stepped into my office and slumped into a chair.

"How'd the kid do?" I asked, looking up.

"Not bad," Boyar answered softly. The muted reply was thoroughly out of character, and his expression told me that the dress rehearsal had not gone well. I called Harvey right away.

"Joe, do you really have to call this kid to the witness stand?" Harvey's voice crackled over the telephone line.

I was in no mood for jokes. "Don't be a wiseass, Harvey. You know I have to call him. Just how bad was he?"

"Well, Joe, buy me a beer at Moe's and I'll tell it to you straight."

"That bad?" I croaked.

On my walk to Moe's, I thought about the tough crew of defense lawyers who'd be trying to pick flesh off the carcasses of my key witnesses, and even try to gnaw at some bones.

Each of my adversaries had his own style in the well. If all their skills had resided in a single one of them, I would have been facing the perfect trial lawyer. Fortunately, each had a weakness that I hoped to exploit.

Forty-six-year-old Gabe Leone, who represented Scott Kern, possessed a rough-and-tumble style that seemed fitting for a man who looked like a longshoreman wedged into a suit and whose basso profundo was rumored to carry an expletive or two. Leone was the former chief of the Queens district attorney's Narcotics Bureau, and I was told that now, as a defense counsel, he "ate young assistant DAs for breakfast." He is to the well what a good club fighter is to the ring: he would take punishment in order to inflict it, betting that he would be the one left standing at the final bell.

Yet if Leone's cross-examination style is to wade in for the knockout, he also exudes a certain charm and sincerity that are not lost on a jury. He had recently won fame representing one Delia Carter, known in the tabloids as "the woman who committed the perfect crime." She made a deal with the Queens DA, promising to testify in her husband's murder trial in return for immunity, and on the strength of her word, the husband was convicted. But after he was sentenced Delia Carter admitted that she was in fact the one who committed the murder. The husband was released, and Delia, because she had been granted immunity, could not be tried for the crime.

After a heavy lunch, Gabe Leone also had a habit in long, tedious cases to doze off. I hoped our jurors would look dubiously at a trial lawyer sleeping on the job.

On the other hand, Bryan Levinson, Jon Lester's attorney, was always wide awake. Levinson's parents had a vaudeville comedy act and he used his inherited sense of theater to considerable advantage. A lifelong resident of Howard Beach, Levinson possessed a quicksilver wit and the ability to ingratiate himself with a jury. At fifty-four, the oldest of the quartet, Levinson would need every one of his comic asides to make his client appear sympathetic. For, by our account, had it not been for Lester's prodding, the racial attack in Howard Beach never would have occurred.

Several years after I left the Brooklyn Legal Aid Society in 1965 to begin a private practice, the office hired a recent law school graduate named Ronald Rubinstein. Two decades later, the forty-nine-year-old Rubinstein, who was defending Jason Ladone, was known along Queens Boulevard as the slickest of the slick. Clothed in expensive Italian suits, or seated behind the wheel of a late-model Mercedes, Rubinstein is the screenwriter's dream (or caricature) of the criminal defense lawyer. My staff was already referring to him as Arnie Becker, after the divorce specialist on the popular television series *L.A. Law*. Appropriately, Rubinstein was skiing at Mount Vail when he read of the Howard Beach attack on page two of the *Denver Post*.

Rubinstein also loved reporters and they liked him, probably because his statements tended toward the inflammatory and reckless. Yet I eventually came to respect him for his considerable trial skills. But his charges in the corridors were so outlandish that I developed a standard answer to reporters seeking reaction: "When Ronnie speaks, you all have to take out your rulers and measure how far his nose has grown."

Finally, there was Stevie Murphy.

And Stevie Murphy was something else.

An elfin streetfighter clad in Kenneth Cole shoes and $600 suits, Murphy would look right at home sitting on an Irish toadstool, guarding a pot of gold. He is the son of a legendary city firefighter who rose through the ranks to become first deputy fire commissioner. The late Stephen Murphy, Sr., was a good friend of mine, a sweet and decent man, and I often wondered aloud to Stevie if he might not have been adopted. I wasn't entirely kidding.

"Joe," Murphy would "scream" in reply (for Murphy rarely just "spoke"), "you only know one side of me. Actually, I'm a very gentle guy."

For this, as for many of Murphy's other statements, he has yet to provide proof. At one point before trial, Murphy requested and received court authorization to search the Howard Beach sewers for the alleged weapons his client said Grimes, Griffith, and Sandiford were wielding. It was a silly order, I told the judge. Even if knives and guns were found, who was to say that they belonged to the victims? Demakos admitted that he had serious doubts about whether Murphy could make the connection, but the search was allowed. No weapons were recovered. Given the neighborhood's reputation, this was a mild surprise to many of us.

Murphy's courtroom etiquette, particularly his cross-examination style, asking questions rapidly and hostilely, was designed to fluster a witness into blurting out answers he or she really didn't mean. And this former assistant district attorney who had worked under Demakos was nothing less than sensational in achieving his end.

My three key witnesses were an admitted drug user and illegal alien who had confessed to having possessed a sawed-off shotgun; a near-catatonic ghetto tough with an extended rap sheet; and a turncoat who had led the attack. Still, as I thought about this Queens Boulevard "crew," I was looking forward to tangling with them.

Then I walked into Moe's and saw the look on Harvey Louie Greenberg's face.

Harvey has an annoying habit of stalling bad news by repeating a phrase. When I asked just how badly it had gone with Riley, he must have said "How about if I tell you" half a dozen times. I began to feel vaguely ill.

"Did you know Riley's been arrested twice before, Joe?" he finally began. "Did you know he used to drive around in his big Buick Electra with a stolen police emergency light? You know, the red cherry light? He would put it on his roof and stop motorists. He'd tell the drivers that they had committed some traffic infraction and then give them a stern lecture. Then he and his friends would howl with laughter and sometimes shoot the poor suckers with a fire extinguisher.

"Did you know that one of the motorists was a woman eight months pregnant? And another was a rabbi on his way to temple to conduct Yom Kippur services? They took down Riley's license plate number and called the police. And did you know that both times he got caught his father and his brother got him off the hook?"

I finished my beer and ordered another.

"So here you have one of the main mutts in the attack," Harvey summed up triumphantly: "He grabs the baseball bat out of Kern's hands. He wants to 'kill the niggers' as much as anybody else. If he wasn't so drunk, Lester probably would have never gotten the bat from him. And as soon as he's arrested, his family comes running to the special state prosecutor looking for a deal.

"Joe, you would give up a month's pay to cross-examine this kid. He's bear meat for any defense attorney with half a brain."

I walked to the back of the bar and grabbed the pay phone. I called Boyar.

"Ed," I boomed into the receiver, "did you know that this fucking kid harassed a pregnant mother and a rabbi and then had his family get him off?"

"Yeah, boss," Boyar replied. "But I didn't think that was such a big deal. It was a prank."

"Bullshit, Ed!" I screamed. "Let me make this clear to you and everyone else. From now on I don't want any more surprises."

I slammed down the phone. Harvey had never seen me so agitated, and I can be a very agitated guy.

"Don't worry, Joe," he said nervously. "Look, I'll work with the kid again. We'll get him ready."

The following day Timothy Grimes was due at the office. In hopes of opening him up, I had had him sit in on my meetings with Sandiford. It hadn't worked. Nothing, apparently, could jog Grimes's memory. By now my entire office was convinced that it was Grimes whom Sandiford had seen on the other side of that fence and had mistaken for Michael Griffith. We were also fairly certain that Timothy had witnessed Cedric's beating. But no one could get through to him.

Mangum made Grimes his special case. "Timmy, things are going to get rough at the trial," Richard would warn him again and again. "If there's anything that you haven't told us about, and if the other side gets hold of it, they'll try to embarrass you."

"I don't know why I even have to testify after what I went through," Grimes replied regularly, and he usually said no more.

The day after the Riley fiasco, I ordered yet another field trip to Howard Beach. "Timmy will ride with me," I told my investigators, instructing them to follow in another car.

"I don't know about this, boss," said Mangum, pulling me to one side. "The kid can get pretty violent."

Good, was my first cynical thought, *maybe he'll put me out of my misery and finally make a contribution to this case.* "Don't worry, Richard, just follow me closely," I said instead, and he and the two investigators followed me to Queens as if attached at the fender.

Midway through the drive, my car phone beeped, I answered, and Grimes, curiously, came alive. "Can you call anywhere on that thing?" he asked me.

"Sure, Timothy."

"Even out of the country?"

"Yes, Timothy. By the way, does your mother know where you are?"

"She don't need to know."

"Don't you think you ought to call her and tell her where you are?"

"Can I do that from here?"

I punched in her number, pushed the send button, and Grimes didn't stop talking for the rest of the afternoon. He spoke to his mother for twenty minutes, and then continued with me, telling me stories about life in the projects in a gentle, singsong tone. He said more during that car ride than he had for the previous nine months. His sentences were connected, although excited. His vocabulary was surprisingly extensive. He was not such a dummy after all.

Whatever else, I thought with relief, *at least I'll be able to get him to tell his story coherently.*

After Grimes attacked Cheryl Sandiford, the District Attorney's Office had deferred the case and allowed Timothy to enter a therapeutic program designed to deal with his tendency toward violence. As he chattered happily that afternoon—about almost everything but Howard Beach—I realized that this young man was seriously disturbed and in need of some long-term treatment. Finally, toward evening, I decided to take a chance.

"Timothy," I asked, "did you or Cedric or Michael pull out a knife in front of that pizza parlor?"

"I told you before that nobody had weapons. What are you always getting on my case for?"

So much for the "new" Timothy Grimes. The kid clammed up when I tried to take him through the scene of the attack, and the drive home passed in silence.

Several days later, when Sandiford arrived for another round of preparations, he appeared to be on edge. Les Smith, one of my investigators, escorted him into the office.

"Cedric," said Smith, "tell Mr. Hynes what you told me coming over here."

Sandiford would not permit his eyes to meet mine. "I feel awful to be the one to be telling you this," he began. "You and your people have been very good to me. The way I see it, we have to be truthful to you or Mike's killers are going to walk free."

I cannot describe the anxiety I felt as Sandiford laid out his preface. It was if an anvil had been surgically implanted on my heart. Finally he got to the point.

"Timmy, he had a knife that night," said Cedric. "I never saw it, but he told me about it last night. He said he's ashamed to tell you."

I had expected this, and nearly breathed a sigh of relief that the confession hadn't been worse. We brought Grimes in that afternoon, and he swore to us that he had pulled his four-inch blade only as a defense mechanism after the whites had come at him with bats and tree limbs. He said he had been too scared to admit to his actions before the grand jury, but decided to tell us now because "it's the right thing to do." Several days later I filed court papers relating this new turn of events and waited for all hell to break loose. I didn't wait long.

HOWARD BEACH BOMBSHELL! screamed the next day's headline in the *New York Post,* and even the great gray *New York Times* played BLACK HAD KNIFE AT HOWARD BEACH above the fold on page one. Rubinstein and Leone both demanded a dismissal based on Grimes's perjured grand-jury testimony—and more knives were out for me than Grimes had owned in his life.

"It changes the entire case, from a racial incident to a confrontation of force on both sides," Rubinstein told reporters. "In other words, a street fight."

"It goes to the state of mind of the young men from Howard Beach," added Murphy. "Now we have them confronted by these three thugs with knives."

There was nothing to do except ride out the storm. Yes, Timothy Grimes had lied to the grand jury, and the contradiction sure as hell wasn't going to make life easier for me. But I felt that my explanation—that a disturbed young man had been confused and frightened by the official proceedings—would preclude a dismissal, and Demakos agreed.

"This admission is not going to have a great deal of significance on the Howard Beach case as a whole," I explained to the media. "Obviously, the jury will take it into consideration when they evaluate Grimes's overall testimony. Grimes only pulled the knife out after he was confronted. He felt threatened."

There wasn't much else I could say.

23

FULL-SCALE WAR

Tuesday, September 8, 1987, was an unusually crisp day for the season. I strolled the one hundred yards across the street from our suite of temporary offices to the Queens County State Supreme Court. Jury selection for the Howard Beach trial of Jon Lester and Scott Kern, charged with second-degree murder, and Jason Ladone and Michael Pirone, charged with second-degree manslaughter, was about to begin.

As far as I was concerned, this first trial *was* the Howard Beach case. These four defendants not only faced the most serious charges (Riley's was a separate case), they also represented the depth of the racial context of that night. I felt completely focused on the need to win. If we lose this one, I lectured the A-Team, our less serious charges will all fall apart, if not on evidence, then certainly in reality. I was apprehensive. Being Irish, however, I was also ready for a down-and-dirty faction fight.

The defense had one big factor going for them: the prevailing school of legal thought was that because of the pace and swirl of events on the night of the attack, it would be nearly impossible to fit Lester's actions, Ladone's actions, Kern's actions, and Pirone's actions into the closely defined degrees of criminal culpability.

"You have to show a state of mind—that the person intended

to act along with the codefendants to commit the specific crime charged," Marvin Kornberg, a prominent Queens Boulevard defense attorney, told *The New York Times*. Norman Siegel, the head of the New York Civil Liberties Union, agreed, saying it was easier to "get the mental state" in a case involving a long-term conspiracy than in a group crime that "spontaneously happens."

I knew that part of the defense strategy would be to urge the jurors to focus on the four teenagers as individual defendants, rather than as a group, and my rebuttal would be short and simple: A chased B to his certain death, and then A turned around and hit C over the head with a baseball bat. Those were the facts. I'd leave it up to the jury to decide about guilt or innocence.

Several weeks earlier Queens County borough president Claire Shulman had volunteered six rooms in the Borough Hall building as office space for us for the duration of the trial. I had never met Shulman, who had succeeded the late Donald Manes. When her offer was proffered, I made it a point to visit her and tell her how grateful I was.

"How kind it is of you not to mention to anyone that I've donated it, Mr. Hynes," she responded. It was a fair indication of where Queens County public opinion rested.

In a last-ditch grope for a positive public image, the four defense attorneys agreed to allow the families of the Howard Beach youths to speak to Wendy Lin, who covered the Queens courthouse for *New York Newsday*. The paper is a staple in Queens. They were all quoted on page one.

"He's trying to be brave, but he's only a kid," Carol Kern said of young Scott. "Why does my son have to go through a nightmare?"

"I wish they'd get off this racial angle," said Joanne Ladone, "it was a confrontation between two groups of people—not black and white, but human beings."

"They're all good kids, and there are worse crimes than a street fight," offered Michael Pirone's sister Donna. "They say this case is going to be as big as Goetz. How can that be?"

"Jon is not a racial person," Jean Lester concluded, mentioning that her son for some time had been dating a black girl. "That's the one thing he isn't."

It was treacle, but it might have been effective had we not long ago prepared for precisely such a blatant assault on the heartstrings. During a midsummer conference in Justice Demakos's chambers we unveiled our media survey, showing him how much publicity The Incident had received, and asked him to take any pre-trial prejudice into account by adopting individual questioning of prospective jurors during voir dire. Defense counsel, particularly Rubinstein, took exception, arguing that the rare procedure would be intimidating to jurors.

The compromise Demakos proposed was, in my opinion, worthy of a Socrates. He would begin with a pool of 250 Queens County citizens, half of whom would be brought to Part K-3. Then twelve would be called by lottery for Demakos to question in general terms. When thirty-six such jurors had been screened and passed on, we would all recess from the courtroom to the judge's eighth-floor conference room for individual voir dire— with an emphasis on specific knowledge of The Howard Beach Incident. Each side would be allowed to submit written, pre-screened questions that would further probe the prospective jurors' knowledge of the racial attack, and Demakos would reject any queries he felt were improper. He would repeat each step until he had a pool of sixty jurors. Then we would return to the courtroom for the traditional lawyers' voir dire. Afterward, Demakos would hear applications for challenges, either peremptory or for cause. When we reached a consensus on the first sixteen—twelve jurors and four alternates—the trial would begin.

All four defense attorneys whined about this arrangement, claiming that this unique form of jury selection, particularly the pre-screened, written questions, violated the rights of the defendants to adequate representation. Demakos disagreed and denied their objections.

As we reached the broad plaza at the entrance to the courthouse, I saw the minicams, still photographers, crowds of reporters, and the ubiquitous protesters. But I looked past them at the eleven words etched in gold script on the courthouse wall: TRUTH, ERROR, TRANSGRESSION, PLEA, INQUIRY, EVIDENCE,

CORRECTION, EXONERATION, REHABILITATION, FAITH, SECU-
RITY.

"Halfway home," I whispered to Richard Mangum. "I'm betting on correction rather than exoneration. Rehabilitation, faith,
and security are somebody else's problem."

The families of a few defendants and a sprinkling of neighborhood supporters were already in seats as I entered K-3. Reporters and courtroom artists followed me in, filing into the first two
rows. I nodded to Stephen Murphy at the defense table to the
left of the well. Matt Greenberg, Ed Boyar, and Mangum joined
me at the prosecution table to the right, beside the empty jury
box.

The tension was palpable, and there was a rustling in the pews
as Judge Demakos took the bench. For the next few minutes the
legal ritual of "appearances" transpired, prosecution first, then
the defense: Hynes, Mangum, Boyar, and Greenberg (whose
final words were nearly drowned out by), Leone, Levinson,
Rubinstein, and Murphy.

Each side had ordered a daily transcript of the day's proceedings from Chief Stenographic Reporter Frank P. Nervo. The first
copy I received was marked "Professor Hynes," and I recognized Frank Nervo as a former student from St. John's Law
School. I don't think this was of any great benefit to our team,
except that some of my saltier sidebar adjectives, muttered out
of hearing range of spectators and jury pool, were mysteri-
ously—and mercifully—deleted.

Demakos began individual questioning of potential jurors by
carefully probing for pre-formed opinions: "Do you consider the
word 'nigger' offensive?" Or, "What about the word 'honky' or
the phrase 'white motherfucker'?"

The early responses were surprising. Potential jurors testified
that they knew very little about the Howard Beach incident,
other than that there had been a fight and that someone had
died. Many had no idea that it was race-related at all. During
phase two in the judge's conference room, a man from Forest
Hills was questioned about his woodworking hobby, and the
mother of two teenage sons from Middle Village admitted that
she would find it hard to convict any teenage boys.

"Do you believe a witness can lie even though he took an oath to tell the truth?" Murphy asked the woodworker, laying the groundwork for later character assassinations.

"In woodworking there are rough exteriors and polished interiors, isn't that correct?" Mangum countered. "Can't people, too, come with those traits?"

Hilly Hoffman, who joined us in the conference room, carefully chronicled each question and response in order to relay them to our recently hired "jury expert," sociologist Jay Schulman, who waited for Hilly's reports every day in our Borough Hall suite. Schulman, who had never before worked with a prosecution team, had been so outraged by the white-on-black attack in Howard Beach that he had volunteered his services to our office.

Schulman developed his skills in the early 1970s, helping antiwar activists and riotous prison inmates obtain more sympathetic juries. "The Father of Jury Consultants" had most recently worked with the group that held up a Brinks armored truck in nearby Rockland County, killing a Brinks guard and two police officers. He also once worked with Rubinstein, who until now considered him a friend. But when Schulman criticized Rubinstein's antics in a newspaper interview during jury selection, the defense attorney refused ever to speak to him again.

Schulman's politics made me uneasy, but the staff, especially Hoffman, welcomed his method, based on the "science" of jury selection. Like a garage mechanic taking a motor apart, he broke down prospective juries by demographic components—age, race, sex, neighborhood, career, salary—each of which was an element that might affect the vote. He studied the background of each prospective juror and gave us his recommendation. I still preferred to choose my jury based on the question-and-answer philosophy, laced with a heavy dose of gut instinct. But I threw Schulman into the chicken soup category: his presence couldn't hurt.

As the selection transpired, Schulman's "science" nearly dovetailed with my instincts. And although we didn't always agree, he was a great help. Sad to say, sixty-eight-year-old Jay Schulman suffered a massive heart attack and died before the Howard Beach trial concluded.

A few days into jury selection, full-scale war was declared. Clearly, defense counsel believed that it wouldn't be possible for their defendants to receive a fair verdict from *any* black juror, and their written questions varied according to the prospective juror's skin color. Whites were queried as to their views regarding street fights. Blacks were asked how their communities would react to an acquittal. When one black woman said she didn't understand the question, Rubinstein remarked aloud that her neighbors would probably throw her a parade if she voted to convict.

The cynicism in this reasoning sickened me, and I let Demakos know it.

"You know, Judge, they're unmistakably trying to challenge every black off this jury, trying to turn this into the goddamn Shea case all over again," I told him at one sidebar up at his bench. "And we both know that that is not going to happen."

His answer was a slight smile and a small shake of his head. I believe he knew what I had in mind.

We had also prepared for the possibility of race-driven challenges to jurors. Late in the spring, Matt Greenberg had introduced us to *Batson v. Kentucky,* a United States Supreme Court case decided in 1986 that represented a major incursion by the court into the once sanctified grounds of prosecutorial peremptory challenges. In that case, named for a black man who was charged with burglary by the State of Kentucky, the prosecutor exercised his peremptory challenges to exclude all four blacks in that particular jury pool.

Justice Lewis Powell wrote the Supreme Court's eloquent decision: "A person's race simply is unrelated to his fitness as a juror," and, "the harm from discriminatory jury selection extends beyond that inflicted on the defendant and the excluded juror to touch the entire community. Selection procedures that purposefully exclude black persons from juries undermine public confidence in the fairness of our system of justice."

In extending the Batson ruling only to prosecutors, the Supreme Court ruled that it was the trial judge's decision to determine whether peremptory challenges were being used by the prosecution to eliminate a certain class of people. Ironically,

Chief Justice Warren Burger wrote in his dissent that the day may come soon when the same standards would apply to defense lawyers. I can't read between the lines as well as my appellate people, but they believed that Burger dissented with tongue planted firmly in cheek, and that he didn't believe for a moment that the ruling would ever be applied to defense counsel. But my eggheads had prepared a memorandum of law to just that effect.

The day Chief Justice Burger referred to arrived on September 19, ten days after jury selection began. Six jurors had been seated, none of them black. I made application demanding that Judge Demakos extend the Batson decision to our case. I recognized the risk involved: a decision in our favor could jeopardize a conviction in the Court of Appeals. Some of my staff, especially Boyar, argued that it wasn't worth risking our whole strategy only to have a conviction overruled on appeal.

"We have enough on these guys to beat them without Batson," Ed protested. "Do we want to risk everything because some Appellate Division rules that our jury selection was unconstitutional?"

It was a point well taken, and I gave it serious thought. But finally I determined that I was not going to sit in a courtroom of the United States of America and watch this racial bias occur. It was abhorrent, and I refused to participate in it. I was willing to take my chances with the Court of Appeals, and we decided to go with Batson.

Demakos reserved his decision, saying he would announce it the following Monday. Ronald Rubinstein walked outside and asked reporters: "If you were Adolf Eichmann, would you have wanted a Jew on the jury?"

On Monday we gathered in the courtroom in a hopeful mood. Demakos's voice was steady and firm. After a public explanation of our request and its entailments, he concluded:

"The question here is whether to apply the Batson decision to this case, where white defendants are charged with crimes against black victims. Does the prosecution have the right to object to the misuse of peremptory challenges?"

The word "misuse" was the key. I felt a wave of euphoria.

"I conclude that, under the reasoning of the Batson decision by the Supreme Court of the United States, the prosecution does have that right. The Court finds that the defense is using their peremptory challenges to strike jurors on the grounds of group bias alone."

From the defense table came a pathetic moan which was picked up by friends and relatives throughout Courtroom K-3. I hardly heard it. I was too elated at getting the chance for a fair trial—not to mention having made a small part of legal history.

The moment Demakos finished his ruling Rubinstein was on his feet, but he seemed more dejected than cantankerous as he approached the bench.

"Your Honor," he said in a hoarse voice, "I respectfully ask you to afford the defense about three hours, time enough to visit the Appellate Division to seek a stay of Your Honor's ruling—which violates the basic concept of constitutional law, due process, and fairness to the defendants in this trial."

"Of course you may," said Demakos, leaving his bench. I thought of *People v. Officer Thomas Shea* and wondered if the memory of the long-dead Clarence Glover had entered into the judge's decision.

The case was heard the following morning in the Appellate Division for the Second Judicial Department, which covered eleven New York counties, including Queens. The Appellate Court ruled that the proper time for the review would be after the trial, if the defendants were convicted. In other words, it decided on purely procedural grounds not to invade the province of a trial judge during trial.

The furious members of the defense team now dug in their heels. Murphy filed court papers charging my office with reverse discrimination, specifically accusing me of "systematically challenging white jurors through the use of peremptory challenges to overload the remaining panel with black jurors."

Demakos told Murphy that his charges were groundless, and when Murphy attempted to press his cause further, Demakos snapped. He called us all into chambers.

"Mr. Murphy, you have made yourself clear in your papers!" the judge shouted. "I have made my decision."

But the defense wouldn't give up. At times I felt they were

cutting off their noses just to spite my face. For example, they selected Mario Olivieri, Jr., a city bus driver who could have passed for black and who admitted during individual voir dire that he believed his college tennis coach had dropped him from the team on the basis of racial bias. They also chose Joseph Ramos, a Puerto Rican-born auto mechanic, who related how as a teenager he had once been chased from a white neighborhood "by some white guys with bats." In their collective concern to bar blacks from the jury, the defense seated both Olivieri and Ramos—as well as Ramjass Boodrham, a Guyanese emigrant of Indian descent who was never asked if he harbored any sympathy for the plight of his fellow countryman, Cedric Sandiford. I certainly did not object to their inclusion.

Two weeks after Demakos's decision, a jury of six whites, two Asian-Americans, two Latinos, one Guyanese, and black housewife Beverly Minor were ready for trial. Of the four alternates, two were Latino, one was white, and one black. A *New York Daily News* banner headline dubbed it THE RAINBOW JURY. I was satisfied, and so, I believe (despite their grumbling), were the defense lawyers.

Eight members of the panel had graduated from college, and of the four who had not—Ramos; Boodrham, a printing press operator; James Spongross, an airline mechanic at Kennedy Airport; and Minor—each impressed me as bright and open-minded. The forewoman was Nina Krauss, a twenty-eight-year-old paralegal. In the seventy or so jury trials I have brought to verdict, I felt that this was easily the "best" jury I had ever chosen.

We would certainly need it.

Several days after jury selection was completed, Murphy began his barrage, announcing to reporters that "Riley told the grand jury he wanted the bat because he was bigger and stronger and could hit the blacks harder. And this is the guy Hynes is basing his case on?"

His voice carried a challenge, one we were ready to accept.

24

911

After nearly ten months of rumor, disinformation, and innuendo, it was time to present the jury with the facts about The Incident at Howard Beach.

Wednesday, October 7, 1987, dawned crisp and clear. I strode into the Queens County Criminal Courthouse with my opening remarks folded under my arm. My argument, which took forty hours to prepare and twenty-five minutes to deliver, was not a simple retelling of events. It was not meant to be. I was making a declaration of war, designed to be fearsome, cold and severe, laced with descriptions of smashed flesh, broken bones, and more spilled blood than these twelve average citizens of Queens County were prepared to hear. We were not talking about a tea party that occurred in Howard Beach on December 19, 1986.

Some jurors winced at the brutality of my descriptions. I wanted them to wince. They had to hear the grisly details in order to understand the brutality of the night.

I virtually screamed the fateful sentence: "There's niggers on the Boulevard, let's go fuckin' kill them!"

I mimicked Scott Kern's shout to drive the point home: "Niggers, get the fuck out of the neighborhood!"

Juror number 10, Mrs. Margaret Van Wart, a gentle widow who worked as a receptionist, turned ashen at my theatrics.

The story of the attack on Howard Beach had to be told graphically and intensely, to blunt the months of propaganda churned out by the four defense lawyers. This wasn't a mere street fight that got out of hand, I told the jury. It was a buzzsaw fueled by ugly racism which snuffed out the existence of one twenty-three-year-old man and left another pleading for his life.

"I will prove in this case that Michael Griffith was killed because he was black!" I thundered, and a murmur spread across the courtroom. "Then, after watching him die, his attackers turned on their heels and began beating and pummeling Cedric Sandiford. As one of his assailants began hitting him with a baseball bat, Sandiford grabbed for the bat, and looking into the eyes of the young man, said, 'My God, I've got a son like you—seventeen years old. Please don't kill me.' His response was to have a baseball bat smashed across his face."

When I finished and returned to my seat, K-3 was as cold and silent as the Alaskan tundra. The defense attorneys looked stunned. My chosen tone had been unmistakable. I believed that the defense lawyers wanted to replay the case of Bernhard Goetz, who felt menaced by four strangers of color in a subway car. Over the course of the trial their strategy would undoubtedly be to ask the jury to presume that twelve healthy adolescents were pressed to resist the menace of three strangers of color in their own backyard. I felt my opening remarks had blunted their design.

"There's no question we have a tragedy here," countered Bryan Levinson in his opening arguments. "Michael Griffith died . . . you'll hear about a fight. But the question is, who initiated that fight? Three lambs walking into Sodom? Or three antagonistic men spoiling for a fight, looking for trouble, and coming across some youngsters?"

Levinson allowed Murphy to pick up, and smash down, the second half of their tactical sledgehammer.

"It's a disgrace that these kids are even here!" Murphy shouted. "If anyone's responsible, it's Riley."

I was out of my chair objecting so often that at one point I decided to stand. But nothing could stop Murphy, who concluded his remarks with a typical distortion. He called Curtis Sylvester a "major drug dealer from Tampa, Florida."

"I assume you're going to prove that, Mr. Murphy," Demakos interjected, after yet another objection.

"I'll prove it," said Murphy. "I'll show you where he keeps his coke."

During the lunch break outside the courtroom, Joe Fried of *The New York Times* confronted me.

"For months you've said that this was going to be a simple homicide and assault trial and nothing more," the Queens-based reporter said angrily. "Now you're heaping this stuff about race onto the top of the case. What's going on here? What happened to A hitting B over the head? What are you trying to prove?"

"It's the jury's duty to decide whether these four kids killed Michael Griffith," I replied. "Not why, just whether."

I left it at that. Fried shook his head doubtfully. I was already locked into my trial mode, with no patience for lengthy explanations. If Joe Fried couldn't figure out what I felt then and what I feel now—that these young punks deserved to have their words thrown back in their faces in a public forum, particularly if those words expressed a motive for their senseless spree—so be it. I was sure the jury saw my point.

After the outraged tenor of my opening remarks, I felt it was time to settle the jury, to allow them to step back, draw a breath, and settle in for what the A-Team had calculated would be at least a month-long test of their attention span. So we called Jean Griffith to the stand. The law requires that the deceased in a homicide trial be identified, and now the solemn nurse's aide was describing in a soft, slow voice her frantic trip to Jamaica Hospital after the heartbreaking phone call from Cedric Sandiford.

"Did you go anywhere after the hospital?" I asked.

"Yes, I went to the morgue."

"Was a body shown to you?"

"Yes."

"Did you recognize it?"

"Yes." Her shoulders began to shake. She took a deep breath. "It was my son. It was my son Michael."

"Thank you, Mrs. Griffith," I said, and I turned to face the defense.

"No questions," the four lawyers shouted in chorus.

Jean Griffith's knees buckled as she walked toward the door. A brace of court officers rushed to her aid. But she was not to vanish from the trial. She attended every session, at times weeping silently or even leaving the courtroom to regain her composure. But she always returned to her third-row seat behind the prosecution, listening with her head held high as the grim details unfolded.

Our strategy included calling more than seventy witnesses after Jean Griffith, and since that disastrous day in the moot court at St. John's their alignment had been meticulously planned. We felt that the jury would need an emotional break after Jean Griffith's wrenching testimony, so a detective was brought to the stand as a technical witness to further acquaint the jury with the streets and avenues of Howard Beach.

The coroner's report on Michael Griffith, with its traces of cocaine, was public knowledge and would soon be placed in evidence. In the press, the defense was portraying Michael Griffith as a violent man who dealt with drugs. We needed to alter that one-dimensional image, to present a softer, more human Michael Griffith to the jury. Before the trial began, Harvey Louie Greenberg had suggested that we play with the idea of calling the dead man's brother, Christopher Griffith, to the stand.

"If he looks halfway straight and has no head problems, figure out a way to get the brother up there," was Harvey's inimitable advice. "The jury will see Michael through him."

Christopher Griffith is handsome and dignified-looking (although we did ask him to remove his earring before his court appearance). A photographer by profession, he possesses a keen eye for details and the clarity of thought to describe them. On the witness stand, Christopher Griffith became his dead brother's "substitute," and his graphic testimony seemed to have a chilling effect on the jury:

"Cedric was sitting on an examination table when I first saw him. He was shivering, although the room was very warm. His eyes were swollen shut and he had a gash in his head which looked about six inches long. The doctor who was stitching Cedric was interrupted by a phone call. He left Cedric sitting there with the dried blood on his scalp and a surgical thread hanging down the left side of his face. He looked so sad."

"Objection!" shouted several of the defense lawyers.

"Overruled," said Demakos.

"He looked like a broken man," continued Chris Griffith in his swaying, West Indian accent.

"Objection."

"Overruled."

On cross, Rubinstein tried an end run.

"Do you know a man named Alton Maddox?" he asked.

It was my turn to object. Since the Marla Hanson trial, Maddox's name had become anathema to all right-thinking people. He was viewed as a troublemaker, and frankly, he was. But this line of questioning had nothing to do with *my* case. Demakos agreed. Rubinstein persisted.

"When did you first speak to Alton Maddox?"

"Objection, Your Honor!"

"Sustained," growled Demakos. "I'm not going to warn you again, Mr. Rubinstein."

Rubinstein flashed an evil grin at the jury and returned to his seat.

The trial continued with Boyar and Mangum laboriously building our case block by block. The tow-truck operator and auto mechanic were called to answer the most irrelevant question of the past ten months: "What were they doing in Howard Beach?"

And because of the many sly accusations alluding to the presence of drugs, the two toll-plaza officers who gave Grimes and Griffith water for Sylvester's radiator were brought in to undercut the defense's contention that drug-crazed *black* men had been marauding through Howard Beach. Both toll collectors testified that they had been trained to observe intoxicated drivers, and that neither Grimes nor Griffith appeared to have been drinking. Again, at Harvey Louie Greenberg's suggestion, we were building a case for normalcy: the black men were doing nothing out of the ordinary.

Officer Daniel McFadden, ramrod straight in the neatly

pressed uniform and spit-shined shoes of the National Park Service, testified that he had observed Curtis Sylvester's disabled Buick by the side of the road in Broad Channel. He had a brief conversation with Sylvester, he said, who informed him that his friends had gone for help, and McFadden had, just minutes before, observed three black men walking north on Cross Bay Boulevard—"walking normally," he noted in his Incident Report.

We were setting the stage for the trial's first dramatic moment, the damning recollections of Theresa Fisher. Despite death threats and obscene telephone calls, Fisher had been able to keep a low profile. She was hinted at in the newspapers only as "Hynes's mystery witness."

As explosive as Fisher's appearance was sure to be, I hoped the recorded tape of her frantic 911 call would cause even more of a detonation. During standard, pre-trial evidentiary hearings, my appellate staff had scored a major victory by persuading Judge Demakos to allow the tape to be entered as evidence. The defense had claimed that the tape was hearsay, which is inadmissible in a trial except for certain stated legal exceptions.

"Why do we have to hear the tapes when we'll hear the witness herself?" Murphy had asked. The eggheads argued that the Fisher tape fell into the exception category, citing a recent decision by the Bronx State Supreme Court (a court of equal jurisdiction to Demakos's) to allow a similar tape, although not a 911 recording, to stand as evidence. We caught the defense attorneys flat-footed. That was the great thing about Brook, Hoffman, and Greenberg: they were constantly checking for changes in the law, and recognized immediately that we could use the Bronx ruling to submit a critical piece of evidence.

Fisher, a thin, attractive woman with a shock of reddish-brown hair, was scheduled to testify October 8, two days into the trial, but the afternoon before her appearance she called to say she wasn't coming to court. I nearly fainted. This was the linchpin of our building-block strategy. With Fisher in person, as well as the recording of her voice, I was going for an early knockout. Her defection would be a major blow. I sent Joe Piccione, one of my more patient investigators, out to her house. Five hours later, at ten o'clock at night, he was back at the doorway of our six-room suite in the Queens Borough Hall.

"Boss," he said, "Theresa is in the waiting room. She wants to be assured by you that nothing will happen to her two kids or her husband . . . or her."

"Done."

"I just want to be yesterday's news," said Fisher, stepping out from behind Piccione's six-foot frame. "I don't want to be dead. I've had to change my phone number three times. I have two little children. I want to be around to enjoy them."

I could see that her argument was directed more at herself than to me, and I allowed the two sides of Theresa Fisher to hash out their differences. The next day, on schedule, Theresa Fisher, mother and housewife, appeared in court in a fashionably tailored gray wool suit. Her nasal New York accent enhanced the air of sincerity about her testimony regarding Sandiford:

"He ran to a fence by the Belt Parkway and tried to get over it. . . . They pulled him down and started beating him. . . . A crowbar was being used, and a tree stump." She went on to describe his pitiful cries for help. The jury was engrossed.

On cross-examination, Murphy's outrageous badgering drew from Fisher the admission that she had withheld several details of the attack from the grand jury.

"I did that because I didn't want to get involved!" she shouted, in a rage. "I did not want to be there. I don't want to be here."

When Levinson pressed her for a precise log of what she had seen, she stumbled over her words before finally beginning to weep, although she still managed to stand up to the defense attorney through her sobs: "I don't know streets. I wasn't worried about minutes. I was worried about the guy's life."

At one point Demakos left the bench to go over to comfort Fisher, to allow her to compose herself. She was the heavyweight champion of witnesses, and I wondered if I had gotten my early KO.

Curtis Sylvester, another early witness, did not pack the same punch. He arrived from Florida dressed in his Sunday best, clearly trying hard to make a good impression, but he looked like an extra from *Miami Vice* in his white linen suit with matching shirt, tie, and hat. I hastily sent Terry Hayes shopping for a blue, crew-neck sweater and a darker tie. We toyed with the idea of dressing Sylvester in a short-sleeved shirt, a subtle hint to the jury that Murphy's "major drug dealer" was free from needle tracks, but decided against it. Sylvester's white suitjacket, tie, and hat remained in our offices as Curtis stepped up to the stand.

Under extremely hostile cross-examination (for what other kind could there be from these *attorneys?*), Sylvester freely admitted to both of his previous arrests, once for sitting in a stolen car, the other the incident with the drugs in Tampa. Although he had never been formally charged, Murphy, firing his usual barrage of questions, wouldn't let that record die.

"On October 2, 1985, were you in possession of a stolen car and did you steal that car?"

"No," said Sylvester. Murphy had seen the police report. He knew someone else had been charged with the theft. He also knew that Sylvester had never been indicted for the cocaine found under the Tampa park bench. That didn't stop him from pandering.

"On November 3, 1986, did you have in your possession thirty-five vials of crack?"

"No."

"Isn't it a fact that you are a major crack dealer?"

"No."

"Your Honor," I cried, "I object to Mr. Murphy's sarcastic performance."

Demakos, who was increasingly ignoring the posturing of both the defense and the prosecution, shrugged and asked Murphy to move on. After several more halfhearted swipes, all of which were met with objections from our table, Murphy finished with Sylvester. The kid was bloodied but still standing. I called it a draw.

We were one week into the trial and Theresa Fisher had departed, but her total impact on the jury was yet to be felt. The taped telephone recording of her call for help was played on Tuesday, October 13. I had my electronics technician, Tony Saraniero, a former detective and eavesdropping expert, wire K-3 with eight stereo speakers, which I had tested the night before. I felt silly sitting in the darkened courtroom, signaling

Tony to throw the switch like some amateur stage manager, but this devastating piece of evidence clearly refuted the "street fight" defense, and I wanted no glitches.

Theresa's trembling, disembodied voice was as emotional as any eyewitness's. I knew I had something powerful, and the next day she again electrified the courtroom.

911 OPERATOR: *"Police Emergency—yes?"*
THERESA FISHER: *"Ah, I live, ah, on 156th Avenue and, ah, they're beating up this guy. There's about twelve guys out here."*
OPERATOR: *"And they're beating him up where?"*
FISHER: *"Beating up on one black guy."*
ANGELA ROMANELLI [*in background*]: *"With a crowbar."*
FISHER [*excitedly*]: *"With a crowbar. It's 156th Street."*
ROMANELLI [*in background*]: *"It's Avenue."*
FISHER: *"Avenue."*
ROMANELLI [*in background*]: *"And 86th Street."*
FISHER: *"And 86th Street. I mean, have somebody here really fast . . . I mean, this kid's screaming out here."*
OPERATOR: *"You're in Queens, ma'am?"*

The 911 operator is trained to be calm and dispassionate while receiving information. Under the dramatic courtroom circumstances, and in stark contrast to the excited voices of the two women, the police aide sounded insensitive. I glanced at the jury. Everyone's attention was riveted. Juror number 3, Michael Sweeney, a young teacher who worked with disabled adults, shook his head in apparent disbelief and looked to the ceiling.

FISHER [*shouting*]: *"This is Howard Beach!"*

The words reverberated throughout K-3. I hoped they seared into the jurors' minds. Not some distant land. Howard Beach. Right here. For the next fifty torturous seconds the 911 operator could not find 156th Avenue and 86th Street.

OPERATOR: *"156th Avenue and 86th Street is not going in . . . location ma'am, One-Five-Six Avenue and Eight-Six Street, that's not valid.*

Here Angela Romanelli grabbed the telephone and began to shout the location of her house.

> ROMANELLI: *"I'm telling you, by the time he gets—"*
> OPERATOR [*in a disinterested voice*]: *"Well, ma'am, if you [sic] reporting an incident you have to give me a location. I don't know where to send the police to."*
> ROMANELLI [*frustrated*]: *"All right. Howard Beach, 156th Avenue in Queens. . . . It's between 84th and 86th Street. The guy's running back and forth."*
> OPERATOR: *"84th Street?"*
> ROMANELLI [*confused*]: *"84th Street?"*
> OPERATOR: *"Yes, 156th Avenue and 84th Street."*
> ROMANELLI: *"They got him in the bushes over there. They're hitting him with crowbars and stuff."*
> OPERATOR: *"One moment, please. These males that's beating him, they're black, white, or Hispanic?"*
> ROMANELLI: *"The guy that's getting beat up is black."*

The 911 operator then asked a question which unintentionally spoke volumes about the state of race relations in New York City.

> OPERATOR: *"And these guys that are beating him are what? White obviously!"*
> ROMANELLI: *"Oh, I don't know. There's about twelve different guys. They're in the bushes. I don't know. I can't see. I know that the guy is black, though. The guy that they're beating up because he's screaming, 'Please don't beat me no more.'"*
> FISHER [*in background*]: *"And the other guys are all white and they're beating him up."*

The tape ended with Angela Romanelli shouting in frustration, "Just get a cop over there!"

Throughout the recording, Scott Kern, Jon Lester, Jason Ladone, and Michael Pirone stared straight ahead with vacant eyes.

Boyar next called to the stand Claudia Calogero and Laura Castagna, whom my staff were to dub "the Sisters of Silence."

Calogero, the young woman in Sal DeSimone's car with Lester and Bollander when the initial confrontation with the black men occurred, was of value simply to corroborate the first meeting between the blacks and the whites. She said she remembered being frightened by the three black men, "and that's about it."

Castagna, too, had developed massive memory problems. Her testimony was a string of I don't remembers. But we were confident the jury would not believe that she couldn't recall the exchange of racial epithets and obscenities in front of the pizza parlor. Castagna was the only female to leave Schorr's party at that time, but she had remained in Riley's car when the mob began its chase. She saw, heard, and said nothing, she testified. But Ed's persistent direct examination finally forced her to admit that after the attack she saw the defendants return to the car, and that one of them, "might have had a bat." Slowly we were building our corroboration.

By Thursday, October 15, the courtroom arena had been prepared to for one of the two surviving Howard Beach victims. I called Timothy Grimes. I led him carefully through his short, violent life, detailing his drug abuse and past bad acts. He showed the jury how he drew his knife and held it in front of him in a fist as the whites approached. He described how he fled from "about ten guys with bats, sticks, and something that looked like an iron pipe."

I was pleasantly surprised by Timothy's performance. He explained that he had been afraid the grand jury wouldn't believe the rest of his story if he mentioned his knife. And at one point, thinking of the two teenaged girls who had spotted the black men walking along Cross Bay Boulevard, I asked him if he had met up with anyone on his walk to the pizzeria.

"Yes," he said.

"What gender were they?"

"Females."

"How old would you say they were?"

"Middle-aged," Timothy answered.

"What is 'middle-aged' to you, Mr. Grimes?"

After a thoughtful pause, he replied: "About twenty-seven, twenty-eight."

The courtroom broke up. Timothy was actually coming across as somewhat credible, as a human being and not some *black* monster who shoved guns into old ladies' ears. After the conclusion of his direct testimony, he even smiled confidently. Actually, his ill-fitting charcoal-gray suit, coupled with that smile, made him look more goofy than sinister.

Gabe Leone got the first crack at him. But the booming foghorn approach didn't faze Grimes, because we had prepared him for it. And Levinson, who followed Leone, did no better. Murphy's and Rubinstein's cross-examinations were postponed until after the weekend.

On Monday morning Stephen Murphy stood on the steps of the Queens County State Supreme Court, where defense counsel held a daily press conference, and boasted that he would, "crack this skell in a half-hour." ("Skell," a street expression used mainly by police, is roughly equivalent to "punk.")

A few moments later Murphy was pacing the well like a bantam rooster before a cockfight. Although Murphy's client, Pirone, had not even been mentioned by Grimes, he was in a mood, he had told reporters, to "work this guy over."

"I'll get the witness into my rhythm," Murphy had bragged, "and then I'll ruin his concentration. If he's not a nice person, then the jury will see. Especially if the witness doesn't have the time or the opportunity to pretend to be someone he's not."

Murphy began slowly, his voice low, his manner and tone exuding sarcasm. At first Grimes sparred with Murphy, responding to his ridicule with sneers. Grimes looked over at me and smiled. And so did Murphy, and I didn't like what that forboded.

The defense lawyer shifted his voice into high pitch and began shouting rat-a-tat questions at Grimes about his drug addictions and criminal record. Then Grimes admitted to robbing the elderly couple in Brooklyn four years before.

"Did you plan this robbery?" screeched Murphy.

"I object, Your Honor!" I shouted.

"Mr. Murphy, please refrain from that line of questioning—you know better than that," Demakos said. But Murphy gratuitously ignored the judge.

"Well, sir," he continued, "are you the type of person who walks down the street, sees a poor victim, and commits a robbery?"

Since Grimes had already admitted to the armed robbery, his actions at any other time were not an issue here. Again Demakos sustained my loud objection. Again Murphy ignored him.

"I'll bet she was really afraid when you said, 'Get over here or we'll kill you.'"

Timothy's head was nearly resting on his chest as Murphy continued to pound him with questions.

"I don't remember," Grimes said in a whimpering voice.

Now Murphy, his face flushed with indignation, moved in for the kill.

"Well, sir, you don't remember if you told this woman you were going to kill her?" he screeched. "How many other people have you told that you were going to kill them?"

"Give him a chance to answer, Mr. Murphy," Judge Demakos broke in.

But there was no answer.

Murphy quickly switched to questions about Grimes's knife.

Finally, Grimes leaped to his feet and shouted, "I'm finished. Finished. I don't even want to testify no more," and he tried to leave the witness stand. A court officer restrained him and Demakos ordered the jury out of the room and declared a recess. Timothy was taken to an office behind the courtroom. Murphy had bragged he would crack him, and Grimes had cracked. At least for now. Father Robert Seay, the Franciscan priest from Brooklyn who was the spiritual adviser to the Griffith family, told me he would speak to Grimes. After several moments, I joined the two in the small office.

"He'll be okay now," said Father Seay.

"Let's go back," added Grimes.

Back in K-3, with the jury recalled and the cross-examination resumed, Murphy immediately launched another assault. Grimes lasted ten minutes before he was again on his feet.

"I'm outta here!" he shouted. "I'm finished with this bullshit—that's it. You can't charge me with nothing, motherfucker."

Murphy beamed. "Nothing seems to embarrass you," he

yelled at the witness. Then he asked Demakos to hold Grimes in contempt.

The judge declined, calling another recess.

Richard Mangum thought perhaps we should call in Timothy's psychiatrist, but I had another idea. "This time," I told Father Seay, "I'll talk to him alone."

As I entered the room, Grimes shouted, "Hynes, I ain't doing that no more." I shouted right back. "Listen, have you ever backed down in a street fight?"

"No."

"Well, what the fuck do you think you're in now? That little prick's breaking you down, after bragging to everyone that that's just what he was going to do. And you're playing right into his hands."

"That's tough."

"Why is that tough, Timothy? Are you *afraid* of him?"

"Listen, Hynes, I'm not afraid of nothing."

"Well, then you listen, Timothy. Don't let this little piece of shit do this to you. Don't let him do it to Michael."

"What does this got to do with Michael?"

"Plenty," I said. "If he can do this to you, and then get lucky with Cedric, those creeps are going to walk."

"Well," Grimes answered, "I don't want that to happen."

The transformation was eerie and unsettling. Grimes was suddenly as placid as Buddha. We sat in silence for a good ten minutes.

Then he said: "Okay, Mr. Hynes, let's go."

Moments later he resumed his testimony, and soon he was finished. Murphy had not pressed him any harder. He knew that another blow-up might shift the jury's sympathy in Grimes's favor. He already had what he needed. He had exposed Timothy as a violent, troubled young man.

But Rubinstein still felt he was owed his pound of flesh. After I objected several times to the repetitive tenor of Rubinstein's questioning (for he was merely spreading the dirt Murphy had already dug), Demakos declared: "I'll tell you what, Mr. Rubinstein. We'll have Mr. Grimes step down and you can step up and you can be the witness." Applause filled the courtroom.

The following day Sharpton, Mason, and Maddox, who had been avoiding the trial, showed up in court after filing a complaint against Murphy with the grievance committee in the Appellate Division of State Supreme Court. They charged that Murphy had "repeatedly and incessantly harassed, argued with, and viciously attacked prosecution witnesses despite repeated judicial warnings and in transgression of legal rules of evidence and procedure." The processing of such complaints is confidential, so the outcome of the charge is not known.

On the courtroom steps, Mason said: "The racist tactics here remind me of what used to happen in Southern courtrooms in the 1940s." He singled out Murphy, saying: "He brutalized Grimes." True enough, but that's the way the game is played, and Mason knew it.

Fifteen yards away, Murphy, surrounded by his own coterie of journalists, pointed to Mason and labeled him a "racial profiteer out to get his name in the papers." They were playing hardball. The television cameras next turned on Sharpton and Rubinstein, who stood on the sidewalk engaging in a bitter debate. Black and white spectators exchanged angry words. I felt a wave of revulsion at both sides, but offered no comment.

In the third week we called Steven Schorr. He, too, was infected by such a convenient case of amnesia that Judge Demakos declared him a "hostile witness." This allowed Boyar, our digger, increased latitude in his questioning. He went after Schorr as if he were cross-examining, and the kid's stutters and stammers about the conclusion of his birthday party left, I felt, an impact on the jury.

The picture of The Incident was being fine-tuned for the jury. The Howard Beach teenagers—Calogero, Castagna, and now Schorr—were obviously stonewalling for their friends. The lone exception was Anthony Mauro, an eighteen-year-old who was present in the Schorrs' paneled basement when Lester issued his call to arms. He identified the four defendants as part of the group that left the party, "mentioning something about a fight." He also testified that, when they returned forty minutes later, John Lester "was holding a bat."

With those words, Mauro, an Eagle Scout, became the latest

of our witnesses who required police protection. Even a death threat "against the jury" had been phoned in to the court clerk, although the court officers had managed to keep this information from the panel and the public. Mauro's testimony was critical, for besides corroborating what Riley was soon to say, he left an indelible impression on a city, and perhaps a jury, that had for months been bombarded by headlines indicting a town. Mauro showed that not all the teens had left the party to join in that mindless charge, and, more important to me, his words finally separated the four individuals on trial from the notion of a monolithic, racist Howard Beach. The jury could now attach a face to the charges on which they would be asked to vote.

Three weeks into the trial, during a lunch break, the jurors sent a note to Demakos complaining that they had to strain to see the witnesses' faces. The overhead lights in Part K-3 had all but burned out. Maintenance told Demakos that the bulbs could not be replaced until the weekend. So he improvised, propping a gooseneck fluorescent lamp on his bench and turning it toward the witness stand.

"It looks like the back of a precinct," I complained when we all returned from lunch, all too aware that Robert Riley, "the rat," was our next witness. Murphy looked critically at the light for a moment, and of course decided he liked it.

"Maybe it should be shined on the attorneys," Demakos said. "They seem to be the performers in the courtroom, rather than the witnesses."

Then he turned to the stenographer: "Don't put that on the record." The light was left on.

25

MURPHY'S GAME

On Thursday, October 22, three days after my wedding anniversary, Robert Riley arrived at our Borough Hall offices at 7:30 A.M. He was trailed by a disheveled platoon of scuffling reporters (who were apparently unused to rising so early). By nine o'clock our suite was ringed by nearly a dozen camera crews. Ed Boyar had spent the final moments putting Riley through his final paces and urging him—unsuccessfully—to relax.

When I reached the courthouse steps, the defense attorneys were conducting four separate press conferences. Murphy's chortle was loud enough for me to overhear: "I'm going to do to this dirtbag exactly what I did to Grimes." I leaned over to Sarah Wallace, who was covering the trial for the local ABC affiliate, and advised her to put ten dollars on Riley. I was being sucked into Murphy's game, finding myself increasingly trying to outshout him in and out of the courtroom (although I have to admit that I wasn't exactly a rookie at this ploy; I didn't have broken knuckles to prove it, but I was a product of the same mean streets). Wallace told Murphy about my line, and he loved it, raising his cackling laugh an octave higher.

"We'll see," he said, and strutted away.

Courthouse officials expected the highest spectator turnout for Riley's appearance since the first steamy days of the Alice Crimmins trial nineteen years before. They were not disappointed. Riley's testimony drew a slew of Howard Beach teens. Most of them shared the feelings of seventeen-year-old John Rosen, who told a reporter the defendants were his friends, and he "came here to watch Riley fry."

Riley arrived in court with his entire family, who seemed to be the only people on earth with any sympathy for the boy. As Doug LeVien had whispered to me on our way in, "If looks could kill, this guy would be dead one thousand times."

On direct examination, Riley testified in low, barely audible grunts. He described Lester shouting through the Schorr house, the caravan to the pizzeria, the subsequent chase, his fight with Lester for the bat, and Michael Griffith's body flying through the air. He said he and Pirone then became sick, and the others turned to find Sandiford. His was a "prequel" to Theresa Fisher's account, and with his description of the tussle for the baseball bat he provided us with our proximate cause for homicide charges.

But Robert Riley was a lousy witness.

His testimony was flat. Under cross-examination, which lasted five hours, he became even worse. By the time he was finished being trampled by the "Four Horsemen of the Apocalypse," he had names and dates and assailants confused and his recollection of the time sequence of the attack was totally off. Bryan Levinson led off with an attempt to undermine Riley's credibility by bringing out discrepancies between Riley's testimony on direct examination and his testimony before the grand jury. He noted, for example, that before the grand jury Riley had not included Lester in a list of white youths who first confronted the black men outside New Park Pizzeria. It had been a simple oversight, as I had pointed out to the jury (there were, after all, a dozen of these kids running about like wolverines on speed), but Levinson pounced on it.

"So you're saying that that was a mistake?" Levinson asked.

"Yes," answered Riley as his cheeks flushed with color.

"Isn't it a fact, Mr. Riley, that it was you leading the chase?" Levinson then demanded.

"No," Riley said.

"Mr. Riley, would you lie to keep from going to jail for the rest of your life?" Levinson continued.

"No," Riley said, as Levinson stalked off and Gabe Leone stepped into the batter's box.

"You cooperated because you didn't want to go to jail for twenty-five-years-to-life, is that correct?" Leone asked.

"That's correct," Riley said, his voice sounding like a moan.

"Did you ever tell anybody you were so drunk that you don't remember what happened that night?" Leone fired back.

"No," said Riley.

"You sure of that?"

"Yes," Riley mumbled.

During Rubinstein's cross, Riley was sullen, and answered the lawyer's questions with an odd little sneer. Finally, as Murphy fulminated, Riley seemed to shrink, appearing by the end to be nearly comatose.

"I got no problem with Riley," Murphy said afterward. "I had the kid agreeing with everything I said. I loved him. I wouldn't mind bringing him back."

Oddly enough, Riley's basic story had not really been shaken. The jury may not have liked Robert Riley, but I felt in my heart that they believed him.

"Boss, there's no way those four defendants are going to take the stand," Ed Boyar insisted. "So the closest the jury can come to getting inside their minds that night is remembering Bobby Riley. I think he worked wonderfully."

For once I was inclined to agree.

Dominick Blum, however, was a different story. The day before he was scheduled to testify, someone had phoned his parents' home and stated simply: "Just tell Dominick Blum that we're going to kill him and his father."

We offered Blum a bulletproof vest to wear into court. He declined.

I had my own problems with Blum's story from the beginning. Given the extensive damage to his car, I wondered how this man could not have realized he had run down something a bit larger than "a tire or a small animal"—such as a human being. Defense counsel was similarly curious. This was their best chance to destroy our argument for the gang's proximate cause of Michael Griffith's death.

It was like shooting fish in a barrel, although I can't say I've ever tried to execute that hoary cliché. Boyar waltzed gently with Blum on direct examination, establishing that there was no way that the forlorn court officer could have been part of the murderous gang. He was, we were telling the jury, simply in the wrong place at the wrong time. Soon it was the defense's turn to pick him apart.

Why hadn't he stopped his car after the accident? Rubinstein wanted to know. And how was it that Paul Blum realized instantly that the accident was more serious than his son, on the scene, had perceived? Why did Blum receive what certainly appeared to be preferential treatment from the police? And why was no breath test administered? Rubinstein was trying to plant the seed in the jury that Blum had known exactly what he had done, perhaps because he had done it on purpose, and the police who investigated had aided a fellow cop's son by absolving him of all intent. Finally, Murphy produced a police report which purportedly quoted the ill-starred Blum.

"I told my father that I hit something on the roadway that might have been a rolling tire or might have been a person," Murphy read aloud. Blum had signed the report. We were aware of this piece of evidence, of course, but during pre-trial prep Blum told us he never said it. He insisted that he signed the statement in a condition of nervous exhaustion.

"Then just tell them your story, tell them the truth" were our instructions. But as Murphy bore in on Blum's inconsistencies, the court officer became embarrassed and flustered. At one point he blurted out, "I don't know if I hit someone."

Murphy roared back: "Sure, Mr. Blum, sure you didn't."

They let him off the stand after raising doubt about intervening cause. Blum slumped from the Queens County State Supreme Courthouse with tears in his eyes. He became our fourth witness—along with Fisher, Riley, and Mauro—to require twenty-four-hour police protection.

It came as welcome news when Demakos announced a day of respite on a Tuesday in late October.

"What's on tomorrow?" Pat asked over a rare eight-o'clock supper, the earliest I had seen my wife for several weeks. Our youngest daughter, Lisa, had just started high school, and Pat had recently returned to the rolls of the work force—as if raising three boys and two girls were some kind of holiday. She was enjoying the experience.

"I've got an early-morning meeting with the A-Team, then lunch with Keating," I replied wearily, and we celebrated the rare off-day with a quiet dinner at home.

The following morning Boyar insisted that Riley and Blum hadn't really damaged our cause, and for the next several hours we kicked around ideas for the summation. Arrangements were made to prepare our medical expert, who was to testify that the tiny amount of cocaine in Michael Griffith's blood could not have impaired his judgment. And Richard Mangum began prepping the detectives who had taken the defendant's statements and would provide further corroboration of Riley.

At a little past noon I met with the Irish Mafia in a restaurant in Chinatown and realized instantly that serious discussion was out of the question. Harvey Louie Greenberg was on the attack, ridiculing our sagging prosecution. And the ever-reliable Keating suggested that there would be a certain historical cachet to an obituary that would read, "Hynes is probably best remembered for his loss in the celebrated Howard Beach case."

After lunch, I was turning the corner of Bowery and Canal streets for the walk back to the office when my beeper made its piercing announcement. Another half-block, another beep. This time the office number was printed out on the beeper's tiny screen. It was obviously important. I hurried to the nearest pay phone.

"Mr. Hynes, your wife has been in an automobile accident." My heart stopped as Catherine Schauf continued. "She's been taken to Brookdale Hospital."

The knot in my stomach tightened. "What happened? How bad is she? Catherine?"

"Mr. Hynes . . . she had a collision with a truck."

"Oh, my God."

"Mr. Hynes, I spoke to the police officer who's at the hospital. He said you shouldn't worry."

"Catherine, get Doug LeVien, tell him to pick me up at the

corner of Bowery and Canal. Right away. What's the name of the cop you spoke to?"

I quickly called the emergency room at Brookdale Hospital and asked to speak to the officer. He told me Pat was conscious, and seemed to be all right. "Just a broken wrist," he said, and of course I refused to believe him. For the next forty-five minutes, on our agonizing (and breakneck) drive to Brooklyn's Brookdale Hospital, I prepared for the worst.

The route that Doug opted for was a reaffirmation that somebody up there likes me. I hung out the passenger-side window, fruitlessly waving my wallet-sized special prosecutor's badge as LeVien ran every red light along Brooklyn's Eastern Parkway. Had we taken a more direct route, along Linden Boulevard, I would have passed the scene and witnessed the results of the accident. I'm not sure I could have handled that.

The tractor-trailer, I learned later, had broadsided Pat's car as she was making a left. The skid marks of the truck's tires measured more than twenty feet, indicating that he was moving at close to sixty miles per hour. The passenger side of Pat's Subaru was slammed against her steering wheel; half the car was crushed, with only the driver's seat remaining. Tire tracks were plainly visible on the hood and roof. I thanked God she was wearing her seat belt.

An emergency room nurse directed me to the X-ray room, where the first thing I saw was a cervical collar ringing Pat's neck. She assured me it was only a precaution. I spent the next three days away from the trial as she recuperated in the hospital. For the first time in nearly a year, The Incident at Howard Beach receded from my mind as I brought Pat her tea and toast and thanked God that she was alive.

Two days after the accident a bouquet of two dozen red roses arrived at our house, accompanied by a handwritten note that read: "Dear Pat, get well soon so you can watch me beat your husband. Best Wishes, Steve Murphy."

It was just past 6:30 P.M., Thursday, November 5, when Matt Greenberg entered our suite in the Queens Borough Hall. I was still optimistic about the case, and my enforced three-day break had given me a little objective distance to judge where we stood thus far. But the A-Team, except for Boyar, was not brimming with confidence. They felt Riley and Blum had hurt our cause badly. A lab technician from the City Medical Examiner's Office was scheduled to testify the following day. Her testimony would include the amount of cocaine discovered in Griffith's blood.

"Mr. Hynes," said Matt, who used that form of address only when he felt a migraine coming on, "we have the laboratory technician in the waiting room, and she has an embarrassing disclosure."

"Like what?" asked Dennis Hawkins.

"Like on the lab report the decimal point regarding the amount of cocaine found in Michael Griffith's body is off."

"By how much?"

"By a factor of ten."

REPORT: GRIFFITH USED MORE COKE, was the headline in *The New York Times* two days later for a story that led, "There was 10 times the amount of cocaine in Michael Griffith's body than originally thought, according to testimony in the Howard Beach trial."

We were reeling from another jolt. There had been a typographical error in the medical examiner's original toxicology report. There had not been 0.1 milligrams-per-liter of cocaine in Griffith's blood, after all. The true amount was 1.0 milligrams-per-liter. The mistake, a clerical error that the medical examiner discovered only as she was preparing her testimony, had been discovered nearly a year after the autopsy.

Still, we had to put the technician on the stand, and we were hurt badly.

"Michael Griffith was so high on coke that it's a wonder he didn't get hit by a low-flying plane from Kennedy Airport," Stephen Murphy screamed to a sea of reporters on the courthouse steps after the lab technician's brief appearance. They then ran to me for rebuttal.

"If you had a grain of sand before, you have ten grains of sand now," I groped, for that was about the extent of my pharmaceutical expertise. "Did he have cocaine before his death? Yes, he did. Did it affect his judgment? I don't believe so."

I added that a medical expert would be called to the stand to explain in finer detail.

A week later, on November 13, our expert took the stand.

"What is your business or occupation, sir?" Ed Boyar began.

"I am a physician and I am a board-certified psychiatrist," replied Dr. Kenneth Tardiff, associate professor of psychiatry and public health at the prestigious Cornell University College of Medicine.

Ken Tardiff, who was unlike any forensic psychiatrist I could recall meeting, was also the answer to our prayers. He had recently completed a detailed study of cocaine-related deaths, with examples numbering in the hundreds. He spoke in easily understood sentences and there was just enough trace of a Brooklyn/Queens accent in his voice to lend him the appearance of a "regular guy."

Nothing the four defense lawyers did could shake Tardiff's conclusion that Michael Griffith's cocaine ingestion had occurred no less than twelve hours, and perhaps as many as eighteen hours, before his death.

Cocaine simply had no effect on Griffith's judgment, Tardiff told the jury, and I could merely hope they believed him, for I was sure the defense would counter with a medical expert of their own.

As the Howard Beach trial entered its third month, our witness strategy was right on target. Following the "down days" of Robert Riley and Dominick Blum, our roster was designed to bounce us back and build up to Cedric Sandiford, our most powerful eyewitness.

Dr. Maria Toscano and her husband, George, were both called to describe the beating they had seen from their second-floor window. Mrs. Toscano began by recalling "a group of white boys" encircling "a black man, one of them was carrying a bat-like object, and one was carrying a T-shaped instrument. Both swung and hit the black man."

Ladies and gentlemen of the jury, I thought to myself as the Toscanos described the gruesome sight, *you might consider Riley a punk and Blum a confused young man. But ask yourselves what Grimes's addiction or Michael Griffith's cocaine use or Sandiford's criminal record have to do with the events these witnesses are describing. The only thing those youths who left the Schorr party knew was that Grimes, Griffith, and Sandiford were "niggers on the Boulevard."*

I scanned the jury, seeking a reaction, as George Toscano gave his testimony. *Remember,* I tried to tell them through some kind of telepathy, *remember when you saw Bobby Riley that he was just what Boyar said he was: one of that gang, one of these four primly suited and neatly coiffed youngsters sitting like angels at the defense table, looking as if they were on line for altar-boy practice.*

26

NO QUARTER, NO RETREAT

From a law enforcement point of view, Cedric Sandiford was a simple victim of an aggravated assault—a felony that occurs about seventy thousand times a year in New York City.

But from my point of view, he was the essence of our case. He was a living, breathing testament to the depraved indifference to human life exhibited by at least three individuals in this courtroom: Scott Kern, Jason Ladone, and Jon Lester. They had chased one man to his death and then turned cold-heartedly to locate, beat, and perhaps kill another. Only Michael Pirone had balked at the sight of Michael Griffith's blood. In the legal context of the Howard Beach trial, assault and homicide were two separate crimes. But in a moral context, they were connected, part of the same lurid drama, and I was sure Sandiford's testimony would convince the jury that the white youths had knowingly committed murder.

Yet for all of Sandiford's importance, his past was not pretty and could get in the way of justice. He had lied to to the Virginia courts years ago when he admitted to the possession of a sawed-off shotgun (which he told me he didn't really have) just to get out of jail. And in the interview he granted Peter Noel of the *Amsterdam News,* he claimed to have seen Michael Griffith crawl through the hole in the fence. Both were certain to be seized upon by the defense attorneys as proof of his unreliability as a witness.

But we had finally convinced Sandiford that his initial story had been wrong, that Michael Griffith must have been dead by the time he himself was cornered on 85th Street. Still, the cross-examination was certain to be brutal, and I figured it would last for days. If one of the defense attorneys managed to knock Sandiford right off the stand, "cracking" him as Murphy had cracked Grimes, our case would lose its foundation.

So on a chilly Saturday in early November, the weekend prior to Sandiford's scheduled court appearance, I turned for reassurance to Arthur Sidney Friedman, the prosecutorial version of Harvey Louie Greenberg. Friedman was my former First Assistant who had been lured away from the Special Prosecutor's Office by a lucrative and prestigious post in private practice. I knew him since my Brooklyn Rackets Bureau days, when he specialized in organized crime. He possessed a special facility for retaining the tiniest details and spotting contradictions. In our rehearsal of Sandiford, I wanted Friedman to use that gift, doing his best to confuse and frustrate our ultimate witness. The defense attorneys couldn't do worse to the witness than would be done by Friedman; I wanted Sandiford prepared for the worst.

During a four-and-one-half-hour mock cross-examination at St. John's on Saturday, November 14, Friedman moved Sandiford to both tears and fury with his shouting, haranguing, and taunting style. It was terrible to watch.

"So when you pleaded guilty to possessing a sawed-off shotgun in the State of Virginia, that wasn't true, right?" Friedman shrieked at Sandiford, ingeniously (and furiously) combining the disparate styles of Leone, Levinson, Rubinstein, and Murphy.

"No, sir," yelled Sandiford.

"Then you lied!"

"No, sir, but—"

"You lied, didn't you?"

"No. I didn't mean to lie."

"But it was a lie, wasn't it?"

"Yes," Sandiford said pleadingly, in the way of a witness caught in an attorney's convoluted snare.

"And you want this jury to believe today the story of a confessed liar—is that correct?"

"No, that's not true," said Sandiford, who looked about to crumble.

"Well, what is the truth, Mr. Sandiford—or do you know the difference between the truth and a lie?"

With every inconsistency, my diminutive friend Friedman bullied Sandiford into a tighter corner. Like a puncher with his man on the ropes, Friedman ripped and slashed. Liar. Liar. Liar.

When he was finished, Sandiford sat up and flashed a broad smile. The two men came together and embraced. The surreal picture of the tall, wiry African-American with his arms thrown around his tiny tormentor gives me a special feeling even to this day.

Because Arthur Friedman had been so brutal and thorough during the mock cross-examination, I felt confident that Sandiford could resist the onslaught when at last I brought him to the courtroom on November 16. I truly believed that there was no way that anyone could "knock off" this witness.

Sandiford breezed through my direct examination as if he were an actor hired to portray himself in a courtroom drama. He told the jury how one of the youths "lashed me in my head, he busted my head open and blood is running down the back of my neck. I felt like my brain busted apart."

"What did you feel?" I asked.

"I felt pain, anguish, and shock," Sandiford said. "As they were beating me with bats and limbs, I turned around and reached up and snatched one of the bats. I was looking in the person's face. He was a white male, about five-two to five-four, one hundred and thirty to one hundred and twenty pounds, blond hair, blue eyes, and round, red cheeks."

Lester had been held in the Rikers Island city jail since January. Now he sat twenty feet from his accuser, his hair darkened considerably by prison's lack of sunlight, the bulge of his "jail muscles" showing under his coat. Sandiford had been wrong about one thing: Lester's eyes were not blue, but a shade of light brown. But for a man who was being beaten when he glimpsed little John Lester, his description was remarkably close.

"Do you see him here in the courtroom?" I asked.

He said he did, stood, and pointed to Lester, who appeared to grow pale, fidgeting with his fingers.

"I tussled with him for a while," Sandiford continued. "I don't know how long. I turned to him and said, 'Please don't kill me, I have a son as old as you.' A blue Olds pulled up and two other white males came out of the car toward me. I released the bat and he lashed me in my head."

Sandiford was righteous now, the jury engrossed. "I broke away and ran across the street. They ran part of the way and was beating me again. They was beating me with bats and tree limbs and I don't know what else. I got hit in the eye with a tree limb. I said, 'Oh God, I'm dead.' I stretched out my hands, covering my face in my arms."

"Did the beatings stop?"

"No, sir," Sandiford said. "They continued beating me for a while. Then they left in cars."

He was magnificent.

On cross-examination, Gabe Leone and Ronald Rubinstein got nowhere with Sandiford, who withstood their expected barrage about the hole in the fence and Michael Griffith's escape, explaining that he had been on the receiving end of an unqualified whipping, and was in no way responsible for the vagaries of his memory. At one point Rubinstein accused Sandiford of "tailoring" his trial testimony to conform to "the prosecution's need." This, naturally, prompted an explosion from me. I was getting sick of these guys and their phony tactics.

"That's objected to, and it's disgraceful," I yelled, and Demakos flashed a sardonic smile.

"I object to *that*," Rubinstein shouted back, "and I demand a mistrial."

Demakos denied the mistrial motion (one of many) and advised us both to calm down.

Then it was Stephen Murphy's turn.

He began in his usual argumentative tone, asking Sandiford if he supported his two children from his previous marriage. Judge

Demakos sustained my objection, and Murphy followed up on Sandiford's previous testimony with what seemed like a non sequitur about joining the U.S. Army in 1968.

"Is that when you developed your drug problem?"

"I did marijuana and cocaine when I was in the service," Sandiford replied, a touch of arrogance in his voice. "At the time I didn't think I had a drug problem."

In contrast to Grimes, Sandiford yelled back at Murphy's belligerent questions, asking on several occasions for "time to let me finish what I have to say, sir." Once his booming voice even disrupted a trial in an adjacent courtroom.

Finally, midway through his two-hour cross, Murphy asked Sandiford about some minor disciplinary proceedings the Army had taken against him. Unexpectedly, Sandiford unfolded from his chair and stood facing Murphy, for just a split second, before turning left toward the judge. "Already?" Murphy shouted, and a wave of acid washed through my stomach and the spectators tensed for another walkout. Even I thought Sandiford was going to quit.

Instead, he slowly pulled off his suit jacket, slung it over the witness chair, sat back down, and smiled.

Demakos look startled, and nervous laughter spread through the courtroom.

"I don't like that remark 'Already,' Mr. Murphy," Demakos said. "It indicates to me that you're up to something you shouldn't be." *Like trying to drive my witness off the stand.* Yet the tenor of Murphy's remaining questions was strangely subdued. Frankly, I was shocked. It almost appeared as if the Screamer of Queens Boulevard was purposely taking it easy on Sandiford.

That afternoon Murphy invited me to lunch for the first time and I accepted (for in spite of myself, I'd taken a shine to him). Over ribs at a Queens Boulevard joint he tried to make me believe that his kid-glove approach had been part of his master plan.

"I already knocked one of your guys off the stand," Murphy "confided" to me. "And this jury's seen me screaming and yelling at everybody you brought up. Sandiford had nothing to do with my guy. Pirone was still puking while Sandiford was getting beat. I go after him, and the jury thinks I'm just a scumbag who wants to beat people up. And they take it out on my client."

There was indeed a method to his madness.

Still, the most dramatic moment of Sandiford's cross-examination was provided that afternoon by Bryan Levinson, who used his wit (where belligerence had failed) to cut effective slices into Sandiford's story. Reminding the witness of his theatrical identification of Lester, Levinson posed a sarcastic follow-up:

"Do you want to look into the eyes of Jon Lester and tell me his eyes are as brown as a cow's?"

Sandiford agreed, and a tense and hushed courtroom watched carefully as Sandiford stepped down from the witness stand, walked through the well, leaned over the defense table, and locked eyes with Lester. They were no more than a foot apart.

"That is the person who was beating me with a baseball bat," Sandiford said, straightening up and pointing at Lester.

"Does he have blue eyes?" Levinson challenged.

"I don't know what eyes he has," Sandiford said calmly on his way back to the box. "Sir, I would know Jon Lester's face anywhere."

When it was over, Stephen Murphy strode over to me in the well and asked if he could say something to Sandiford. I nodded, and Murphy edged closer to Cedric.

"Mr. Sandiford, you're all right," Murphy whispered with a big grin.

Cedric was smiling when he looked up from some papers. "Mr. Murphy, you're all right, too."

The two warriors, Murphy and Sandiford, had taken each other's best shot. And like battle-weary campaigners, a bond of respect had formed in the well of K-3. Or, as the headline in the following morning's *New York Newsday* put it: NO QUARTER, NO RETREAT.

I drove home late that night in a state of mental and physical exhaustion. Our case was nearly through, the facts were in, and Pat sensed immediately how I felt.

"So I take it that whatever the jury decides, you've got the feeling they've already made up their minds," she said.

"We have shot our load," I said. "And I have no idea what that panel is thinking."

Over the next four days Richard Mangum used the testimony of several detectives to put the various admissions of the defendants at the precinct before the jury, thereby corroborating Riley's testimony. Ed Boyar introduced certain technical evidence regarding the 911 tapes, the sequence of which—showing Griffith being chased to the highway before Sandiford was attacked—further established our claim for proximate cause. Penultimately, we requested that Demakos allow the jury to visit the scene. The judge said he would rule on the field trip to Shore Parkway and 90th Street in the near future. (He denied our request several days later.) And while the placement of these statements and exhibits on record was a necessary facet of the legal construction of our case, it all seemed so anticlimactic on the heels of Sandiford's dramatic appearance. Even the rows of reporters and chanting demonstrators outside the courthouse seemed to feel the energy drain. The defense hadn't even begun to present their cases yet, and I felt everybody was already awaiting a verdict.

The jury had heard the extent of the terror that morning in Howard Beach: it had not been a fight between two groups, it had been a lynching. And all the legal theorems in the universe would not make one-tenth the impression on these jurors' minds as the testimony of Fisher, and Grimes, and Riley, and Sandiford.

But just in case, on November 21, 1987, two and a half months after jury selection began and six weeks after opening statements, I rose to enter my last exhibit, the pictures the police Crime Scene Unit had taken of 90th Street on the day I had met the Howard Beach citizen who cursed me on his way to church. The perspective of the photo exhibit was facing down 90th Street, toward the Belt Parkway, and each juror could clearly see the tunnel effect, the fencing and garages that had hemmed in Michael Griffith. I needed the jury to remember those photos.

Then, at last, I turned toward Judge Demakos:

"May it please the court," I said. "That is the case for the People of the State of New York."

27

THE DEFENSE

Then it was the turn of the defense. Their presentation was rather brusque, not intended, as Bryan Levinson told reporters, "to be a razzle-dazzle kind of thing." I expected this. Their strategy from the beginning had been to destroy *our* case. So they counterpunched. They pummeled our witnesses. They tried to prove that there had been no racial assault, but merely a midnight confrontation that led ("alas, tragically") to Michael Griffith's accidental death, for which, of course, their clients bore no responsibility. When they couldn't call our witnesses liars, they said almost nothing.

Over the next four days they summoned only thirteen people to testify, as opposed to our seventy-two, and their effort was as halfhearted as their witnesses were pedestrian. Several Howard Beach all-night service station managers told the jury that Sylvester could have certainly stopped at their garage for mechanical assistance, implying a sinister motive for his failure to do so. And a sixteen-year-old girl, who said she was driving along Cross Bay Boulevard with her mother on the night of the attack, recalled seeing four black men near a broken-down car, one wielding "what appeared to be a gun."

By the time Boyar finished destroying her half-remembered and jumbled story on cross-examination, it wasn't even clear what borough, much less what street, she had been riding through.

For comic relief, we were treated to a performance from Jerold Levine, Esq., a Queens Boulevard lawyer whom the Ladones retained to represent their son, Jason, immediately following The Incident, while Rubinstein was skiing in Vail.

On cross-examination, Boyar countered Levine's notion that Jason Ladone had been illegally detained at the 106th Precinct by asking the lawyer if the youth had in fact been arrested.

"Arrested? Well, he was detained," answered Levine, who paused for a moment to think. "In my opinion, arrested. But no charges were leveled against him. I learned that he was being detained, which under my understanding of the legal law is an arrest when you lose your freedom."

Heads were scratched and eyes blinked at the logic and syntax of Levine's scrambled testimony; it was what the sports writers used to call Stengelese. Matt Greenberg leaned over the prosecution table and offered in a stage whisper, "as opposed to the illegal law."

Nevertheless, in two instances I worried that the defense counsel's tactics were reaching "my" jury (as I had come to think of it) and giving our case serious problems. My first fear was personified by Dr. Thomas Manning, who was brought in to support Murphy's claim that Michael Griffith was "so coked out he could have been hit by a jet." My second was embodied by Harold Kern, whom Leone called to fight for his son's life.

Our strategy was simple. Ed Boyar would take on their medical witness, in hopes of negating Manning's expertise with his technical trial skill. And I was to cross-examine Harold Kern, the most uncomfortable job I have ever had. Throughout the trial we had categorized each witness loosely, and I had given out direct- and cross-examination assignments based on those categories. Mangum, for instance, a former Queens County prosecutor, has a subtle rapport with the law-enforcement types, and he basically handled the cops. Boyar, on the other hand, possesses a much better grasp of scientific miscellanea, which is how I determined that he would deal with the "experts." I also chose Boyar as my designated "hit man," the attorney to crack any witnesses sympathetic to the defense. Thus he had handled "the Sisters of Silence" and several of the other

Howard Beach teens. If the jury focused on any one prosecutor as an ogre, we didn't want it to be me, the man who would soon be asking for their help in obtaining a conviction. When we rolled out our big guns, our Fishers and Sandifords, it was only natural that the jury see the special state prosecutor take charge of his case. Thus, when we learned that Harold Kern would be taking the stand to fight for his son's freedom, I decided that I would have to face him in the well; their last, best shot should be taken at me.

Dr. Manning was first. Under direct examination, he testified that Michael Griffith's judgment was so affected by cocaine that he caused his own death. The witness was convincing. He carried himself with an air of scientific authority, and his list of credentials was awesome: chief toxicologist for the Nassau County Medical Examiner's Office; master's degree in physiology and doctorate in pharmacology; numerous teaching positions in toxicology; published in several fields; and he had been declared an "expert" witness in forensic toxicology by the New York State courts, testifying in more than a hundred cases. Jurors eat that stuff up.

Bryan Levinson moved to have Judge Demakos declare Dr. Manning an "expert" for the Howard Beach jury. Given his résumé, we would have appeared foolish to object.

Dr. Manning testified that he had spoken to the New York City toxicologist who prepared Michael Griffith's lab report, and at this point Levinson asked his witness to step down to a blackboard in the center of the court well.

I immediately requested a sidebar and reminded the judge that *my* medical "expert" had been forbidden to use a pre-prepared chart. This trial had been a series of psychological battles to win the hearts and minds of the jury, and the last thing I wanted was "Professor" Manning giving the panel a short course on toxicology. Demakos ruled in our favor.

However, shortly after this small victory, Levinson led his witness through a carefully prepared—and effective—narrative, constructing a theory that Griffith had ingested a "near lethal" dose of cocaine somewhere between fifteen minutes and two hours prior to his death. Levinson concluded with a flourish that pierced the heart of the matter concerning the exact cause of Michael Griffith's death: "Then at the time of death, would you say with a reasonable degree of scientific certainty that he was under the influence of cocaine?"

"Yes," answered Dr. Manning.

The emphasized words "certainty" and "cocaine" had my head reeling. The doctor looked very smug as he glanced in my direction.

"Your witness," said Levinson.

Boyar stood up and whispered to me and Richard Mangum. "Don't worry, boss, I'm going to nail this guy." I mustered a weak smile for the consistency of my favorite cockeyed optimist.

But Boyar wasn't kidding. He quickly established that Dr. Manning had not reviewed the coroner's work sheet, and was thus unaware of the date that the tests were performed on Michael Griffith's body. The defense expert had no idea, in fact, if the autopsy and report were done on the same day, nor how to explain a number of factors that could have affected the report.

"Have you ever studied how quickly it is that the body loses heat, loses body temperature, after death; how fast it cools off?" asked Boyar, subtly making his point about the body temperature's effect on ingested drugs.

Manning sheepishly admitted that the question was out of his "area of expertise," and that a pathologist might better answer that. With the doctor off guard, Boyar pressed. And his intent was not lost on the jury when he enumerated the previous witnesses who had testified to seeing Michael Griffith acting normally that night.

Would not a trained Park Police officer, or two toll-booth collectors, recognize a man on a lethal dose of cocaine? Boyar wanted to know. And then he jumped to the topic of the drug's side effects, specifically as an appetite suppressant, while reminding the jury of Griffith's stop for pizza.

Dr. Manning's responses were unsteady. Better than that, he gave *our* "expert" an inadvertent boost.

"Wouldn't the appetite be suppressed?" Boyar asked.

"I can give you the general pharmacology of cocaine," replied Dr. Manning, "but I can't tell you what a particular individual would be—because I don't do this kind of thing. This is for a forensic psychiatrist."

"Like Dr. Kenneth Tardiff," Boyar said under his breath.

Boyar had done a masterful job, and when it was over I felt certain we had won the "battle of the experts."

As their final witness, the defense called the father of Scott Kern. Harold Kern claimed that the detectives had not read his son his rights that night in the 106th Precinct. And while Mr. Kern's testimony, if believed, would strike only the admissions of his son, the three other defense attorneys obviously hoped that the jury would become so angered by the "Gestapo" tactics of the police that they would reject all of the defendants' statements as evidence. As the senior Kern marched determinedly toward the stand, I was touched by a twinge of pity and a sense of admiration for the man fighting for his kin.

His direct testimony recounted the story of being awakened by detectives in the wee hours of December 22, 1986, two days after the attack. The investigators, he recalled, wanted to speak to Scott. The cops advised Mr. Kern that he could drive with his son to the precinct. Once there, the youth made his statements.

But it was not until Scott had been interrogated several times, Harold Kern said, that he was read his Miranda warnings. Kern said that he complained to the investigators that his son's right to remain silent should have been given earlier. Nevertheless, both Scott and Harold Kern had signed the Miranda card, which by law requires the signature of a suspect before questioning can begin.

On the surface Harold Kern's story seemed implausible, yet I wouldn't have been shocked to learn that events had actually transpired that way, given the shaky manner in which the entire Howard Beach investigation had been handled. However, it was my job to show the jury that Harold Kern's account was extremely unlikely.

The art of cross-examination is perhaps the second-hardest lesson for a trial lawyer to learn. The most difficult is when to say, "No questions." A cross-examiner will nearly always fail in a direct confrontation with an adversarial witness. Harold Kern was never going to say, "But of course, Mr. Hynes, on reflection,

I see the events I testified to never occurred." So the point of a "cross" is to illuminate the possibility that through bias, or faulty memory, or even the desire to look good, a witness has colored his testimony. With Harold Kern, that last was the most difficult. For while a juror might believe that he lied for his son, no juror wants to see a father called a liar.

I was delicate with Mr. Kern as I asked him about the first time he had heard of the incident at Howard Beach, and his answers were sadly tentative. Despite the media blitz of that first, foul weekend, Harold Kern testified that it was the 106th Precinct detectives who initially informed him of the attack.

"So to your recollection there were no television or radio reports about the Howard Beach incident?" I asked.

"That's correct."

"Did you read anything?"

"No, I didn't read anything in the newspapers."

Next I began to ask Mr. Kern about when he felt the need to call a lawyer for his son. He replied that, when a detective informed him that there was a death involved, he asked if Scott was under arrest. The detective said he wasn't.

"Did you ask him if your son was somehow involved, and how he was involved?"

"He said we have to bring him down to the precinct," Harold Kern said.

"At the time of that response from the detective, you did not feel it necessary to ask for an attorney, is that correct?"

"That's correct."

And then Harold Kern testified that on the drive to the station house he never asked his son why detectives would want to question him about a black man's death.

"I said, 'Scott, why didn't you tell me that something happened?'" Harold Kern said on the stand, and I thought I could hear several jurors' hearts breaking. "And he said, 'I didn't know nothing, so I felt I didn't have to tell you anything.' Like that."

"What did you say to your son, sir?"

"I said, 'Don't worry about it, then, just tell the truth.'"

"And you did not ask him any further questions about whether he might be involved?"

"No, not really."

During that same car ride to the 106th Precinct, Harold Kern said Scott had told him, "Daddy, I don't know anything about someone getting killed." Yet at the station, as I told the jury, in Harold Kern's presence, Scott Kern told detectives about Sal DeSimone's statement: "I told you that the black guy got killed."

"At that point, Mr. Kern, when you heard your son tell the detectives about his conversation with DeSimone, did it concern you that in fact he did hear about someone getting killed?"

"Objection!" shouted Gabe Leone.

"Overruled," said Demakos. I continued. "At that point did you have any concern about perhaps the need to get an attorney to advise your son?"

"No, I did not."

As I backtracked Harold Kern through his direct testimony, I continually questioned him about his decision to find a lawyer for his son. Finally, we reached the point where he said his son was tardily read his rights, followed by Harold Kern's direct testimony that he felt he had been duped.

"But did you say, 'Hey, Detective, I want to get an attorney?' "
I asked.

"No, I did not."

"Why did you sign the card?" I asked, referring to his son's Miranda rights.

"I told him, 'I'm signing under protest.' "

"Did you write, 'Under protest'?"

"No, I did not."

"You did not?"

"Like I say, I was confused. We were there nineteen and one half hours."

"Not at that point you weren't. At that point you were there from about three-thirty A.M. to eight A.M."

I was finished, and Judge Demakos ordered a recess. As I reached the large vestibule to K-3, where the defendants' families often gathered to speak to their lawyers, I caught a glimpse of Harold Kern out of the corner of my eye. His back was to the wall, and he was nervously lighting a cigarette. He looked as sad as I imagined a man could look. I had not destroyed him—as I could have—and I believe he knew that. I had merely raised questions to let the jury decide. I walked over and extended my hand. He took it.

"You did okay, Mr. Kern."

He looked at me through eyes filled with tears. "Thank you, Mr. Hynes."

28

CLOSING ARGUMENTS

Helman Brook was jogging when it occurred to him that each staff member should draft a summation. This was on a chilly morning right before the trial began. He wanted time for the process to mesh. I agreed.

Hilly Hoffman, for instance, would undoubtedly hand in a detailed and thorough appellate analysis. And Richard Mangum would contribute his lilting, evangelical cadences to the rhetoric. Pamela Hayes's draft would undoubtedly contain a personal passion that might otherwise be lacking. And we could count on Matt Greenberg and his assistant, Virginia Modest, for a scholarly legal draft. Dennis Hawkins's pragmatism would ensure that we covered every point. And, finally, Ed Boyar's dispassionate skill in the well of the court would translate into logic on paper. Brook served as editor in chief, and my final draft passed through numerous appellate reviews by the A-Team.

When I was finally through tinkering, perhaps two weeks before we rested the case, this composite was the best summation I had ever seen.

I thought of the hands that contributed to the work as I fidgeted at the prosecution table one week after my grilling of Harold Kern. I was waiting to deliver my closing remarks. A summation is a lawyer's signature, and electric currents can fill a courtroom when an attorney delivers the final plea. Some lawyers—including me—favor the high drama of literary allusion and biblical reference. Others—Stephen Murphy and Harvey Louie Greenberg spring to mind—prefer to hammer home facts in a more pragmatic manner, dropping in references to specific laws.

I was proud of my contribution and I was proud of my staff. A camel is said to be a horse designed by a committee, yet I felt privileged to be the instrument of the combined ideals and hard work of the A-Team. It was Wednesday, December 9, 1987, three hundred and fifty three days since The Incident at Howard Beach, and four defense lawyers and a prosecutor were prepared to make their final invocations.

Bryan Levinson was precise and analytical. And both Gabe Leone and Ron Rubinstein were professionally thorough and hard-hitting. But it was Stephen Murphy who stole the show for the defense. As I sat at my table, watching him work, I confess to experiencing more than a few pangs of envy. The guy was brilliant.

Originally, the defense strategy was to allow Murphy to speak first in order to set the tone. None of the others could assault a prosecution's case like the Screamer of Queens Boulevard. But after three months of high-decibel workouts, Murphy's vaunted vocal cords had finally failed him. He arrived in court with a mild case of laryngitis and sucked on lozenges while Levinson and Rubinstein delivered their remarks. By the time he rose to speak, his voice had barely returned.

"You're lucky in one respect," he told the jurors, rasping over the rail that separated the panel from the wall of the court. "I have a sore throat and a cough, so I can't yell very much today. But on the other hand, I will get close to you, and you may catch whatever I have."

The jury reacted. James Spongross was smiling, Michael Sweeney broke into a grin, and even Felicia Chapman, a black city housing manager and alternate juror who had replaced Beverly Minor (whose son had taken ill), allowed the corners of her mouth to turn up. The jury was charmed by Stephen Murphy, a difficult man not to like. I could see instantly that my work was being cut out for me.

"Let me just look at what happened here during this trial,"

Murphy said as he began with the fundamental technique of reminding the jurors that they had promised to be fair. In a hoarse and squeaky voice he asked them how they would feel if they were in his defendant's shoes, or if in fact anyone would "want to be in the position that Michael Pirone has been put in."

An honorable technique: ask the jury to identify with the client. He then moved rapidly into an assault upon our witnesses, raising the obvious (and expected) questions:

"We have here a situation where the prosecution has said that carrying a shotgun with the intent to do something to somebody, to cause harm, that's okay. Assaulting your wife is okay," he continued. "Robbing an old lady is okay. Burgling is okay. Using crack is okay. Taking your mother's and your girlfriend's money is okay. Stabbing your girlfriend is okay," Murphy said, as I gave silent thanks that his voice had worn out. *"Everything* seems to be okay."

For more than two hours Murphy dissected our case against Pirone, ridiculing our witnesses and repeating over and over that his client's legs had been injured so horribly in a 1985 automobile accident that he could not possibly have run after either Griffith or Sandiford.

He ignored Riley's testimony, although it tended to exonerate his client. And by the time he hit his stride our case against Pirone seemed to be crumbling into dust. His final appeal carried a soft eloquence as he leaned close to the jurors and reminded them again of their oath to be fair. He pointed to his client, who looked so young and vulnerable, and urged the jury to see his side.

"He has been through an ordeal sitting over there for the last three months. Are you going to listen to the prosecutor when he gets up and bangs the table and tells you to forget about the fact that there is no evidence against Mr. Pirone? Can you forget what he's suffered—for *nothing?*

"I ask you this: Is there anyone here who wants this to happen to him? Would you want to be convicted on this evidence? You all promised me at the beginning that you would give the same fair trial that *you* would want."

Murphy then turned his back to the jury, bowed his head

solemnly, and began to walk back to his table. Abruptly he halted and turned back to the panel. From my seat at the prosecution table, his eyes appeared to be glistening with tears.

"My God, I would hate to think that I would be convicted because I got into a car with somebody and went to a pizza place when I can't even run," he pleaded emotionally. "Nobody gives a damn whether I can run. Nobody gives a damn whether I'm guilty or innocent."

The blacks in the spectator section, some of whom had heckled Murphy during his previous remarks, fell mute. They had obviously not seen Michael Pirone (as I had) skip across Queens Boulevard, dodging lunchtime traffic, during several breaks in the trial.

"Nobody did anything to prove this kid was guilty," Murphy concluded, thrusting his hands into brown suitpants and staring at each of the jurors. "That would be a travesty. He had nothing to do with all of this. I hope you will give him the same fair shake you would want.

"My God, would you want to be convicted on this? I don't think any of you would. If you convict Michael Pirone, somehow we will all suffer."

He was finished.

And I knew Michael Pirone was free.

Between recesses, a lunch break, and several short breathers, Gabe Leone completed the defense's final remarks at almost 5:30 P.M. Now Judge Demakos turned to our table and said, "Mr. Hynes, are you ready? We will take a fifteen-minute recess and then prosecution will proceed."

I was on my feet in a flash, asking to approach the bench. Demakos denied me that chance. And I was angry and not doing much to conceal it.

Throughout the trial, Judge Demakos had found time to regale us all with his "war stories," some concerning his Alice Crimmins prosecution, and more than a few about the Thomas Shea case. One in particular dealt with the defense's summation for officer Shea, which had ended at six in the evening. Judge George Balbach forced Demakos, the prosecutor, to sum up in front of an exhausted jury, and he had carried those scars to the bench. Now he was doing the same thing to me.

I tried to appeal to him, on the record, in front of the jurors, "Judge, don't you think the jury could use an overnight?"

"No, Mr. Hynes, they'll be fine," he replied as he rose to leave the bench.

Court officers began escorting the jurors from the room, and I stormed through the well of K-3.

"Tom"—it was the only time during the entire trial that I dropped a respectful title in addressing the judge—"what the fuck are you doing?"

His only response was a wave of his hand. It might as well have been a red flag.

"You've bitched about George Balbach for twenty years," I exploded, "and now you're doing the same fucking thing."

But it was no use. He was out the door before I was finished. Demakos told me later that he thought the jurors deserved the "continuity" of each side's closing remarks. All I could think about was exhausted jurors falling asleep during my summation. I was steamed. As I strode angrily through the lobby, I brushed off reporters who had witnessed the exchange. Suddenly I spotted Pat, with our youngest daughter, Lisa, standing off to the side of the steps. It was my wife's first appearance in court since the accident. She'd come in the hope of either seeing my summation or helping me to relax over dinner. Dennis Hawkins told her what happened in court. She hugged me and offered a suggestion:

"Why don't we just get this thing over with."

"May it please the court, Mr. Justice Demakos, counsel for the defense, Madam Forelady, ladies and gentlemen of the jury:

"I think it's fair to say that early last September, as you entered this building, not one of you could have imagined that you would spend more than a quarter of a year as jurors in the service of the State of New York. And yet each day you reported here to this courthouse and you showed the very same attentiveness, interest, and patience as you did the day before—all the while showing where it was appropriate that you have not lost your individual or collective sense of humor. I find that truly remarkable, so for myself, my colleagues, and for all the lawyers, I want you to accept our sincere gratitude and appreciation."

It was Wednesday night, December 9, and I was fulfilling a pro forma, textbook obligation which is by no means gratuitous. I have the utmost sympathy for a juror's travails, or, as I tell my law students, "Stop by a central jury room someday and visit the cattle cars they call jury pools." Murder suspects are treated with more dignity. Like Murphy and his associates before me, I wanted to thank the jury.

"From the beginning of the voir dire—the jury selection phase of the trial—through the various opening statements, promises were made in this trial. You promised to listen to all of the evidence, and I remind you that evidence came only from the testimony given by witnesses who took this stand, and from physical evidence—exhibits, photographs, and maps.

"I remind you that testimony from the witness stand became evidence only when both the question and the answer were permitted by Justice Demakos. So if a question was asked and the judge sustained an objection, that question was not evidence. The judge has reminded you of that many times during the trial. To put it another way, nothing a lawyer said—not me, my colleagues, or any of the defense lawyers—nothing we said was evidence."

As I uttered those words my eyes swept the jury box, trying for contact with each individual juror. It had been a contentious trial, rife with charges and countercharges, and what I felt was a subtle racism bubbling just below the surface. I've learned from long experience that, whatever occurs during a trial, it is always best to relate it back to the promise a jury makes in the beginning: to listen with an open mind before reaching any conclusion. Experience has taught me that jurors have difficulty violating this oath.

"Each of you said you would accept Justice Demakos's instruction about the law as it applies to this case, and then, after you deliberate, to render a verdict. You promised that the verdict would not be influenced by prejudice, fear, sympathy, or anything other than the evidence and the law. And you promised this because that is what the law demands. The law applies to and protects us all; it protects you and me and all citizens regardless of our gender, our color, our origin, our religion or absence of religious belief. It applies to and protects the poor, the sick, the homeless, and each of these four defendants seated before you here on trial.

"And, yes, it applies to and protects Michael Griffith, Cedric Sandiford, and Timothy Grimes.

"From the beginning, every society has established rules of conduct, rules of law, without which it could not exist. Principal among these laws are those designed to protect life and property. And it does not matter whether a member of society has run afoul of the law in the past, because the law and its protection is for everyone.

"To breathe, to smile, to laugh, to cry, these are gifts we all share. No one has a right to take those precious gifts away from any of us. And the God who gave us those gifts also, in the words of Thomas Jefferson, 'gave us life and gave us liberty at the same time.' Liberty to come and go as we please, liberty to travel freely, is essential to our human dignity. Without it we are less than human. We travel freely between continents on this planet, and we travel freely to work and to recreation. There are no borders in our land that we cannot freely cross.

"Many years ago our nation established the principle that the color of a person's skin cannot determine where one sits on a bus, or where one attends school, or where one sits in a restaurant. It also cannot determine where one travels to, or when it is time for a person to die."

I hit that phrase hard and stared at the jury for several seconds before spotting Sandiford in the spectator section of the courtroom. It was his first time in court since his testimony, and I noticed that several of the jurors were also staring, not back at me, but rather at him.

A young man was murdered because he was black in a white man's neighborhood, I was telling these people. My mind raced back to Boyar's phrase: "Joe, they didn't need a passport." I was banging home the crux of the matter, that these white defendants had killed Michael Griffith strictly because he was "a nigger" in their neighborhood. No matter how many questions defense counsel raised about Griffith's background, or Sandiford's criminal record, or what these black men were doing in white Howard Beach, no one decides when it is time for a person to die. *Pause for a moment,* I cautioned myself, *and let that idea sink in.*

We are not here to excoriate the community of Howard Beach, I had reminded these jurors time and again. This crime could have occurred in any community in the world. The basis is distrust, and hatred for people who are different. It happened in the Holocaust, and it still happens in South Africa. It occurs in the northernmost province of my ancestors' country and I'll be damned if I'm going to let them get away with it in mine.

"For centuries, commentators have written of the sanctity of human life," I continued, "and the common interest we share in protecting it. Perhaps no one has spoken more eloquently of the relationship of one life to another than the preacher and poet John Donne. More than two hundred and fifty years ago, Donne wrote: 'No man is an island, entire of itself; every man is a piece of the continent, a part of the main. Any man's death diminishes me, because I am involved in mankind; and therefore never send to know for whom the bell tolls; it tolls for thee.'

"And of death, Petrarch said, 'A good death does honor to a whole life.' He could have added that a bad death does dishonor to us all.

"And so no matter how the lawyers for the defendants sought to destroy the character of Michael Griffith, Cedric Sandiford, and Timothy Grimes, the law, as well as fundamental principles of life and human dignity, say they were entitled to walk the streets of Queens County freely, without fear of violent attack, humiliation, or death.

"Michael Griffith had a right, under our law, to live his life to full term; not to have it cut short when he was a vigorous twenty-three years old. In the book of Ecclesiastes we are told, 'To every thing there is a season, and a time for every purpose under heaven. A time to be born, and a time to die.' Who were these four defendants that they should decide for Michael Griffith that it was his time to die?

"So what do you have to decide? After all the evidence you have seen and heard during the past eight weeks, I tell you now that there are really only a few questions that you have to answer: Who killed Michael Griffith? Who beat Cedric Sandiford so severely with a bat, tree limbs, and a tire iron that he, too, might have died had he not pretended to be dead? Who rioted in the quiet, residential streets of Howard Beach during the holiday season of 1986?"

I turned and pointed to the defendants, who appeared to physically recoil from my finger. I allowed my arm to remain vertical to my torso as I moved my hand in a slow arc, like a gunfighter sighting four victims. I had the jury now, rapt, almost blocked in stone. A summation is like a pyramid, tediously constructed brick by brick, and I had just laid the foundation.

My nervousness was gone, the butterflies in my belly replaced by a fire, a fire to convince this jury, to make them see and understand what had happened to Griffith, Sandiford, and Grimes—not in some alien nation where repression is routine, but in the United States of America.

My summation, forty typewritten pages, was much longer than what I was accustomed to delivering. Some lawyers will tell you that nine-hour closing remarks are par for the course, but I am always reminded of Edward Everett, who spoke for three hours at Gettysburg on November 19, 1863, and was never heard from again.

As I stood at the podium pointing to the defendants and searching the jury's eyes, I was struck by an ironic notion. I don't like to use a podium, as I believe a prosecutor should be able to carry the logical analysis of his case in his memory. But I had decided that this summation was so long and complicated that I would need the podium for the first time in my career.

Oddly, I now realized, I had been wrong, for the words flew from my mouth as if I were reliving the entire past year: the horror of the attack; the meticulous investigation; the hatred, and bigotry, and demagoguery. I thought of Melville's Ahab, and the obsession which had torn his "body and soul until they bled together."

The sociologists—not to mention defense counsel—had explained Michael Griffith's death away in terms of a flawed social structure. But I took this killing more personally. The twisted mentality that blazed forth in Howard Beach that brutal night was a hidden menace to our society. There were really only a few questions for these jurors to answer. Right now, in this cavernous courtroom, it was more than my duty to ensure that they were answered correctly. In a way, I felt it was my calling.

"Ladies and gentleman of the jury, the evidence gives you these answers: Scott Kern, John Lester, Jason Ladone, and Michael Pirone killed Michael Griffith.

"Kern and Lester are charged with murder and manslaughter, and Ladone and Pirone are charged with manslaughter. Justice Demakos will instruct you on the elements of each crime. But make no mistake about it. These four killed Michael Griffith.

"Defense counsel would like to point you in the wrong direction. They want you to answer the most irrelevant questions that have pervaded this trial. What were 'they'—Michael Griffith, Cedric Sandiford, and Timothy Grimes—doing in Howard Beach? The people have presented evidence about this matter, but I tell you that the bottom line is that it doesn't matter. That's not what this case is about.

"This case is about murder, manslaughter, assault, and riot. And if you get distracted by the smokescreen, justice will not be served.

"Remember, please, that Cedric Sandiford and Timothy Grimes are not on trial here—any more than is the memory of Michael Griffith or the community of Howard Beach. None of these are on trial. The only ones on trial are these four defendants.

"Examine the evidence and review what happened on the night of December 19 and the morning of December 20, 1986."

From this point I led the jury through a factual reconstruction of our case that took the better part of an hour. I did my best to defuse and deflate the various defense proclamations. I reminded the panel of our medical expert, who said Michael Griffith was not high on cocaine, and added that he had not run through a hole in the fence but had been chased up a "tunnel." I exhorted them to forget about Dominick Blum, a victim of circumstance, and laid out the times of the 911 calls.

I forced them to think about the nature of a society that kills and maims strangers for invading their turf, and from the looks on their faces I felt I was getting through. Did this gang of youths know about Cedric Sandiford's conviction or Timothy Grimes's addiction when they piled into their cars? I asked them. Of course not, I said, these white kids just wanted to fight.

"Michael Griffith turned onto 90th Street and was helplessly propelled down a tunnel, a chasm of death. And the force, the power, and the fury that propelled him ever closer to the Belt Parkway was Lester, Ladone, Kern, and Pirone.

"Ladies and gentleman of the jury, the force, the dynamics of the impact were secondary to the real power behind Michael Griffith's death. The terror, the horror, caused by the wanton, callous, and brutal conduct of the defendants: Lester, Ladone, Kern, and Pirone.

"They want you to believe that Michael Griffith, Cedric Sandiford, and Timothy Grimes were violent and aggressive men, that they came to Howard Beach looking for trouble. That is absurd, and their version of events will not stand up. When you review all the evidence, make your decisions based on fact and not on innuendo.

"A lot has been said by defense counsel about Robert Riley. That he's a deal-maker, a liar, a drunk, and ultimately a rat for selling out his friends. The only thing I agree with—and the defense has said it often enough—is that Robert Riley killed Michael Griffith. He did. So did these defendants. Scott Kern and Jon Lester killed Michael Griffith as surely as Robert Riley did. Jason Ladone and Michael Pirone killed Michael Griffith as surely as Robert Riley did. The only difference between him and them is that he decided to cooperate, to once and for all tell the truth about that awful night when he and the defendants killed a stranger who had the audacity to come into *their* neighborhood.

"Ladies and gentlemen, I want to bring up something that may be on your minds as you look across the courtroom to where these four defendants sit. Maybe some of you, perhaps all of you, have looked at them and said, 'But my God, they're so young. How could they have done something so vicious? How could they have chased Michael Griffith to his death? And how could three of them have turned from that and beaten Cedric Sandiford until he, too, appeared to be dead?'

"As you ask yourself these questions, please recall how

Theresa Fisher saw the attack, how she described the fury and brutality."

And here I replayed the tape of Fisher's 911 call. While the hysterical phone call played I looked at Cedric Sandiford and Jean Griffith in the courtroom, and their faces were as impassive as granite. As the tape ended I turned again to face the defendants.

"You see them now sitting over there. They could be attending a high school graduation or waiting for a job interview. There isn't even a hint of anger now, a hint of hatred or viciousness.

"I urge you, when you deliberate, to think of them not as they look now, but as they looked on the night of December 19, 1986, and the early morning of December 20, 1986.

"Use your individual and collective abilities as you deliberate. Use the evidence to picture what really happened that night. You will see these four defendants not as they look today but as they looked then, with faces twisted with hate, screaming filthy racial epithets, shouting threats of violence, racing through the streets of Howard Beach, pursuing and driving Michael Griffith to a horrible death.

"Then, not satisfied, three of the four—Kern, Lester, and Ladone—pursued Sandiford, surrounded him, and brutally pummeled him into the ground, stripping him of his very dignity as he pleaded for his life.

"Ladies and gentlemen, I submit to you that the prosecution has proven the guilt of the defendants beyond a reasonable doubt.

"Don't try to be detectives, nor social scientists. Nothing you can do can roll back the clock. Nothing you can do can change anything that happened on December 19 and December 20. But there is something you can do as jurors.

"Your verdict can be the spark to light the candle of justice, a candle that will be seen for decades to come."

29

THE VERDICT

By the time Judge Demakos began to read his charge to the jury at 10:00 A.M. the following day, the courthouse lobby was jammed with black activists, defense supporters, reporters, curious onlookers, and interested attorneys. They all lined up to enter K-3. Extra court officers were assigned to the area outside the first-floor courtroom, and a platoon of thirty uniformed police officers—"just a precaution," one patrol sergeant told me—snaked down the building's steps and onto Queens Boulevard.

I couldn't predict what the jury would do. It was too late now to do anything about it. We'd all had our say, and now it was in their hands. Demakos delivered his charge, the legal explanation of the facts the prosecution and defense had presumably laid out over the past three months. I had not, for instance, uttered the word "corroboration" during trial, but had instead tried to show the jury that Riley couldn't have been lying. There were simply too many pieces of testimony and evidence, however minute, that proved his story. It was up to Demakos to define the law for them. He spent the entire morning and most of the afternoon clarifying his instructions, and the panel alternately fidgeted and sat attentively as he discussed the fine legal points of corroboration, or explained that when someone, through a series of actions, puts into motion a course of conduct that that person should have known would result in serious physical injury or death, then theirs is the proximate cause of that crime.

Demakos dissected each count of the indictment—ranging from murder to riot—and instructed the jury how to consider culpability, telling them, for instance, that if they found Kern and Lester not guilty of second-degree murder, they should then move on to consider the question of manslaughter. To find the defendants guilty of murder, he said, "you must determine whether the circumstances were so brutal, so callous, so completely dangerous and inhuman that it shows an utter disregard for the endangered person."

Before retiring for deliberations, the jury asked to go to Howard Beach to see the scene of the attack. They also requested a list of the exhibits, a blackboard, and the plea agreement Robert Riley had signed. I took that to mean that they wanted to see just how easily Riley was getting off, a request that didn't thrill me. At 4:28 in the afternoon of December 10, 1987, the Howard Beach jury went out. Two hours and twelve minutes later, without reaching a verdict, it was sequestered for the night in a Queens motel. At that moment, in the Borough Hall suite where the A-Team had gathered, my investigators blew out the wax votary light they had dubbed the Candle of Justice. It would burn whenever the jury deliberated.

On Friday, Demakos denied the request to visit the scene, and the jury asked to again hear the statements the defendants had made to detectives. As they filed back into K-3 to listen to the stenographer's redaction, Forewoman Nina Krauss sat down and, I was sure, caught my eye, shot me what I can only describe as a Mona Lisa smile, and nodded her head several times. Incredulous, I turned to Mangum: "Did you see that?"

"I saw it," he said. "What does it mean?"

I had no idea, but when she continued her facial contortions over the next several readbacks I began to suspect she was sending me a message.

"We're going to have an early verdict," I told the trial team during a Saturday-afternoon break from a readback of Theresa Fisher's testimony. "Nina Krauss gave me another one of those looks. We're in."

But as the days melted into a week with still no verdict, and Krauss's tics continued unabated, she became the subject of animated speculation in our Borough Hall suite.

"Why are they taking so long if she's giving us these signals?" everyone wanted to know. I had no answer.

On the third day of deliberations the panel asked to hear the Toscanos' testimony again, and by the fifth day (with our Candle of Justice having burned for twenty-eight and a half hours) the defense attorneys were acting spry. "The longer they're out, the more problems they're having with Hynes's case," Murphy told a friend. "And the longer it gets, the better it looks for the defense."

By the seventh day, I was in agony, benumbed by the interminable readbacks. There would be one at eleven in the morning, and then another at five, with nothing but dead time in between. Some of the investigators brought Woody Allen movies into our temporary offices. But I was much too antsy to sit in front of the VCR. "Relax," Jean Griffith told me, for she and Sandiford spent much of the vigil in our offices, "whatever the jury does is one thing, but the Lord will provide, and do what He has to do in his own good time." Pat, meanwhile, knew enough about my nature to let me sweat this one out in peace.

But the days still ran together, and we all became giddy with a kind of courtroom cabin fever. Although I got to know and like many of the reporters now virtually living in the courthouse pressroom (which I entered unannounced on day eight, shouting "Verdict!" just to see them scramble), their repetitive questions and predictions were driving me nuts. But on the morning of day eleven, the first anniversary of The Incident at Howard Beach, I would have welcomed still another columnist's speculative fantasy rather than the headline I read in the *Daily News:* BEACH JUROR TO SELL STORY.

The paper reported that Forewoman Krauss's boyfriend, Mark Friedman, a field producer for a local television news program, had been authorized to sell her ringside view of the trial to the highest bidder. That cleared up the mystery of Nina Krauss's facial tics. Friedman sat directly behind me during the trial and readbacks, and the signals Krauss was sending went

literally over my head. Friedman claimed in the story that the
New York Post offered $7,500, and *Newsday* $10,000, although
editors for both papers denied the figures. But they did not deny
the fact that Friedman was shopping Krauss's story, and all four
defense lawyers demanded a mistrial. Momentarily furious, I
calmed down when Demakos refused to even hear their motion.

At 8:30 P.M., December 21, 1987, a year and a day after the
attack in Howard Beach, Doug LeVien blew out the Candle of
Justice for the final time. After twelve days of deliberation, the
twelve men and women filed into the jury box as a flurry of
reporters squeezed into the front rows of the courtroom. Seconds later, each member of the A-Team, surrounded by investigators, crowded into stone-silent K-3.

Nina Krauss's hands trembled as she clutched the slip of
paper, listened to the court clerk, and, in a cold, steady tone,
pronounced the verdicts:

"To the charge of manslaughter in the second degree, how
does the jury find Scott Kern?"

"Guilty."

"To the charge of manslaughter in the second degree, how
does the jury find Jason Ladone?"

"Guilty."

"To the charge of manslaughter in the second degree, how
does the jury find Jon Lester?"

"Guilty."

"To the charge of manslaughter in the second degree, how
does the jury find Michael Pirone?"

"Not guilty."

Kern, Ladone, and Lester were also judged guilty of assault;
Michael Pirone was acquitted of all charges. For those who believe, with Disraeli, that circumstances are the creatures of men,
instead of vice versa, the Howard Beach verdict was a reaffirmation of faith. We hadn't gotten the murder conviction, but
what we had got was damn good enough.

As the verdicts were read, Kern's mother, Carol, collapsed in
a heap, and Jean Lester seemed to turn gray before my eyes.
Several leather-jacketed members of the Revolutionary Com-
munist Party disrupted the verdict reading by scattering leaflets

throughout the courtroom. They chanted "Murderers! Murderers!" as court officers dragged them away. Venerable and gothic
Part K-3, ill-lit and swathed in ominous shadows for the past four
months, was now awash in the piercing white light of television
cameras, which Demakos had allowed into the courtroom for
the climax.

The three guilty defendants stared straight ahead stoically as
Pirone and Murphy embraced and wept through the pan-
demonium, an island of muted happiness in an ocean of grief.
Juror Ramjass Boodrham said several days later that Murphy's
client should light a daily votive candle for the rest of his life.
Maybe he does.

The A-Team was led out the back door of the courtroom by
court officers and investigators. Jean Griffith and Cedric Sandiford were at my side. I embraced Pat in a back alcove of the
courtroom. I was elated, of course, but I was also oddly numb.
I never truly enjoy putting people behind bars. I have always
found it difficult to rejoice over convictions, the way, say, a
defense attorney can celebrate an acquittal. I have known defense lawyers who say they hear a trumpet crescendo accompanying the words "not guilty," but the song I think of in victory
is "Taps." I believe my staff feels the same way, which accounted
for our somewhat subdued celebration.

Once back in our suite, Jean Griffith kissed me, and Sandiford
hugged me, and someone broke out champagne and bottles of
Heineken beer. Christopher Griffith appeared more or less
dazed, asking the lawyers to explain to him the meaning of the
verdict, especially Pirone's acquittal, and I supposed that in the
emotion of the moment he was feeling quite overwhelmed. I
called Governor Cuomo, who offered congratulations, and then
I waited for the press to arrive. After the verdict, the defendants
and their families remained in the courtroom, where Demakos
had given their lawyers permission to hold a news conference,
and most members of the media were still there.

"These young men were the scapegoats of a nation that has
neglected its minorities," said Rubinstein, and Levinson said he
felt "terrible, just terrible, but Jon Lester is doing well, he's a
very tough kid." At this point it was all rhetoric. Although the

defendants had been acquited of the most serious charge, second-degree murder, we all felt the verdict fair and just. Personally, I experienced mixed emotions about the role of my office:
vindication for my diverse group of lawyers and investigators,
who had now established a very high standard of excellence
within the criminal justice community; and sadness that it was
all over and we'd never work together on anything like this
again for the rest of our lives.

But my strongest feeling was of relief; I was just glad it was
over, glad that we had won, glad that justice had triumphed.
There was some backslapping and handshaking, and many hugs
and big smiles, and then the media arrived.

"Our society, represented by a Queens County jury, has ruled
that it won't tolerate hatred based on anything that makes us
different," I told the reporters. "And now that this jury has
convicted these defendants, they have been stripped of any
pretense of innocence. The brutality and callousness of what
they did that night has been revealed for all to see."

During the session a young newspaper reporter asked Sandiford if the convictions "said something about the value of black
life in America."

"No, sir," he replied. "It says something about the value of
human life in America."

Hearing that, I felt like cheering.

At the same time, I understood that our victory had come
ultimately at the expense of Michael Griffith. He had died for
this trial. As happy as we were at that moment, one glance across
the room at Jean Griffith and her surviving son reminded me
that all of this had happened because a man had been killed for
no good reason. That's why a pall hung over the verdict: our
success was rooted in a human tragedy.

The following day, Wednesday, December 23, the Special
State Prosecutor's Office held its annual Christmas party. It was
the most festive one I have ever attended. Amid clinking glasses
and holiday toasts, one by one the A-Team came up to me, first
Hawkins, then Hayes, then Brook, Greenberg, and Hoffman.
Boyar was not yet off to the hinterlands, and he followed Mangum, who'd walked in behind Hershey. Finally, I shook hands

and embraced Mike Nadel. Hardly any words were passed among us as I thought about the day Mario Cuomo called me and asked me to do a job for the People.

The maximum sentences for second-degree manslaughter and first-degree assault—the most serious felonies Scott Kern, Jon Lester, and Jason Ladone were convicted of—are each five to fifteen years. In New York State it is customary for a judge to order convicted felons to serve such sentences concurrently. I am not a vindictive man, but I didn't think that was a lot of prison time for someone who had killed another human being. Once the dust from the verdict had settled, I ordered my appellate staff to find the legal rationale to support an argument before Judge Demakos for consecutive sentencing, a rarity in New York.

"Impossible, you can't do that," Helman Brook argued. "No judge ever gives consecutive sentencing. Plus, we virtually admitted during trial that these crimes were concurrent, what with how we kept connecting Griffith's death to Sandiford's assault."

"Of course I relied on Sandiford at trial," I said. "But now we're at the sentencing stage, and they're separate, violent felonies, and we've got to get this judge to agree to send these people away consecutively. Find it for me, please."

Over the next several weeks, they did. On Friday, January 23, 1988, I appeared for the final time in Courtroom K-3, making my plea for the maximum incarceration for Jon Lester, the first of the defendants to be sentenced. I asked Demakos to "send a very clear message that this will not be tolerated, that people will know that if they can't respect one another, and if that lack of respect moves them to violence, then they will be punished severely."

Levinson, flanked by a haggard and drawn Lester and Lester's mother, Jean, asked the judge not to be moved by "those who would rather see a scaffold built on Queens Boulevard and see my client hung." Earlier, Jean Lester had told her son's attorney that "there's nothing left to exact from him, they've squeezed every pound of flesh and every drop of blood."

This, I felt, was also part of the tragedy of Howard Beach: the broken lives of the Kern family, the Lesters, the Ladones. During a quiet moment before Lester's sentencing, Jean Griffith told me that she often cries for the mothers of the teenagers who killed her son. "But at least they can visit them in jail," she said. "I have nothing to visit except a patch of black dirt."

After all pleas were heard, Demakos spoke, saying he had received over fifteen hundred letters since the verdict, and all but two (one from from Mayor Koch) asked that he be lenient.

"Now, what disturbs me about all these letters is that there is no remorse," Judge Demakos announced, "that many treat this case as a political entity, an unwarranted conviction of the community of Howard Beach, that this event was just a fight between a group of boys. Well, this is not a conviction of the community of Howard Beach. This is a conviction of three young white men who recklessly chased a young black man into a parkway where he was struck and killed by a car. And after having seen this, they continued to chase another black male so that they could assault him. And all this just because they were black.

"Although I agree with the jury verdict of reckless manslaughter, I find that Lester's actions following the death of Griffith, showing no remorse, no sense of guilt, indicated a mind to me that is pretty close to evincing a depraved indifference for human life.

"What kind of an individual do I have before me who, after witnessing a young black man get crushed by a car, continues his reckless conduct by savagely beating another black male with a bat?"

Then Demakos sentenced Jon Lester to the maximum ten-to-thirty years in prison—two consecutive five-to-fifteen-year terms.

As Lester left the courtroom he told his supporters, "I will be acquitted on appeal. I just wanted to say that. Thank you, everybody."

The packed courtroom gave him a standing ovation.

Jon Lester was sentenced to ten to thirty years in prison.

Scott Kern was sentenced to six to eighteen years in prison.

Jason Ladone was sentenced to five to fifteen years in prison.

In two subsequent Howard Beach trials handled by my staff:

Salvatore DeSimone and Harry Buonocore pleaded guilty to riot in the first degree and were sentenced to five years' probation and two hundred hours of community service.

John Saggese and Thomas Gucciardo were found not guilty of all charges.

William Bollander, James Povinelli, and Thomas Farina were convicted of riot in the second degree and were sentenced to four-month, intermittent prison terms (which they served on weekends), two hundred hours of community service, and three years' probation.

As part of his plea-bargain arrangement, Robert Riley pleaded guilty to felony assault in the second degree. He was sentenced to six months in prison.

EPILOGUE

In late August 1989, one week before Robert Riley began serving his prison sentence, as I was in the middle of a heated campaign race for the Brooklyn District Attorney's Office, three black teenagers from the East New York section of Brooklyn walked off a subway train in the predominantly white Bensonhurst neighborhood of the borough. One of the blacks, sixteen-year-old Yusef Hawkins, had asked two friends to accompany him while he went to Bensonhurst to look at a used car.

As the three walked down the main thoroughfare of the neighborhood, they were accosted by a gang of white boys carrying baseball bats and screaming, "Niggers, get out of the neighborhood!" The blacks were attacked, and Yusef Hawkins was shot dead.

This incident followed by four months the brutal rape of a white woman in Manhattan's Central Park by a gang of rampaging black youths, a "wolf pack" as the media dubbed them. Before she was dragged to a desolate culvert and gang-raped, the woman's head was stove in with bricks and wooden sticks. One of the suspects, in a statement to police, said the gang had roamed that night with a specific purpose, that they were "out to fuck up white people."

Like The Incident at Howard Beach, what occurred in Central Park in April 1989 and what happened in Bensonhurst in August 1989 reflect a reality of urban life that will threaten the existence of every American unless we make greater efforts to understand why these incidents happen. In neither Central Park nor Bensonhurst were drugs or poverty the obvious cause. Instead, it was violence for the sake of violence, fueled by racial dynamics.

Tough talk and being tough are two different things. Teenage violence is not a new phenomenon, but it seems to have gotten worse. Teenage gangs are no longer content to fight one another over turf, they have graduated to shootings and homicide, and attack innocent citizens in all parts of the country.

I have felt a father's pain rushing to an emergency room twice in the last two years. On one occasion my eldest son had been slashed with a beer bottle, leaving a permanent, nine-inch scar on his forearm. On another my youngest son was kicked in the face, breaking his jaw in two places. I felt rage after seeing their spilled blood, and I can confess that had I caught either attacker and not been restrained, the intellectual debate over the death penalty would not have been a factor for me.

Yet I yearn to know why those thugs violently assaulted my two boys, just as society needs to know why the young woman in Central Park was brutally defiled and the young man in Bensonhurst was blown from this earth. Why was Michael Griffith killed? Why was Cedric Sandiford brutally beaten?

I watched the funeral ceremonies for young Yusef Hawkins at a campaign stop, surrounded by black and white citizens of Brooklyn. As black ministers and politicians exited the church, the camera zeroed in on their angry faces, the television announcer reported that black leaders were organizing a march through the Bensonhurst neighborhood.

"What the fuck do they want with us now?" said a white voice to my rear. I didn't even turn around. I didn't have to. I envisioned that Boston firefighter, in that Berkshire hotel nearly three years before, with that red tide rising in his cheeks.

Why were Michael Griffith and Yusef Hawkins killed? Why was that woman brutally raped? I don't know, and I don't think society knows. But as I write this, eleven years before the end of this century, I am sure of one thing: we had all better damn well find out.